Deborah Kamen
Greek Slavery

Trends in Classics –
Key Perspectives on Classical Research

General Editors
Franco Montanari and Antonios Rengakos

Series Editors
P. J. Finglass, S. J. V. Malloch, Christos Tsagalis

Associate Editors
Anna Marmodoro and Elena Isayev

Volume 4

Deborah Kamen

Greek Slavery

—

DE GRUYTER

ISBN 978-3-11-063759-5
e-ISBN (PDF) 978-3-11-065476-9
e-ISBN (EPUB) 978-3-11-065123-2
ISSN 2626-1030

Library of Congress Control Number: 2023936262

Bibliographic information published by the Deutsche Nationalbibliothek
The Deutsche Nationalbibliothek lists this publication in the Deutsche Nationalbibliografie;
detailed bibliographic data are available on the Internet at http://dnb.dnb.de.

© 2023 Walter de Gruyter GmbH, Berlin/Boston
Cover image: Domenico Spinosa, Fondo Marino, courtesy of Nicola Spinosa
Printing and binding: CPI books GmbH, Leck

www.degruyter.com

For SLR

Preface

In keeping with the aims of the *Trends in Classics: Key Perspectives in Classical Research* series, this book is designed as a guide for anyone wishing to undertake research on Greek slavery or to familiarize themselves with the current landscape of Greek slavery studies. It is thus not an introduction to Greek slavery so much as an introduction to the *study of* Greek slavery, providing a point of entry to the major themes that have shaped recent scholarship on the topic. For this reason, I focus primarily on scholarship from the past twenty to twenty-five years, citing earlier work only when it is especially formative or when it remains the most recent treatment of a given topic.

Whenever possible, I try to talk about slavery using the helpful guidelines provided in the community-sourced document "Writing about Slavery/Teaching About Slavery: This Might Help."[1] Although these guidelines were designed by scholars of color to discuss racialized slavery in the modern world, I believe that they can apply, *mutatis mutandis*, to antiquity. In short, this document suggests that we shift the language we use to talk about slavery, with the aim of destabilizing the problematic assumptions that underlie our usual vocabulary. Thus, for example, if we use the phrase "enslaved person" rather than "slave," this superficially small change allows us to acknowledge the humanity of the person in question, as well as to emphasize that being enslaved is a *condition*, something that happens to a person, rather than an inherent feature of their identity. Similarly, it is best for us to avoid words like "master," which adopt the perspective of the enslaver. Preferable is that we refer to these individuals more frankly and descriptively: namely, as individuals who have enslaved other human beings, treating them as if they were their property. Following most (if not all) of the document's guidelines, I use terms like "master" or "slave" in this book mainly in contexts where I am attempting to preserve the viewpoint of our ancient Greek authors.

After many delays caused by the pandemic, I was able to write the bulk of this book in Edinburgh in the spring of 2022. I thank the University of Washington for granting me a much-needed sabbatical, and the University of Edinburgh (in particular my hosts Douglas Cairns, Mirko Canevaro, and Lucy Grig) for providing such an intellectually rich environment in which to write. Conversations with colleagues over the years (especially Sarah Brucia Breitenfeld, Naomi Campa, Sara Forsdyke, Steve Hodkinson, David Lewis, Toph Marshall, Jason

---

1 Foreman n.d.

Porter, Ulrike Roth, Lene Rubinstein, and Rachel Zelnick-Abramovitz), as well as the insights of the students in my graduate seminar at the University of Washington in the winter of 2022, have clarified and enriched my thinking on the topic of Greek slavery. I am also grateful to Patrick Finglass, Simon Malloch, and Christos Tsagalis for the invitation to contribute to this series and for their feedback on my manuscript. Finally, I am indebted, as always, to my friends and family, and especially to Sarah Levin-Richardson for all of her love and support.

Contents

Preface —— VII
Abbreviations —— XI

1 Introduction —— 1
1.1 Historiography of ancient slavery —— 1
1.2 Monographs on Greek (and Roman) slavery —— 2
1.3 Edited volumes, encyclopedias, and handbooks —— 6
1.4 Defining slavery —— 9
1.5 Slave societies? —— 12
1.6 Conclusion —— 14

2 Epichoric Slave Systems —— 16
2.1 Slavery in the Mycenaean and Homeric worlds —— 16
2.2 Slavery in archaic Athens —— 18
2.3 Slavery in Sparta —— 21
2.4 Slavery in Crete —— 24
2.5 Slavery in classical Athens —— 27
2.6 Conclusion —— 30

3 Economics of Slavery —— 32
3.1 Supply of enslaved people —— 32
3.2 Numbers of enslaved people —— 36
3.3 Roles in the economy —— 38
3.4 Prevalence of slave labor —— 44
3.5 Conclusion —— 46

4 Treatment of Enslaved People —— 47
4.1 "Slaving strategies" and household management —— 47
4.2 Types of violence and its effects —— 50
4.3 Institutionalized violence —— 53
4.4 Protection from (extreme) violence? —— 57
4.5 Conclusion —— 59

5 Sex and Gender —— 61
5.1 Gender —— 61
5.2 Prostitution —— 64
5.3 The sexual use of non-prostituted enslaved people —— 66

5.4	Enslaved people as sexual subjects —— 70	
5.5	Conclusion —— 71	
6	**Agency, Resistance, and Revolt —— 73**	
6.1	Agency —— 73	
6.2	Resistance —— 76	
6.3	Revolt —— 79	
6.4	Conclusion —— 82	
7	**Manumission —— 83**	
7.1	Modes of manumission —— 83	
7.2	*Paramonē* and its implications —— 93	
7.3	The status of formerly enslaved people —— 96	
7.4	Conclusion —— 99	
8	**Representations, Metaphors, and Legacies —— 101**	
8.1	Representations in literature —— 101	
8.2	Representations in art —— 107	
8.3	Metaphors —— 109	
8.4	Legacies of Greek slavery —— 113	
8.5	Conclusion —— 117	
9	**Epilogue —— 118**	

Works Cited —— 119
Index Locorum —— 141
General Index —— 145

Abbreviations

Ael.	Aelian
VH	*Varia historia*
Aesch.	Aeschylus
Cho.	*Choephoroe*
Aeschin.	Aeschines
Ag. Inv.	Agora Inventory Number
Andoc.	Andocides
Antiph.	Antiphon
Anecd. Bekk.	I. Bekker, ed., *Anecdota Graeca*, 3 vols. (Berlin 1814–21)
Ar.	Aristophanes
Eq.	*Equites*
Ran.	*Ranae*
Vesp.	*Vespae*
Arist.	Aristotle
Ath. Pol.	*Athēnaiōn politeia*
Pol.	*Politica*
[Arist.]	Pseudo-Aristotle
Oik.	*Oikonomika*
Athen.	Athenaeus
BNJ	Brill's New Jacoby (Leiden 2007–)
Cic.	Cicero
Orat.	*Orator*
CID	*Corpus des inscriptions de Delphes* (Paris 1977–)
Dig.	*Digest*
D. S.	Diodorus Siculus
D. L.	Diogenes Laertius
Dem.	Demosthenes
[Dem.]	Pseudo-Demosthenes
Ephor.	Ephorus Historicus
GDI	*Sammlung der griechischen Dialektinschriften* (Göttingen 1884–1915)
Harp.	Harpocration
Hdt.	Herodotus
Hellanic.	Hellanicus Historicus
Hes.	Hesiod
Op.	*Opera et Dies*
Hom.	Homer
Il.	*Iliad*
Od.	*Odyssey*
Hyp.	Hyperides
IC	*Inscriptiones Creticae* (Rome 1935—1950)
IG	*Inscriptiones Graecae* (Berlin 1873–)
Is.	Isaeus
Jensen	C.C. Jensen, ed., *Hyperides: Orationes sex cum ceterarum fragmentis* (Leipzig 1917)

Lys.	Lysias
Men.	Menander
Her.	*Hērōs*
ML	R. Meiggs and D.M. Lewis, *A Selection of Greek Historical Inscriptions to the End of the Fifth Century B.C.* 2nd edition (Oxford 1989)
Paus.	Pausanias
Philoch.	Philochorus
Pl.	Plato
Grg.	*Gorgias*
Leg.	*Leges*
Resp.	*Respublica*
Plut.	Plutarch
Lyc.	*Lycurgus*
Sol.	*Solon*
Poll.	Pollux
Polyaen.	Polyaenus Historicus
Schol.	Scholia
Smyth	H.W. Smyth, *A Greek Grammar for Colleges* (New York 1920)
Sol.	Solon
Theopomp.	Theopompus Historicus
Thuc.	Thucydides
Vita W	*Vita Aesopi Westermanniana*
West	M.L. West, *Iambi et Elegi Graeci.* 2nd edition (Oxford 1989–92)
Xen.	Xenophon
Hell.	*Hellenica*
Hier.	*Hiero*
Oik.	*Oikonomikos*
[Xen.]	Pseudo-Xenophon
Ath. Pol.	*Athēnaiōn politeia*

1 Introduction

This chapter begins with a brief survey of work on the historiography of Greek slavery (and ancient slavery more broadly) before turning to the major monographs and edited volumes that have been published on the topic over the past twenty to twenty-five years. I then address two of the major definitional debates currently at play in the field of ancient slavery studies: namely, 1) how best to define "slavery" and 2) whether the concept of "slave societies" is a useful one. As a whole, the introduction lays the groundwork for recent scholarly debates about specific aspects of Greek slavery, which I turn to in the chapters that follow.

1.1 Historiography of ancient slavery

Even today, one of the biggest names in ancient slavery studies remains the twentieth-century Greek historian Moses I. Finley.[1] Among Finley's many contributions to the field is the eponymous first chapter of his *Ancient Slavery and Modern Ideology* (1980), a historiography of scholarship on ancient slavery from the seventeenth to the early twentieth century.[2] Other historiographies include Paul Cartledge's "Greek Civilization and Slavery" (2002), which surveys Anglo-American scholarship on Greek slavery from 1950–2000, highlighting one key work from each decade, and Niall McKeown's polemical *The Invention of Ancient Slavery?* (2007), each chapter of which addresses key examples of a particular approach or school of thought in ancient (and in particular) Roman slavery

---

[1] For Finley's work on ancient slavery, see especially Finley 1981 and 1998 [1980], but the bibliography is voluminous. For recent critiques of aspects of Finley's work on slavery, see Vlassopoulos 2016a, Lenski and Cameron 2018a and b, Lenski 2018b, Lewis 2018a, Vlassopoulos 2021. On Finley's influences and his intellectual/political context, see especially the scholarship of Daniel Tompkins (e.g. Tompkins 2013, 2014); see also Shaw 1998, Harris 2013, Lenski 2018a. On the impact of Finley on his contemporaries and on later scholars, see Jew, Osborne, and Scott 2016; for his impact specifically in France, see the essays in *Anabases* 19 (2014) 11–129.
[2] Finley 1998 [1980], ch. 1; he argues that this scholarship was characterized by three sometimes-overlapping approaches: the moral/spiritual (often Christian); the antiquarian; and the economic. But see Vlassopoulos 2016a, 76 and 2021, 15, who rejects Finley's historiography as "misleading."

https://doi.org/10.1515/9783110654769-001

studies.³ More recently, Kostas Vlassopoulos, in the second chapter of his *Historicising Ancient Slavery* (2021), has provided a clear overview of work on ancient slavery up to 2021, with the aim of investigating why the field has developed in the ways it has. Laying out three major debates that have shaped the modern study of ancient slavery (what he calls the modernist, the humanitarian, and the class struggle debates), Vlassopoulos shows how Finley's approach to ancient slavery responded to, and reshaped, these debates and ultimately became the dominant paradigm in ancient slavery studies — a paradigm that Vlassopoulos himself finds problematic.⁴ To demonstrate the value of new, post-Finleyan avenues for studying ancient slavery, Vlassopoulos surveys the lessons we can learn from global studies of slavery — including how slavery differs over time and space — as well as other developments in the study of ancient slavery over the past forty years that challenge older approaches and debates.⁵ The usefulness of global and comparative slave studies in particular has recently been stressed by scholars of Greek slavery.⁶

1.2 Monographs on Greek (and Roman) slavery

Monographs published in the past twenty-five years have illuminated various aspects of Greek slavery, as well as ancient slavery more broadly. To move in roughly chronological order, Peter Hunt's *Slaves, Warfare and Ideology in the Greek Historians* (1998) makes the important argument that the reason the Greek

---

3 Cartledge 2002a; his list includes Finley 1981, 97–115 (originally published in the 1950s); Davis 1966; Jameson 1977–78; de Ste. Croix 1981; and Hunt 1998. Only ch. 7 of McKeown 2007 focuses on Greece; here he discusses Johnstone 1998; Hunt 1998; duBois 2003.
4 Vlassopoulos 2021, 15–24; see also Vlassopoulos 2016a. Briefly, the modernist debate was between those who thought ancient societies were based on slavery and those who did not; the humanitarian debate between those who thought ancient slavery became more humane over time and those who thought it was always oppressive and cruel; and the class struggle debate between those who thought enslaved people in antiquity were a class and those who who thought they were not.
5 On the usefulness of global slavery studies, see Vlassopoulos 2021, 24–31 (see also Vlassopoulos 2016b); on (other) recent developments in the field of ancient slavery studies, see Vlassopoulos 2021, 31–38. See also Doddington and Dal Lago 2022, which draws together historiographical, theoretical, and methodological approaches to slavery across time and space (including Greece and Rome).
6 See Ismard 2017b and Lewis 2022b on the benefits (and potential pitfalls) for Greek historians of engaging with global/comparative slave studies. For recent work on Greek slavery making good use of comparative material, see Harrison 2019 and Forsdyke 2021.

historians (Herodotus, Thucydides, and Xenophon) do not mention slave participation in warfare is not that enslaved people did not participate, but that their involvement conflicted with the ideology of the citizen-soldier.[7] Hans Klees' comprehensive *Sklavenleben im klassischen Griechenland* (1998), in turn, was one of the first works to attempt to access the *experiences* of enslaved people, now a burgeoning trend in ancient slavery studies.[8] In *Slaves and Other Objects* (2003), Page duBois contends that while enslaved people were ubiquitous in antiquity, embedded in all aspects of Greek life, they have been mostly invisible to moderns, from laypeople to classical scholars.[9] Next, in *Slavery: Antiquity and its Legacy* (2009), duBois turns to the ways in which ancient slavery (primarily Roman but also Greek) can provide us with models not just of dominance but also of resistance.[10] And Kelly Wrenhaven's *Reconstructing the Slave: The Image of the Slave in Ancient Greece* (2012) looks at how the Greeks' literary and visual representations of enslaved people served to naturalize and justify the institution of slavery.

Other monographs on Greek slavery have focused on the intersection of slavery and politics. Paulin Ismard's *La démocratie contre les experts: Les esclaves publics en Grèce ancienne* (2015), published in English as *Democracy's Slaves: A Political History of Ancient Greece* (2017), represents the now-standard work on public slaves in Athens — i.e., enslaved people owned by the state — showing how their labor, and in particular their expertise, allowed for the run-

---

7 Hunt 1998. On enslaved people in the Greek military, see further Hunt 2006; Akrigg 2019, 99–105; Ducrey 2022 (on Greece and Rome).
8 Klees 1998, with chapters on the process of enslavement; the supply of materials (clothing, food, etc.) to enslaved people; morale and working conditions; property ownership by enslaved people; slave families and sexual relationships with owners; punishments; training, education, and cultural participation; manumission; and the position of enslaved people in the state and society. For more recent work on the experiences of enslaved people in the Greek world, see Forsdyke 2021; in the Roman world, see Joshel and Petersen 2014. See also Kamen and Levin-Richardson 2022a and 2022b, who use Saidiya Hartman's methodology of "critical fabulation," developed in the context of her work on trans-Atlantic slavery (Hartman 2007 and 2008), to explore the lived experiences of enslaved people in Greece and Rome.
9 duBois 2003.
10 duBois 2009; slavery in Greece is covered on pp. 54–66 (slavery in Greek political theory) and pp. 78–94 (slavery from Homer through Hellenistic literature). This book is part of a reception-studies series on "Ancients and Moderns," edited by Phiroze Vasunia; the series looks at how various aspects of antiquity, e.g. slavery, race, gender, sex, war, religion, etc., have shaped the ideas, society, and culture of later periods, including our often complicated investments in these issues today.

ning of the Athenian democracy.¹¹ Ismard continued this work in his *La cité et ses esclaves: Institution, fictions, experiences* (2019), which explores the relationship between slavery and democratic ideology in Athens.¹²

Manumission in the Greek world has been another area of growing interest, with Rachel Zelnick-Abramovitz's *Not Wholly Free: The Concept of Manumission and the Status of Manumitted Slaves in the Ancient Greek World* (2005), the first English-language monograph on the topic, paving the way.¹³ In this book, Zelnick-Abramovitz lays out a comprehensive account of how enslaved individuals could be freed in ancient Greece, including the various ways in which manumission delivered only an incomplete form of freedom. Sara Zanovello's *From Slave to Free: A Legal Perspective on Greek Manumission* (2021 [2017]), in turn, takes an explicitly legal approach to the subject, aiming to uncover how the Greeks themselves understood manumission as a legal institution — namely, as an extinguishing of the enslaver's right of ownership, resulting in a change in legal status of those who were manumitted.¹⁴

Recent years have also seen the publication of a handful of introductions to Greek (and Roman) slavery. Jean Andreau and Raymond Descat's *Esclave en Grèce et à Rome* (2006), translated into English as *The Slave in Greece and Rome* (2011), provides an impressionistic survey of ancient slavery, with chapters on definitions, the earliest forms of slavery, demographics, the economy, and ways of escaping slavery.¹⁵ *Sklaverei und Freilassung in der griechisch-römischen Welt* (2009), by Elisabeth Hermann-Otto, is designed for interested laypeople and

---

11 Ismard 2017a [2015].
12 Ismard 2019.
13 Until Zelnick-Abramovitz 2005, the main studies on the topic were Calderini 1908 and Rädle 1969. Zelnick-Abramovitz's book includes chapters on definitions and approaches to slavery and freedom; evidence for different types of manumission; the nature of manumittors and manumitted slaves; the procedures underlying the act of manumission; laws and legal actions pertaining to manumission; and the reality of freedom for formerly enslaved individuals. For a more detailed summary of the book, see Kamen 2005.
14 Zanovello 2017 (a PhD dissertation subsequently published as a monograph: Zanovello 2021) has chapters on the origins of manumission (starting with Homer), manumission and sale in the Delphic inscriptions, manumission and consecration in central Greece (focusing on the inscriptions from Chaeronea), the Athenian evidence for manumission and *paramonē* (i.e., post-manumission obligations), and "public" manumission (i.e., manumission by the polis) in classical Greece.
15 Andreau and Descat 2011 [2006]. But see Hunt 2012, who points out the inconsistent citation of both primary and secondary sources (making it hard to evaluate some of the authors' more "eccentric" claims) and the authors' sometimes "too credulous" approach to the ancient sources.

students as an introduction to slavery (and manumission) in both Greece and Rome, with a considerably greater focus on Rome.¹⁶ Much more accessible to the general reader or undergraduate student, however, is Hunt's *Ancient Greek and Roman Slavery* (2018). Hunt devotes each chapter to a major issue in the study of slavery, including definitions and evidence, enslavement, economics, politics, culture, sex and family life, manumission, everyday conflict, revolts, and representations of enslaved people.¹⁷ Similarly geared toward students is Eftychia Bathrellou and Kostas Vlassopoulos' *Greek and Roman Slaveries* (2022), a thematically organized sourcebook equipped with study questions and suggested bibliography.¹⁸ And Sara Forsdyke's *Slaves and Slavery in Ancient Greece* (2021) provides a highly readable introduction to Greek slavery, suitable for advanced undergraduates, graduate students, and educated general readers, that explores "how individuals became enslaved, how they worked and lived, and the nature of their relations with other slaves — as well as their masters."¹⁹ She stresses throughout her book the degree to which Greek culture was dependent on enslaved labor, aiming to give enslaved people their due by reading against the grain and by making ample (but careful) use of comparative evidence.

Finally, two recent paradigm-shifting monographs are of particular note. David M. Lewis' *Greek Slave Systems in their Eastern Mediterranean Context, c. 800–146 BC* (2018) looks at what he calls "epichoric slave systems"; indeed, one of his key arguments is that there is not one monolithic "Greek slavery." He contends, convincingly, that these slave systems must be looked at alongside contemporaneous Near Eastern societies, which he argues did not differ radical-

---

16 Hermann-Otto 2009; only one chapter (ch. 2) focuses on slavery in the Greek and Hellenistic world. The others examine the "problem" of ancient slavery in modernity, including definitions and terminology; Roman slavery; and practices of manumission, focusing on late antiquity. For a critical review of this book, see Schipp 2010; for a brief discussion of problems with ch. 2 in particular, see Fischer 2010a.
17 Hunt 2018b. On the usefulness of this work as an undergraduate textbook, see Huemoeller 2018.
18 Bathrellou and Vlassopoulos 2022, which includes chapters on definitions, the evidence for slavery, the consequences of slavery for slaveholders; slaving strategies; relations between "masters and slaves"; the distinction between free and slave; enslaved persons and their communities, slaving and no-slaving zones; experiencing and resisting enslavement; manumission and freed slaves; slavery and historical change; and comparing ancient slaveries. This work is a very good substitution for Wiedemann 1981, the only sourcebook on this subject until recently; in addition to containing some errors and being outdated in terms of methodological approaches, Wiedemann 1981 is primarily a collection of literary and documentary texts, whereas Bathrellou and Vlassopoulos 2022 also includes material evidence.
19 Forsdyke 2021, quotation at p. 2.

ly from the Greeks in their conceptions of slavery and freedom. Lewis also reaffirms the case that slavery is best understood as a property relationship (see further ch. 1.4) and critiques Finley for the distinction he drew between "slave societies" and "societies with slaves" (see further ch. 1.5).[20]

A second major recent work is Vlassopoulos' *Historicising Ancient Slavery* (mentioned above), which draws together the influential work he has done over the past fifteen or so years (much of which I discuss in the chapters that follow). After sketching out trends in scholarship that have produced (apparent) paradoxes, Vlassopoulos seeks to resolve these paradoxes by suggesting new tools and new approaches for studying ancient slavery. Stressing both change over time and the agency of enslaved people, he argues that slavery should be conceptualized as a historical conglomerate of 1) different symbolic systems (i.e., slavery as property; as a distinct legal and social status; as a cluster of related modalities: e.g. as a relationship of domination, an instrumental relationship, an asymmetrical negotiation of power, an asymmetrical relationship of benefaction and reward, etc.); 2) different "slaving strategies" (i.e., the varying techniques used by enslavers to maximize what they derived from the institution); and 3) different dialectical relationships (i.e., between enslavers and enslaved, free and enslaved people, and members of the various communities enslaved people participated in).[21] As Nino Luraghi has noted in his review of this book, this is very much not a textbook or a general introduction to the topic, but "a combination between a manifesto or program for future research, and an interpretive exploration of the modern historiography of slavery."[22]

1.3 Edited volumes, encyclopedias, and handbooks

In addition to monographs, edited volumes on ancient slavery have been published in recent years. Every year, GIREA (Groupe international de recherches

---

20 Lewis 2018a; this book has been reviewed positively: see, e.g., Kamen 2021. The work is divided into four parts: Part I is prolegomena (definitions of slavery, freedom, slave societies, etc.); Part II, epichoric slave systems of the Greek world (including chapters on archaic Greece, helotic slavery in classical Sparta, classical Crete, and classical Attica); Part III, slave systems of the wider Mediterranean world (with chapters on Iron Age II Israel, Assyria in the eighth and seventh centuries BCE, Babylonia in the seventh to fifth centuries BCE, the Persian Empire, and Punic Carthage); and Part IV, an attempt to understand regional variation in slaveholding.
21 Vlassopoulos 2021. For the term "slaving strategies," see Miller 2008.
22 Luraghi 2022. Some small criticisms aside, Luraghi concludes that Vlassopoulos 2021 is a "must-read for this subject."

sur l'esclavage dans — now, depuis — l'Antiquité) holds a conference and publishes its proceedings.²³ Among the many notable volumes published in this series, two embody particularly well the trends found in recent scholarship on ancient slavery. One is Anastasia Serghidou's edited volume *Fear of Slaves — Fear of Enslavement in the Ancient Mediterranean* (2007), which addresses free people's fears both of enslaved people and of being enslaved themselves.²⁴ The other is Antonio Gonzales' *La fin du statut servile?* (2008), which adds to the growing bibliography on manumission by exploring the movement of individuals from enslaved to free, and the limitations thereon. While the focus is primarily Greece and Rome, a few chapters address slavery and manumission in other time periods.²⁵

One trend found in recent edited volumes, and alluded to above as a trend more broadly in ancient slavery studies, is an explicitly comparative agenda. For instance, the essays in Thomas Wiedemann and Jane Gardner's edited volume *Representing the Body of the Slave* (2002) examine how the enslaved body is written about and depicted in art in Greece, Rome, early medieval Britain, the Ottoman Empire, North America, the Caribbean, and Brazil.²⁶ In *Slave Systems: Ancient and Modern* (2008), edited by Enrico Dal Lago and Constantina Katsari, each chapter takes a comparative approach to "slave systems" in the ancient Mediterranean and modern Atlantic.²⁷ In the same year, Dal Lago and Katsari published another edited volume, *From Captivity to Freedom: Themes in Ancient and Modern Slavery* (2008), which applies a comparative lens, albeit in a slightly different way than *Slave Systems*; within each thematic section (e.g. "captives and slaves," "female slaves," "slave rebellions," etc.), there are two paired papers — one ancient, one modern — on a particular theme.²⁸ Stephen Hodkinson and Dick Geary's *Slaves and Religions in Graeco-Roman Antiquity and Modern Brazil* (2012) examines the roles of enslaved people in religion — and in particular their agency (including resistance and the formation of identities and com-

---

23 E.g. Garrido-Hory 2002; Alvar and Hernández Guerra 2002; Anastasiadis and Doukellis 2005; Serghidou 2007; Iriarte Goñi 2007; Gonzales 2008; Arcuri, Caliri, Pinzone 2012; Compagno, Gállego, García Mac Gaw 2013; Reduzzi Merola 2014; Beltrán, Sastra Prats, Valdés Guía 2015; Cortadella Moral, Olesti Vila, Sierra Martín 2018; Martínez Lacy 2018; Gonzales 2019; Alvar Nuño 2019; Reduzzi Merola, Caravaglios, Bramante 2020; Pałuchowski 2022.
24 Serghidou 2007.
25 Gonzales 2008.
26 Wiedemann and Gardner 2002.
27 Dal Lago and Katsari 2008.
28 Katsari and Dal Lago 2008.

munities) – in both antiquity and modern Brazil.²⁹ And John Bodel and Walter Scheidel's *On Human Bondage: After Slavery and Social Death: A Comparative Study* (2017) provides a critical re-examination of Orlando Patterson's groundbreaking sociological study *Slavery and Social Death* (1982) (see further ch. 1.4),³⁰ with chapters ranging from Greece and Rome to the societies of early modern Europe, Han China, colonial Brazil, and others.³¹

Other edited volumes have focused on particular approaches to, or themes in, ancient slavery. For example, *Reading Ancient Slavery* (2011), edited by Richard Alston, Edith Hall, and Laura Proffitt, aims to recover the voices and agency of enslaved people from both literature and art.³² The contributors to *Penser l'esclavage: Modèles antiques, pratiques modernes, problématiques contemporaines* (2012), edited by Gonzales, seek to apply to ancient slavery methods for studying modern slavery, and moreover to look at slavery alongside other forms of subjection and dependence.³³ Ben Akrigg and Rob Tordoff's *Slaves and Slavery in Ancient Greek Comic Drama* (2013) addresses various aspects of slavery in Greek Old and New Comedy, a topic that has received considerably less attention than slavery in Roman comedy.³⁴ And most recently, C.W. Marshall and I co-edited a volume on *Slavery and Sexuality in Classical Antiquity* (2021), exploring the relationship between sex and slavery in Greece and Rome and calling attention to the ways in which enslaved people were not only sexual objects but also subjects with agency.³⁵

Finally, a couple of handbooks to ancient slavery have been published in recent years, as well as brief overviews of Greek slavery in various handbooks and encyclopedias.³⁶ Keith Bradley and Paul Cartledge's *Cambridge World History of Slavery*, vol. 1: *The Ancient Mediterranean World* (2011), is the first volume of a four-set series that tracks slavery from antiquity to today, with chapters covering the ancient Near East, classical Greece, the Hellenistic world, and

---

29 Hodkinson and Geary 2012.
30 Bodel and Scheidel 2017; Patterson 1982.
31 Chapters on Greece: Lewis 2017, Hunt 2017b; Greece and Rome: Harper 2017.
32 Alston, Hall, Proffitt 2011.
33 Gonzales 2012.
34 Akrigg and Tordoff 2013.
35 Kamen and Marshall 2021. The chapters on Greece are Gaca 2021, Glazebrook 2021a, Marshall 2021, Matuszewski 2021, Porter 2021, Wilson 2021, and Wrenhaven 2021.
36 For brief surveys of Greek slavery, see duBois 2012 [2009], Lewis 2015, Hunt 2015a (ancient slavery including Greek), Tordoff 2017, Kamen 2020 [2013]. For an annotated bibliography of scholarship on Greek slavery, see Zelnick-Abramovitz 2014.

Rome.³⁷ Also quite useful is *The Oxford Handbook of Greek and Roman Slaveries* (2016–), edited by Stephen Hodkinson, Marc Kleijwegt, and Kostas Vlassopoulos.³⁸ Currently online and eventually to be published in print, this handbook contains short chapters on particular types of evidence (e.g. epigraphic, papyrological, visual, material) and particular themes (e.g. gender and slavery, slaves as active subjects, slaves and religion), with most chapters addressing their topic in both the Greek and Roman worlds.

1.4 Defining slavery

As mentioned above, one of the major debates about ancient slavery today is the question of how to define slavery.³⁹ Scholars of Greek slavery – and slavery more generally – have long held that slavery is best understood as a relationship of property. Indeed, this idea can be traced back at least as far as Finley, who defined the slave both as property (from a legal perspective) and as an outsider (from a sociological perspective).⁴⁰ Aristotle himself wrote that the slave is "a sort of animate piece of property (*ktēma ti empsuchon*)" (*Pol.* 1253b33) (see further ch. 8.1).⁴¹ This is, moreover, the definition laid down by the League of Nations in 1926: "Slavery is the status or condition of a person over whom any or all the powers attaching to the right of ownership are exercised."⁴²

Nonetheless, not everyone has deemed this definition of slavery adequate, including Patterson, who offered up his own definition in 1982: namely, that slavery is best understood as *social death*. In Patterson's often-quoted words, slavery is "the permanent, violent domination of natally alienated and generally dishonored persons."⁴³ This definition has long been widely influential, but it

---

37 Bradley and Cartledge 2011. On Greek slavery, the relevant chapters are Braund 2011 (slave supply), Cartledge 2011 (Helots), Golden 2011 (slavery and the family), Hunt 2011 (slavery in literature), Rihll (slavery in classical Athens), Kyrtatas 2011 (slavery and the economy), McKeown 2011 (slave resistance), Morris 2011 (slavery and archaeology).
38 Hodkinson, Kleijwegt, Vlassopoulos 2016–.
39 On defining slavery in a global perspective, see Lewis 2022d.
40 Finley 1968.
41 For this translation of *ktēma ti empsuchon*, see Greenwood 2022, 338; on the importance of translating the indefinite *ti* here, see Greenwood 2022: 343–346. See also Arist. *Pol.* 1254a14–18, where the slave is said to be property (*ktēma*) belonging by nature to another human being.
42 League of Nations, Slavery Convention, 25 September 1926, Article I.
43 Patterson 1982, 13; Patterson has since revised his definition (see below). See also Ismard 2019, 23–35, who finds the property definition insufficient in and of itself (while still arguing that it was an important part of how the Athenians conceived of slavery).

has recently been called into question by scholars of slavery, including scholars of Greek slavery. Vlassopoulos, for example, does not find Patterson's concept of social death entirely satisfactory, in part because (Vlassopoulos argues) viewing enslaved people as socially dead does not give them their due as agents with their own subjectivities (see further ch. 6).[44] He does agree with Patterson, however, that the property definition is insufficient. At least for the Greeks, Vlassopoulos argues, the conception of slavery as a relationship of *domination* was most salient.[45] He contends that Aristotle's definition (on which most scholars build implicitly or explicitly) is not in fact the conventional way that Greeks thought about slavery: rather, Aristotle's ideas were idiosyncratic, rooted in his opposition to the idea that slavery was only by convention and to Plato's idea that all forms of rulership were the same. Dismissing Aristotle, then, Vlassopoulos builds his case for the Greeks' conceptualization of slavery from their own vocabulary of slavery, arguing that because *doulos* — the most common word for slave — is used in opposition to *eleutheros* (typically translated as "free," but the primary meaning of which, he asserts, is "in control of oneself"), *doulos* must have the primary meaning of "under another's control." This implies, he says, that at least when the Greeks use *doulos* (and related nouns and verbs), a relationship of domination is always meant, as it is when we see the word used metaphorically.[46]

To Vlassopoulos' mind, shifting how we think about and define slavery has important ramifications. As opposed to focusing on the binary relationship between "master" and "slave," that is, the relationship that is predicated on ownership, thinking of slavery in terms of domination makes it possible to situate the enslaver-enslaved relationship within a larger web of power relations. It also allows us to view slavery as ever-changing and always under negotiation,

---

44 See Vlassopoulos 2018 and 2021 (esp. ch. 7 on slavery from the enslaved person's perspective).

45 On slavery as a relationship of domination: Vlassopoulos 2011a; see also Vlassopoulos 2011b, which draws on Aristotle's concept of *koinonia* ("community") as a model that existed in conjunction with the property model. This conception of slavery, Vlassopoulos says, allows us to recognize that enslaved people formed parts of communities (not only of other enslaved people but also of metics and citizens), fashioning identities and building support networks apart from their enslavers.

46 Vlassopoulos 2011a argues further that this helps explain why the Greeks were often imprecise in distinguishing between different types of slaves: from their perspective, all slaves were dominated, thus all were *douloi*. Moreover, he says, it helps explain the Greeks' inability to imagine a world without slavery, since they could not conceive of a world without power relations. On the metaphor of slavery, see Brock 2007; Hunt 2011, 23–25; and ch. 8.3.

characteristics that the property definition does not fully accommodate.⁴⁷ Vlassopoulos has therefore advocated for a new approach to slavery, namely, that we view it as a non-static phenomenon composed of three interrelated conceptual systems: a definitional one (namely, slavery as property); a prototypical one (slavery as a distinct legal and social status); and, most innovatively, a cluster of related modalities (e.g. slavery as a relationship of domination, an instrumental relationship, an asymmetrical negotiation of power, an asymmetrical relationship of benefaction and reward, etc.).⁴⁸

Lewis' criticism of Patterson is different from Vlassopoulos', targeting in particular Patterson's dismissal of property as the primary definition of slavery.⁴⁹ Arguing that Patterson's understanding of property is overly broad, Lewis demonstrates that the legal definition of ownership proposed in 1961 by the jurist A.M. Honoré perfectly describes slavery in societies across time and space.⁵⁰ Lewis does, however, find some aspects of Patterson's social death definition useful, especially in trying to understand slavery from the enslaved person's perspective, rather than the enslaver's. He concludes, then, that the property definition should be used *along with* Patterson's definition.⁵¹ A complementary solution has been proposed by Noel Lenski, who suggests adding property to Patterson's definition of slavery to form a definition of "ideal slavery" (i.e., slavery is in its most complete form): thus, "slavery is the enduring, violent domination of natally alienated and inherently dishonored individuals (slaves) that are controlled by owners (masters) who are permitted in their social context to use and enjoy, sell and exchange, and abuse and destroy them as property."⁵² Forsdyke, too, has proposed an emended definition: "The state of being controlled by force and/or by social consensus (as expressed by laws,

---

47 Vlassopoulos 2011a.
48 Vlassopoulos 2021.
49 Lewis 2015, 2017 (for an extended criticism of Patterson), and 2018a. See also Harris 2012, 352–354, on whom Lewis draws.
50 See Honoré 1961, for whom the key components of ownership are the right to possess, right to use, right to manage, right to income, right to capital, right to security, absence of term, transmissibility, prohibition of harmful use, and liability to execution.
51 Lewis 2017, 48: "Instead of a zero-sum standoff between Patterson's definition and the traditional property definition, we should move toward a more productive synergy. Accepting the property definition as a taxonomic tool, we can proceed to use Patterson's variables (permanence, violent domination, natal alienation, and dishonor) as an analytical strategy to understand the most basic and cross-culturally consistent *social effects* of slave ownership. This shifts the perspective to the slave himself (or herself), allowing us to gain a more rounded understanding of slavery as a historical phenomenon."
52 Lenski 2018b, 51.

institutions, and other cultural practices) by another human being who makes use of one's labor and has total power to use, enjoy and abuse one as they see fit."[53] Like Patterson and Vlassopoulos, she stresses domination more than legal ownership, but she omits Patterson's focus on natal alienation and dishonor, on the grounds that not all enslaved people in Greece were displaced from their homelands and some do seem to have had (at least some) honor.

Patterson himself later revised his definition of slavery, developing a new definition that he felt better applied to slavery of all periods (including today), namely, "*the violent, corporeal possession of socially isolated and parasitically degraded persons.*"[54] Since modern slavery is not always permanent (in the sense of being inherited), he removed that aspect from his definition. The addition of "possession" alludes to the ownership dimension, with "corporeal" hinting at the frequently carnal aspect of the enslaver's domination of his slave's body. Patterson's other changes included replacing the term "natal alienation" with the broader "social isolation" (since modern-day sex slaves might be enslaved within their own communities) and adding "parasitical degradation" to emphasize the fact that the enslaved person "parasitically" aggrandizes the power and honor of their enslaver. These revisions yield a definition that addresses many, if not all, of the concerns leveled by scholars in recent years. While there is not yet consensus, it does appear that a hybrid definition best encapsulates the various facets of slavery.

1.5 Slave societies?

A second issue of debate centers on Finley's famous distinction between "slave societies" and "slave-owning societies." In what he called "slave societies," slaves make up a certain percentage of the population (roughly 20%) and are fundamental to the economy, with their labor producing a surplus for the elites; in "slave-owning societies" or "societies with slaves" (as they have come to be called), slaves do not reach the requisite percentage and play a less fundamental role in the economy.[55] Finley asserted, moreover, that there were only five

---

53 Forsdyke 2021, 39–40.
54 Patterson 2012, 329; italics original.
55 Finley first drew this distinction in 1968, 308. On the background for Finley's ideas on this subject, see Vlassopoulos 2016a and 2021, 15–24; Lenski 2018a, 2018b, 16–18. That enslaved people must represent over 20% of the population to qualify as a slave society, see Hopkins 1978, 99; on Finley's refusal to play the "numbers game," see Finley 1998 [1980], 147–148. On the criterion of surplus wealth generation for the elite, see Finley 1998 [1980], 150 (a criterion

genuine slave societies in world history: classical Greece (except Sparta), Rome, Brazil, the Caribbean, and the United States.[56] Although these tenets were long accepted, they have recently come into question. In the edited volume *What is a Slave Society? The Practice of Slavery in Global Perspective* (2018) — an example of the type of global slavery studies mentioned above (ch. 1.1) — the editors Noel Lenski and Catherine Cameron challenge the binary of "slave society" versus "society with slaves" (although some of the volume's contributors continue to find it a useful heuristic).[57] Exploring the binary's applicability (or in most cases, lack thereof) to a wide range of societies, the volume also challenges the premise that only five societies qualify as "slave societies," even by Finley's own definition. The volume thus shows that there are many more "slave societies" than Finley thought, including non-Western ones — a conclusion that has ramifications in turn for how unique we think Greek slavery was.[58]

Lenski himself has pointed out two key problems with Finley's model: its ethnocentrism (i.e., its Western focus) and its "categorical imprecision." By the latter phrase, Lenski refers to the model's too-rigid use of binary categories; the lack of clear-cut boundaries to the notion of "society"; the model's being built on observations derived entirely from Western social, political, and economic structures; and its emphasis on similarities and its glossing over differences.[59] Lenski therefore proposes an alternative to Finley's model, one focusing on the "intensity" of slaveholding practices, measuring these practices against an

---

adopted by Hunt 2018a, but see the criticism of Vlassopoulos 2016a, 95–96; 2016b, 8; 2021, 177). For a challenge to the connection between slave numbers and the economic and cultural importance of slavery in a society, see Hezser 2016. For a challenge to the connection between the economic importance of slavery and its cultural, social, and political importance, see Vlassopoulos 2016a, 96; 2016b, 8–9; 2021, 177–178. For less economic (and more social) criteria for determining a slave society, see Andreau and Descat 2011 [2006], 13–16.

56 He omits Brazil in Finley 1968 but includes it elsewhere (e.g. Finley 1998 [1980], 148). Although Finley includes "classical Greece" on this list, Lenski points out that Finley himself said he meant primarily classical Athens by this (2018b, 40–41).

57 Lenski and Cameron 2018b and many of the chapters in Lenski and Cameron 2018a. For other challenges to this binary: Heszer 2016; Vlassopoulos 2016a, 95–97; 2016b, 8–11; 2021, 176–183; Lewis 2018a (esp. ch. 4) and 2018c. That the concept of "slave society" is in fact useful, see Hunt 2018a (on classical Athens); see also Hunt 2018b, 50–51. Although Lewis 2018a challenges the validity of the term "slave society," he does use it to evaluate whether each society he studies would fit the bill for a Finleyan "slave society."

58 See similarly Lewis 2018a (esp. ch. 4).

59 See Lenski 2018b, 24–38 on Finley's ethnocentrism (see also Vlassopoulos 2021, 178–179 for a critique of Finley's focus on Western societies); Lenski 2018b, 38–46 on categorical imprecision.

"ideal" form of slavery (see his definition above in ch. 1.4) that is maximally advantageous for the slaveowner (thus drawing on the property definition) and maximally disadvantageous for the enslaved person (thus drawing on the social death definition).[60] In this scheme, societies would be classified not as a "slave society" or "society with slaves," but instead with regard to how well they conform to various elements of an "ideal" slave society, the most "intensive" ones being those that most closely map onto the ideal.

Vlassopoulos, too, finds many faults with the dichotomy "slave society" versus "society with slaves" and proposes getting rid of it entirely.[61] For him, the model focuses too much on how the *elites* derived their surplus (omitting other, non-elite types of slaveholders) and fails to distinguish between different kinds of slaving strategies.[62] More useful, Vlassopoulos says, would be to set out various axes for measuring similarities and differences between societies. For example, one axis would measure the extent of slave ownership in a society (that is, whether it was limited to the elites, or not); another axis would gauge whether a society had other sources of revenue and labor; and a third axis would measure how the language of slavery was used figuratively to refer to other kinds of relationships. His solution, then, is different from Lenski's, but the two models are compatible, as he himself acknowledges.

1.6 Conclusion

Much recent scholarship on Greek slavery has been a response to the influential work of Finley from the mid- to late-twentieth century, including his definition of slavery and the distinction he drew between slave societies and slave-owning societies. Indeed, two of the most recent monographs on ancient slavery, those of Vlassopoulos and Lewis, are explicitly framed as criticisms of Finley's approach and many of his conclusions, with many other works implicitly engaging with the ideas of Finley in one way or another. The specific topics explored in monographs the past twenty-five years include the roles of enslaved people in Greek warfare, the reception of Greek (and Roman) slavery in the contemporary world, the practice and conceptualization of manumission in Greece, and the importance of public slaves in classical Athens. In addition, a handful of gen-

---

60 Lenski 2018b, 47–57. This model is cited approvingly by Lewis 2018c; Vlassopoulos 2021, 182–183; Forsdyke 2021, 49–50.
61 Vlassopoulos 2021, 176–183.
62 For these "slaving strategies" (e.g. working in mines, working independently, etc.), see Vlassopoulos 2021, ch. 4.

eral introductions to the subject of Greek (and Roman) slavery have been written for audiences of lay readers or students, and edited volumes and handbooks on various aspects of Greek and Roman slavery have proliferated, with an increasing emphasis on looking at these slaveries in a comparative or global context.

2 Epichoric Slave Systems

Slavery was not the same at all times and at all places in Greece. Rather than treating "Greek slavery" as a monolith, then, a recent move, pioneered by Lewis, has been to think in terms of "epichoric slave systems," which differ from place to place and from time to time.[1] In this chapter, I trace recent trends in work on a set of distinct epichoric slave systems, namely, those found in the Mycenaean and Homeric worlds, archaic and classical Athens, Sparta, and Crete. This is meant not to be a comprehensive survey, but instead to give a sense for the range of "Greek slaveries" that scholars have studied.

2.1 Slavery in the Mycenaean and Homeric worlds

Our earliest evidence for slavery in the Greek world comes from the Mycenaean period, in the form of bureaucratic clay tablets from the poleis of Pylos and Knossos.[2] These tablets were administrative records of palace operations, recorded by scribes in Linear B (an early syllabary for writing Greek), which include details about the manufacture and distribution of commodities.[3] The tablets frequently refer to the status category *do-e-ro* (masculine) / *do-e-ra* (feminine), a word that later becomes *doulos* (the most common classical Greek word for slave).[4] Unfortunately, however, there is not enough evidence to determine the precise status of these people. Although they appear to have been bought and sold — in fact, two contracts of *do-e-ro* sales survive from Mycenaean Knossos — scholars tend to view them not as chattel but as something else.[5] Dimitri Nakassis, for example, renders the term as "servant" rather than "slave," pointing out that many of them are high-ranking servants of the gods.[6] Indeed, while a small subset of these individuals' names are paired with the names of other people (most likely their owners), the majority are paired with the name of a god or gods (also likely their owners).

---

[1] Lewis 2018a; Vlassopoulos 2021 (esp. ch. 8) also argues against viewing Greek slavery as a monolith but instead as a system of different slaveries.
[2] On Mycenaean slavery, see Fischer 2008, Andreau and Descat 2011 [2006], 17–19.
[3] See Nakassis 2013 for a rich accounting of what these tablets can tell us about Mycenaean society.
[4] On the etymology of *do-e-ro* and *doulos*, see Gschnitzer 1976, 2–8.
[5] That they are not chattel, see Andreau and Descat 2011 [2006], 17–19. On the contracts of sale, see Olivier 1987.
[6] Nakassis 2013, 14–15.

We are on slightly stronger ground when it comes to understanding "Homeric" slavery.[7] Although the poems of Homer are set in the Mycenaean period, they were orally composed over many centuries and only set down in writing in the 8th century BCE. What we have in these poems, then, is a blend of details from different eras, with social institutions that are probably most similar to those of the 8th century.[8] In Homer, the most common terms for "slave" are *dmōs* (masculine) and *dmōiē* (feminine), referring to an enslaved man and woman of the house respectively and stressing their close connection with the household. *Dmōs* therefore has some semantic overlap with the Homeric word *oikeus*, which refers to a "person of the household" in general, sometimes free and sometimes slave; the term *amphipolos*, by contrast, specifically designates an enslaved woman waiting on the mistress of the house. *Andrapodon*, literally "man-footed creature," appears only once in Homer to refer to human war booty (the term becomes more common in classical Greek); also rare is *doulos*, which refers specifically to unfree legal status, though it may have been used more frequently outside of epic.[9] Although slavery features in both of Homer's epics, the depiction of the institution is not identical in the two poems: in the *Iliad*, the story of the Trojan War, we generally find people being enslaved through war (i.e., facing their "day of slavery," *doulion ēmar* [*Il.* 6.463]); in the *Odyssey*, people are already enslaved. Odysseus' estate, albeit on a larger scale than average, provides a glimpse into the types of domestic labor (including wet-nursing, cooking, cleaning, and spinning and carding wool) and agricultural labor (primarily animal husbandry, cereal farming, and arboriculture) performed by enslaved women and men, with the wet-nurse Eurycleia and the swineherd Eumaeus serving as paradigms of "good slaves" (see further ch. 4.1).[10] Dating to around the same time as the first writing down of Homer's poems are the poems of Hesiod. In his *Works and Days*, which treats the subject of agriculture, Hesiod states explicitly that a slave, and in particular a female slave, is a necessity for working a medium-sized farm, along with a house and an ox (403–406). There are also scattered references in the *Works and Days* to enslaved people laboring

---

[7] On Homeric slavery, see Andreau and Descat 2011 [2006], 19–25; Lewis 2018a, ch. 5; Harris 2012 and 2020; Van Wees 2021.
[8] This was first argued most compellingly by Morris 1986, and is now followed by most scholars (see Lewis 2018a, ch. 5).
[9] For the meaning of these terms in Homer, see Gschnitzer 1976, 46–72 (*dmōs*), 16–19 (*oikeus*), 22–32 (*amphipolos*), 14–15 (*andrapodon*), 8–13 (*doulos*).
[10] On the enslaved labor found on Odysseus' estate, see Lewis 2018a, 114–117. Eumaeus famously states that on the day of slavery, Zeus removes half of a man's virtue (*aretē*; *Od.* 17.322–323).

in the fields, suggesting that in addition to being employed by the elite on a relatively large scale, they were also used as well as on a lesser scale by the sub-elite.[11]

Until recently, the conventional wisdom was that the slave system we find in Homer and Hesiod was not one of chattel slavery: that is, one in which enslaved people were owned as property. This argument is predicated, implicitly or explicitly, on the observation that the relationship between enslaver and enslaved is generally represented in Homer as one of intimacy, with the enslaved person considered part of the family.[12] It is, however, a mistake to treat Homer (or Hesiod, for that matter) as a straightforward window onto the reality of slavery in 8th century Greece; after all, his poems are literary representations shaped by generic and ideological concerns (see further ch. 8.1).[13] Moreover, Edward Harris, followed by Lewis, has shown that enslaved people in Homer were indeed considered property who could be bought and sold and over whom all rights of ownership were exercised.[14] Harris and Lewis have also argued, relatedly, that these individuals played an important role in the economy of Homeric society, since they bolstered the prestige and dominance of the elite.[15] We have no reason to doubt, then, that a form of chattel slavery existed at this time – even if the nature and scale of the institution looks different from what we find in the late archaic and classical periods.

2.2 Slavery in archaic Athens

In the early 6th century BCE, Athens was torn by civil strife between rich and poor citizens. Many of the poor had become *hektēmoroi*, literally "sixth-parters" or sharecroppers, who paid rich landowners a portion (likely one-sixth) of the produce they harvested. Other poor people were in debt bondage to their creditors, to be released only when they had paid off their debts. Still others were enslaved for debt and sold abroad as slaves by their creditors. It was in this context, in 594/3 BCE, that the Athenian lawgiver Solon made reforms referred to as *seisachtheia*, literally "shaking off of burdens" (Arist. *Ath. Pol.* 6.1, 12.4; Plut. *Sol.* 15.3).[16] This entailed releasing all those Athenians who were in debt

---

11 Lewis 2018a, 117–118; Van Wees 2021.
12 See Andreau and Descat 2011 [2006], 25.
13 See Thalmann 1998.
14 Harris 2012 and Lewis 2018a, ch. 5; see also Van Wees 2021.
15 Harris 2012, followed by Lewis 2018a, ch. 5.
16 For various approaches to Solon, see the essays in Blok and Lardinois 2006.

bondage, bringing back to Athens those who had been sold abroad as slaves, and preventing the enslavement of all Athenians to their fellow Athenians in the future. While conventional wisdom holds that Solon abolished debt bondage, Harris has argued that Solon abolished only enslavement for debt (also known as debt slavery); debt bondage, he argues, did continue.[17] Other scholarship has added to this argument by positing that the threat faced by Athenians before Solon's reforms went beyond slavery for debt and debt bondage, both of which were legal at the time, and extended even to extra-legal enslavement by force. For this reason, Solon had to revise not just the laws themselves but also how people *thought about* the law, and did so by enforcing the idea that the rule of law was supreme.[18]

If, as nearly all scholars agree, Athenians could not be enslaved to their fellow Athenians after Solon's reforms, what were the ramifications of this for the institution of slavery? Finley famously argued that it was Solon's reforms, at least in part, that led to the development of chattel slavery. More precisely, he argued that three conditions produced the demand for chattel slaves: 1) the concentration of land in a limited number of hands, thus requiring this land to be worked by individuals outside the family of the landowners; 2) "sufficient development of commodity production and markets"; and 3) a negative condition, the lack of an internal labor supply, compelling landowners to turn to outsiders for labor.[19] All three conditions, he says, were met in Athens after the reforms of Solon, which precipitated "the advance, hand in hand, of freedom *and* slavery" — a now-famous formulation.[20] That is, it was the newfound freedom of all Athenians — and relatedly, the proto-democracy of post-Solonian Athens — that drove the development of chattel slavery. While Finley could not claim that the same set of factors found in Athens were present in all archaic poleis, the linking of freedom/democracy and slavery has in fact been observed

---

17 For the argument that Solon abolished debt bondage, see Finley 1981, ch. 9 and more recently Hunt 2018b, 71. For the argument that Solon abolished debt slavery: Harris 2002. The distinction between these two modes of exploitation is that enslavement for debt makes someone the slave of their creditor (who thus has rights of ownership over them), whereas debt bondage is a status arising from pledging one's services as security for a debt: it is not permanent and the creditor does not have all of the rights of an owner.
18 Lewis 2004.
19 Finley 1998 [1980], ch. 2; for these conditions, see p. 154.
20 Finley 1981, 115.

elsewhere.[21] For instance, the Chians were believed (correctly or not) to be the first of the Greeks to employ "purchased slaves" (Athen. 6.265bc), doing so on a large scale (Thuc. 8.40.2); we also know they embarked on democracy very early, as attested by an inscription from 600–550 BCE discussing a council of the people (ML 8).

Finley's model for the development of chattel slavery was for many years accepted, receiving its first serious challenge in a 1996 article written by Tracey Rihll.[22] Although Rihll shares with Finley the belief that Athens became a slave society only in the archaic period, she disagrees with him on several points, including his premise that demand for slaves drove the supply. She details Greece's early expansion into peripheral territories, through which captives were produced, and the growth of the slave trade, by which these captives were distributed to the core of the Greek world from the margins.[23] It was this supply, she suggests, that drove the demand for chattel slaves, rather than vice versa. Correspondingly, she argues (contrary to Finley) that freedom/democracy arose out of slavery, rather than vice versa, with the presence of enslaved people generating an awareness among free people of constraints they might have imposed on them.[24] While Rihll's essay was significant for challenging the status quo established by Finley, it has not been adopted in full by most scholars.

Certain points, however, have gained traction. Harris, for example, has advanced Rihll's argument that the practice of acquiring chattel slaves from outside was not an innovation of Solon's, demonstrating that we find it as early as Homer (see ch. 2.1). He does concede, however, that the importing of slaves may have increased after Solon's reforms.[25] Lewis, in turn, demonstrates that it was not the *fact* of importing slaves but the *strategies* for acquiring them that changed after Solon, including a turn toward trade rather than raiding and debt bondage; there was also a change in the ways the Athenians chose to exploit enslaved labor (e.g. turning toward commerce, manufacturing, and mining; see ch. 3.3).[26] We should always keep in mind, moreover, that the patterns of devel-

---

[21] Cf. Rihll 1996, 93–94, who argues that Finley's model is specific to Attica and does not work for other states, some of which had chattel slaves without a *seisachtheia* to create the "negative condition."
[22] Rihll 1996. For a brief recent summary of the problems with Finley's model, see Lewis 2022c, 71–73.
[23] Rihll 1996, 102–106.
[24] Rihll 1996, 106–111.
[25] Harris 2012; see also Van Wees 2021.
[26] Lewis 2018a, 120–121.

opment of chattel slavery found in Athens do not represent a universal: rather, the slave system of each polis evolved in its own distinct way.

2.3 Slavery in Sparta

A very different epichoric slave system is found in Sparta.[27] One issue of continued debate among scholars is the origins of the Spartans' slaves, the Helots, who worked the lands that neighbored Sparta, namely, Laconia and Messenia. It used to be conventional wisdom that the Helots were the descendants of preexisting free populations in these territories who had been conquered by the Spartans in the ninth and eighth centuries BCE.[28] In fact, according to some ancient sources, the Helots (*Heilōtes*) are so-called because of the conquest of Helos, a town in Laconia.[29] But this is likely a false etymology: among other reasons, it is hard to explain on linguistic grounds the spelling of *Heilōs*, which includes a letter (i.e., iota) not found in the place name *Helos*. It has also been suggested that the name might be derived from the Greek verb *haireō* (aor. *heilon*), "to catch," or *haliskomai* (aor. *healōn*), "to be caught," but that too presents challenges, since neither verb perfectly accounts for the morphological form *Heilōs*.[30] Both of these etymologies presuppose the conquest of a population, but the long-held view that the Helots were a conquered people has been challenged in recent years, in particular by Luraghi. More specifically, Luraghi argues that the conquest of Messenia and Laconia was not a reality but instead an ideologically and politically motivated fiction.[31] Rather than the enslavement of local populations in situ, he argues that what happened was a standardization in the seventh century BCE of various forms of dependent labor into one servile status (namely, "Helot"). The shared identity of Helots, then, had to do not with a shared ethnicity or origin but rather with their shared condition of enslavement under the Spartiates (full Spartan citizens).[32] A compatible suggestion,

---

[27] For overviews of current debates about Spartan slavery, see Cartledge 2011 and more recently Lewis 2021. See also Luraghi and Alcock 2003, an edited volume devoted to the major questions and approaches in the study of Helots.
[28] For this view, see Van Wees 2003; see also Cartledge 2003 and 2011, 76–78 (though he points out that the ancient sources themselves differ).
[29] See Hellanic. BNJ 4 F 188; Ephor. BNJ 70 F 117; Theopomp. BNJ 115 F 13.
[30] For *Heilōs* coming from a Greek verb meaning "catch" or "capture," see Cartledge 2002c [1973], 83. For a discussion of the debated etymology of *Heilōs*, see Ducat 1990, 8–11.
[31] Luraghi 2003.
[32] Luraghi 2002; see also Luraghi 2009, 270–274.

proposed by Jean Ducat, is that the system of helotage seen in the classical period evolved over time out of a system of slavery akin to what we see in Homer.[33] While both of these theories have found support, the conquest explanation continues to have strong adherents, and the question of the Helots' origins remains one that is hard to answer definitively.[34]

Another important issue debated by scholars is the status of Helots. The second century CE grammarian Pollux famously classified Helots, along with a handful of other dependent populations of the Greek world, as "between slave and free" (Poll. 3.83).[35] But what was this status, precisely? For a long time, scholars interpreted the Helots as serfs, and this is a view that is still held by some.[36] Other scholars, however, have pointed out the ways the term "serf" does not neatly map onto the Helots' status.[37] Recently, there has been a move, articulated most strongly by Lewis, to view Helots as chattel slaves. In addition to the fact that our classical sources consistently refer to Helots as *douloi* ("[chattel] slaves"), Lewis demonstrates that Helots meet the criteria of property, and thus should be considered chattel.[38] In fact, Lewis has argued that we should consider classical Sparta a genuine "slave society" (*pace* Finley; see ch. 1.5), and perhaps the most extreme one in the Greek world, since the Helots' agricultural labor not only provided the elites' wealth but allowed all economic classes the capacity to provide their required contribution to the public mess halls.[39]

A related debate exists over whether Helots were owned by individuals or by the state. Unsurprisingly, those who espouse the former view are those who consider Helots to be chattel slaves, whereas those holding the latter view argue that the Helots, while owned by the state, were assigned to individual Spartiates. The best evidence we have on this question is unfortunately ambiguous. Ephorus says that Helots were "slaves (*doulous*) on certain terms (*epi taktois tisin*)," namely, that "the one who holds (*ton echonta*)" a Helot could not man-

---

33 Ducat 2015; see similarly Welwei 2006, Lewis 2022c.
34 See Lewis 2021.
35 Following Pollux' classification of Helots: Finley 1981, ch. 7; cf. Lewis 2018a, 143–146, who deems Pollux' statement an inaccurate representation of helotage and other types of "helotic" slavery.
36 Helots as serfs: see de Ste. Croix 1981, 149; Fisher 2001 [1993], 23–32 ("community slaves or serfs"); Hunt 2017b and 2018a, 77–84.
37 See Forsdyke 2021, 45, who says that "chattel slave" does not neatly fit their status either.
38 Helots as chattel slaves: Ducat 1990 (esp. 19–29); Luraghi 2002, 230–235; Patterson 2003, 289–299; Lewis 2018a, ch. 6. Cf. Cartledge 2011, 75, who says that "Helots both were and were not *douloi*."
39 Lewis 2018a, 142–143.

umit or sell that Helot "outside the boundaries of Sparta" (BNJ 70 F 117).[40] Some scholars have taken this as evidence that Helots were individually owned, since the implication is that their "holders" could sell them *within* the city's boundaries.[41] However, this same passage has been taken to mean that the Helots were owned by the state, since only the state could manumit them.[42] But the capacity to manumit is not in itself evidence of state ownership; after all, other poleis were able to free (privately owned) chattel slaves under certain circumstances (see ch. 7.1).

Another issue under discussion has been that of Helot numbers, with current estimates trending toward a lower ratio of Helots to Spartiates than used to be thought. Our best direct testimony is Herodotus, who says that each Spartiate who fought at the Battle of Plataea (479 BCE) was accompanied by seven Helot soldiers (9.10.1, 28.2, 29.1). Taking the 7:1 ratio of Helots to Spartiates as an *upper* limit and drawing on both textual sources and topographical evidence (e.g. how much land each *klaros*, or "allotment," contained), Thomas Figueira estimates that in c. 480/79 BCE, there were 75,000–118,000 Helots, which represents three to five times the number of Spartiates (who at that time were at their highest number).[43] Scheidel, by contrast, downplays the ancient evidence (including the testimony of Herodotus) and designs what he calls a "simplified model" for determining Helot numbers, focusing on two key factors: production (i.e., how much food the Spartans' land likely produced) and consumption (i.e., how many citizens and Helots that land could have supported). Although this model does not yield a definitive answer to the question of Helot numbers – no model can – it does provide a few sets of possible numerical ranges (of which 113,983 is the lowest proposed number, 218,756 the highest) based on hypothetical carrying capacities of the land.[44]

Finally, one methodological trend that has developed in the past twenty years has been to study Helots alongside similar (better-understood) status groups in other historical societies. Thus, for example, Hodkinson looks at serfdom in Russia, slavery in the American South, and slavery in pre-colonial Africa, in order to hypothesize about what Helot-Spartiate relations might have

---

40 Lewis 2018a, 137–139 argues that underlying this restriction (and the restriction on manumission, below) was a desire to preserve the slave supply, especially since Sparta did not engage in foreign trade like other large poleis did.
41 See Ducat 1990, 21–22; Luraghi 2002, 230–231; Lewis 2018a, 128–129.
42 Cartledge 2003, 17–20 and 2011, 81–82.
43 Figueira 2003; for these figures, see p. 220.
44 Scheidel 2003; for these figures, see p. 243.

looked like.⁴⁵ Hans Van Wees, in turn, uses the parallel of the Spanish domination of native Central Americans to make his case for viewing the Helots as "conquest serfs" akin to many other subjugated populations.⁴⁶ And Luraghi discusses various comparative approaches to helotage, examining the ways that ancient authors compared slavery in Sparta to that in other Greek poleis (e.g. Crete, Thessaly, Chios) as well as evaluating the cross-cultural comparisons that scholars like Hodkinson and Van Wees have made. Ultimately, Luraghi finds the comparative approach useful for understanding the historical development of helotage, in particular in helping us see the ways that Spartan slavery is a less unique system of exploitation than both the ancients and modern scholars usually hold.⁴⁷

2.4 Slavery in Crete

We have a surprisingly large amount of information about the slave system in Crete, due primarily to the enormous law code preserved at Gortyn (*IC* IV 72), inscribed ca. 450 BCE (but whose laws seem to date back much earlier, namely, to the sixth or even seventh century BCE). These laws reveal a spectrum of statuses in Gortyn ranging from free citizens, to free non-citizens or second-class citizens (*apetairoi*), to foreigners, to those in debt bondage, to people of servile status.⁴⁸ Particularly striking is that the law code reveals different penalties for crimes committed by and against different status groups, although fine-grained distinctions between intermediate categories are not always made in these cases. For example, when it comes to rape, if the victim is an enslaved person, the penalty is 1/40th the penalty for a free victim, and if the rapist is an enslaved person, the penalty is twice as high as for a free rapist.⁴⁹ Our picture of Cretan slavery can be supplemented by the insights we get from Aristotle's discussion in the *Politics* of Cretan society, which he compares and contrasts to Sparta.⁵⁰ For example, Aristotle points out that whereas Helots repeatedly revolt in Sparta, this does not happen in Crete; according to Aristotle, this is because Cretan

---

45 Hodkinson 2003 (= 2008).
46 Van Wees 2003.
47 Luraghi 2009.
48 On the range of status groups of Gortyn, see Link 1994, 9–51; Gagarin and Perlman 2016, 77–84.
49 The penalties for rape represent an oft-cited example: Gagarin 2010, 17–18; Lewis 2018a, 152; Gagarin and Perlman 2016, 82.
50 Sparta: Arist. *Pol.* 1269a29–1271b19; Crete: Arist. *Pol.* 1271b20–1272b23.

cities do not engage in war with poleis outside of Crete, and when they are at war with one another, they refuse to ally themselves with their neighbors' deserters — thus disincentivizing enslaved people from deserting (*Pol.* 1269a36–b5, 1272b16–22). Lewis thinks a more likely explanation has to do with the distribution and management of Cretan slaves: the proximity of farms to their owners (as compared to the situation in Sparta) meant that managing slaves was easier and that enslaved people did not have the same opportunities to revolt.[51]

A couple of issues related to Cretan slavery have attracted scholarly attention in recent years. One has to do with the terminology used for unfree labor and its implications for the types of servile status that existed in Crete.[52] The Gortyn Law Code uses both *dōlos* and *woikeus* for unfree people, and it is not entirely clear what distinction (if any) exists between these two terms. Michael Gagarin follows the scholars who argue that *dōlos* refers to imported chattel slaves, *woikeus* (the older term) to indigenous serfs, though he notes that these two groups are most often treated the same under the law.[53] *Dōlos*, he adds, can also be used in a broader sense (i.e., encompassing *woikeus*) in order to designate servile as opposed to free status. Lewis, by contrast, drawing on a point made over a hundred years ago, argues that *dōlos* and *woikeus* are actually synonyms, both meaning chattel slave. Since the two terms never appear side-by-side in the code, they must be interchangeable. The only reason for the variation in their use, he suggests, is the compositional history of the code: the laws were assembled over many years and their original language was preserved when the code was inscribed. He concludes that there is no such thing as a "serf" in Crete and that all servile people were considered chattel.[54]

Another scholarly debate has to do with the question of the seemingly privileged status of enslaved people in Crete, at least in comparison with elsewhere in Greece. For instance, it appears from the law code that they were permitted to

---

51 Lewis 2018a, 159.
52 The extensive vocabulary for slavery in Crete is hard to unpack. In addition to the terms attested epigraphically (e.g. *dōlos*, *woikeus*), we also find references in literature to *klarōtai*, *mnoïtai*, *chrusōnētai*, *amphamiōtai*, among other terms. On the Cretan vocabulary for slavery, see Link 1994, 30–48, 2001; concise summaries can be found in Lewis 2018a, 150n10; Pałuchowski 2018, 4.
53 See Willetts 1967; Gagarin 2010; see also Gagarin and Perlman 2016, 81–82; Bile 2019. For a reconstruction of the development of chattel slavery and serfdom in Crete, see Pałuchowski 2018.
54 Lewis 2013; 2015; 2018a, 150–153; forthcoming. On the synonymous status of these two terms, see also Finley 1981, 135–137; Link 2001.

marry, own property, and participate in litigation.⁵⁵ And as Adam Pałuchowski has pointed out, they were apparently not subject to corporal punishment for their offenses, as enslaved people were elsewhere (see ch. 4).⁵⁶ Indeed, Aristotle says, albeit hyperbolically, that the Cretans grant their slaves (*doulois*) "all the same things" (*talla tauta*) they grant to free people, except for gymnastic training and possession of arms (*Pol.* 1264a21–22). Lewis contends, however, that we should view these not as *rights* but *privileges*, arguing further that they were designed less for the enslaved person's advantage than to enhance the property rights of the slaveowner. Allowing marriage, for example, was a means of incentivizing good behavior, and even more importantly of increasing the enslaved population.⁵⁷ Moreover, some of the apparent rights (and obligations) turn out to be mirages if the code is read carefully: Lewis argues that although the code refers (in what he says is a sort of shorthand) to enslaved people paying fines and having damages paid to them for a variety of offenses, it is more likely, based on the laws about enslavers' liability for enslaved debtors, that the enslaver paid and received money on behalf of enslaved people in other circumstances too.⁵⁸ However, this does not mean that slaves could not *de facto* own money or belongings — they probably could, even if they could not do so *de iure*.⁵⁹

A final issue has been whether to consider Gortyn and other Cretan cities as "slave societies" in the Finleyan sense (see ch. 1.5). In the past, scholars — to the extent that they devoted attention to Cretan slavery at all — denied Cretan *poleis* this title, primarily because they assumed that the agricultural labor was performed not by slaves but by serfs. As noted above, however, Lewis has shown that all Cretan slaves fit the criteria of chattel, and moreover that they played a key role in the economy. Indeed, their performance of agricultural labor is what allowed all Cretan citizens to pay their required tithe (a percentage of their produce) to the common mess halls, thus guaranteeing their membership in the civic community. Having their slaves perform this labor also freed up the Cretans to devote themselves to military pursuits. In this way, Gortyn and many other Cretan cities can indeed be considered "slave societies."⁶⁰

---

55 See Garlan 1988 [1982], 100; see also Gagarin 2010, who argues that *woikeis* may have had greater rights than *doloi*.
56 Pałuchowski 2017.
57 Lewis 2013; 2018a, 157, 160.
58 Lewis 2018a, 154–155; Lewis 2020.
59 Lewis 2020, 82–83.
60 Lewis 2018a, ch. 7.

2.5 Slavery in classical Athens

I turn now to one last epichoric slave system, namely, that found in classical Athens. Classical Athens has historically formed the center of most Greek slavery studies, and in fact much of the evidence I discuss in the chapters that follow does come from Athens. However, looking at classical Athenian slavery here as simply one epichoric system among others — as Lewis does in his book — will allow us to decenter Athenian slavery, at least to some extent.[61]

One issue that scholars have recently explored with respect to slavery in Athens is how enslaved people — usually referred to as *douloi*, *oiketai*, or *therapontes*, among other terms[62] — fit into the broader picture of Athenian status. A major development of the past fifteen or so years has been a recognition that status in Athens was more complex than the rigid binary of slave/free, or ternary of slave/metic [i.e. resident foreigner]/citizen, that we find in most of our ancient sources.[63] Such binary and ternary divides were in fact reinforced by both law and ideology, but a closer look at our evidence reveals that there were in fact a multiplicity of status groups. Thus, for example, in my book *Status in Classical Athens*, I argue, drawing on Finley, that we might best view status in Athens as a spectrum of (at least) ten statuses, ranging from the basest chattel slave to the most elite male citizen.[64] However, the metaphor of a spectrum has not won universal favor.[65] Ismard, for example, prefers to think of status in terms of "overlapping layers," with Athenian society taking "the form of a multidimensional social space, traversed through and through by a kaleidoscope of statuses."[66] Peter Davies similarly argues that the spectrum model is too uni-

---

61 On classical Athens as one epichoric slave system, see Lewis 2018a, ch. 8. For an overview of slavery in classical Athens, see also Rihll 2011.
62 On the meaning of the term *oiketēs* in classical Greek, see Lewis 2018a, 295–305.
63 See Vlassopoulos 2007, 2009; Kamen 2013a; Ismard 2017a [2015]. Cf. Trevett 2017: "every individual necessarily belonged to one of three distinct status groups: citizen, metic, or slave."
64 Each chapter is devoted to a relatively distinct status group: chattel slaves, privileged chattel slaves, freedmen with conditional freedom, metics, privileged metics, bastards, disenfranchised citizens, naturalized citizens, female citizens, and male citizens (Kamen 2013a). On the spectrum of statuses, see Finley 1981, 98 (see further pp. 116–149), though he claims that the spectrum was not visible in the classical period, only in the early archaic period and the Hellenistic period (p. 132).
65 Criticisms of Finley's spectrum model go back at least to de Ste. Croix 1981, 92–93, who argued that the idea of a spectrum has no explanatory force.
66 Ismard 2017a [2015], 61 and 78. For the idea that status was "multidimensional" rather than "unidimensional," see also Taylor 2015, 37, Davies 2017 *passim*, Vlassopoulos 2021, 106. See further Lewis 2018a, 76, who argues that status "should be considered as a miscellany, not as a

dimensional to reflect the multidimensional nature of Athenian status. By this, he means that status in Athens (as in many societies, ancient and modern) consisted not only of "societal" or institutionalized status — namely, one's legal status (e.g. slave, metic, citizen) or position (e.g. a priesthood or magistracy), along with its associated legally defined rights — but also of "sub-societal" or interpersonal status, which accrues from other sources (e.g. wealth, attractiveness, education, friendships, etc.). The former has to do with one's standing vis-à-vis society as a whole, the latter one's standing vis-à-vis people one normally interacts with. Both aspects, he says, are germane in determining one's (overall) status, and a single spectrum cannot capture both.[67] I agree with these scholars that a unilateral spectrum has its flaws, but if we view it as a schematic model rather than an encapsulation of all of the aspects of status, I believe it helps us break out of the trap of viewing Athenian status as binary (or ternary). Future work, following the lead of Davies, will need to be done to sketch out what a multidimensional model of status might look like, one that can take into account the contexts or arenas in which individuals operated and how that affected their sub-societal status.[68]

Another debate about Athenian status centers on the degree to which distinctions between status groups were "blurred."[69] Edward Cohen was among the first to argue that status distinctions in Athens were often slippery and hard to identify, so much so that one's legal status was in many cases not actually very important.[70] Vlassopoulos added to this discussion by demonstrating that the blurring of status identities happened especially in what he calls "free spaces" (e.g. the agora, workplace, tavern, and trireme), and that this was a side-effect of the inclusiveness of the body politic in democratic Athens.[71] However, Diego Paiaro and Mariano Requena, while acknowledging that some status blurring

---

spectrum," since in a true spectrum, one color gradually shades into the next, something that is inapplicable to Greek status groups. Even Finley admitted that "spectrum" was an imperfect metaphor and a bit too neat (Finley 1973, 68 and 1981, 132).
67 Davies 2017. On the need to take into account both institutionalized and non-institutionalized aspects of status, see also Lewis 2018a, 78–79, and similarly Vlassopoulos 2021, 106–107.
68 Davies 2017, 32: "status is performative and contextual: the elements of one's status which are important change depending on the circumstance and on those with whom one interacts." See also Vlassopoulos 2021, ch. 5 on slave identity and how it varies by context.
69 Cf. Lewis 2018a, ch. 2, who finds the language of "blurring" misleading; see esp. p. 78.
70 E. E. Cohen 2000.
71 Vlassopoulos 2007. See also Vlassopoulos 2009, where he argues that it was often hard to tell enslaved from free because they held many of the same occupations, and that many enslaved people took advantage of this ambiguity.

did occur, stress the real effects that one's status had on one's role in the city, arguing that some of our evidence for "blurring" comes from pro-oligarchic sources that over-emphasize the participation of non-elites in the Athenian polis.[72] Forsdyke, in turn, has called attention to the tension that existed between, on the one hand, the blurriness of status categories, especially in certain contexts where it was hard to tell enslaved from free (e.g. at work, in battle, in civic religion), and, on the other hand, the city's simultaneous attempts to draw strict distinctions between status groups in a variety of legal ways (e.g. through slave torture for testimony and differential punishments for free and enslaved people; see further ch. 4.3).[73]

A related topic of interest has been the question of movement, lawful or otherwise, between status categories. Vlassopoulos, for example, has explored the phenomenon of enslaved people exploiting the blurriness of status to try to pass as metics or citizens.[74] He even suggests that the (surprisingly frequent) use of citizen-attested names by enslaved people can be explained, at least in part, as one way they tried to disguise their actual status.[75] Forsdyke has likewise argued that enslaved people in Athens regularly tried to pass as free, as suggested by Athenian courtroom trials over identity and by laws designed to prevent status transgression from happening, and corroborated by comparative evidence from other slave societies.[76]

Some enslaved people in Athens did, however, succeed in legitimately attaining their freedom and even, in exceptional cases, their naturalization (see further ch. 7). Claire Taylor has argued that the social networks that some enslaved people formed helped them build social capital, and through that, social mobility.[77] She clarifies that social mobility in this context "ought to be conceptualized in terms of relative functionings" — that is, what one's capabilities allow one to do — "rather than solely in terms of wealth or freedom (though of course these affect the range of choices available)."[78] Davies, in turn, suggests using the term "status crystallization" rather than "social mobility" to describe what happens when the different elements of one's status — societal and sub-

---

72 Paiaro and Requena 2015. See further Trevett 2017 on the fundamental importance of status differences in most areas of public/civic life.
73 Forsdyke 2021, ch. 4. On this tension in the context of Greek and Roman slavery more broadly, see duBois 2021.
74 Vlassopoulos 2009.
75 Vlassopoulos 2010 and 2015.
76 Forsdyke 2018 and 2021, 189–192. On Athenian identity trials, see also Lape 2010, ch. 5.
77 Taylor 2015.
78 Taylor 2015, 38.

societal — come into alignment.⁷⁹ Status crystallization was not easy to achieve, however, since formerly enslaved people continued to be viewed by many as (still) slaves, and naturalized citizens (whether servile in origin or not) often faced difficulties in having their new status socially recognized (see further ch. 7.3).⁸⁰

Finally, a long-running debate about slavery in classical Athens has to do with the degree to which Athenian society was (broadly speaking) dependent on enslaved labor. This question is related to, and sometimes part of, a larger scholarly debate about Greek slavery and agriculture, which I discuss in more detail in ch. 3.3. For now, it suffices to note that the profound impact of slavery on Athenian society has in recent years been strongly reaffirmed. In Forsdyke's words, "without slave labor, it is unlikely that the Athenians would have enjoyed the quality of life — the material prosperity and the opportunities for civic engagement — that they clearly did during the classical period."⁸¹ In fact, Lewis has shown how heavily the Athenian elite relied on slave labor, thus qualifying Athens as a "slave society" by most definitions, even if its dependence was not as extreme as in Sparta. At the same time, because the Athenians could acquire slaves relatively cheaply, slaveholding was open to a broad swath of citizens and metics — not just the elite — with the result that slavery permeated the lives of average Athenians more so than that of free people in other poleis.⁸² In short, then, slavery in Athens affected nearly everyone and everything.

2.6 Conclusion

This chapter has showcased the range of slaveries that existed in the Greek world. Rather than viewing the key distinction as one between chattel slavery in some poleis and something else (e.g. serfdom) elsewhere, many scholars (and in particular Lewis) have turned in recent years to viewing all enslaved people in the Greek world as chattel, that is, as the property of enslavers. By this reasoning, the major difference between poleis (and sometimes over time in the same polis) is in the *ways* in which chattel slavery operated, with variations in the degree to which enslaved people were integrated into the house-

---

79 Davies 2017.
80 On the persistent stigma faced by formerly enslaved people, see Kamen 2013a, ch. 3. See Deene 2011 and Kamen 2013a, ch. 8 on the challenges faced by naturalized citizens in Athens.
81 Forsdyke 2021, 160.
82 Lewis 2018a, ch. 8. On classical Athens as a slave society, see also Rihll 2011.

holds and societies of their enslavers, whether they were mainly imported or mainly indigenous, and where they fell on a hierarchy of statuses within a given society. As we have seen, however, these are all matters about which there is not yet scholarly consensus.

3 Economics of Slavery

Enslaved people formed an inextricable part of the economies of most Greek poleis, even if their precise economic impact has been debated. To get as full a picture as possible of the debates surrounding the economics of slavery, it is helpful first to address how the Greeks acquired their slaves and in what numbers before we turn to the types of labor these individuals performed. I conclude by surveying recent scholarship that has sought to explain the prevalence of slave labor as compared to free labor in Greece.

3.1 Supply of enslaved people

The supply of enslaved people in the Greek world has long been of interest to scholars, with the focus of the discussion shifting over time.[1] Unfortunately, we have little direct evidence for the "slave supply," as it is usually called, but we can sketch a picture on the basis of Greek literature (especially drama and historiography) and material culture (especially epigraphy).[2] In trying to determine the nature of the slave supply at Athens, for example, scholars regularly turn to the Attic Stelai, the inscriptions recording the property confiscated from the Athenian citizens convicted of defaming the Eleusinian Mysteries and mutilating the city's Herms statues in 415 BCE.[3] Amongst this property is human chattel, listed along with the enslaved person's ethnicity and how much they were sold for at auction. These records are therefore valuable for tracking both the origins of enslaved people and their cost, though it is important to keep in mind that these individuals represent only a cross-section of all enslaved people in Athens.

Scholars have also tried to ascertain the sources of enslaved people on the basis of their names, relying particularly on "ethnic" names (e.g. Thraitta, "Thacian") or "foreign" (i.e., non-Greek) names (e.g. Daos or Manes). Recently,

---

[1] A good overview of the slave supply in Greece is Braund 2011; see also Klees 1998: ch. 1; Wrenhaven 2013a; Hunt 2018b, ch. 3; Forsdyke 2021, ch. 2; Van Wees 2021 (specifically on the supply in archaic Greece); Lewis, Morton, Parkin 2022 (on Greece and Rome). On the slave trade and its relationship to Greek ethnography, see Harrison 2019.
[2] Other genres of evidence are also helpful: e.g., on the archaeological evidence for the slave supply, see Thompson 2003, ch. 1. See also Lewis 2022a, who argues that Attic oratory (specifically Dem. 34.10) provides a testimonium to the transport of enslaved cargo by sea.
[3] See Braund 2011, 123–124. On the Attic Stelai, see Pritchett 1953, 1956, 1961.

however, it has been shown that names should not be taken as definitive indications of an enslaved person's origins, for a couple of reasons. First, ethnic and foreign names do not necessarily match their bearer's origin; they may simply be the owner's best guess as to the enslaved person's ethnicity.[4] However, even if names cannot be taken as proof of any *individual*'s origins, they can still give us a broad-strokes picture of where enslaved people in a given polis were coming from.[5] Secondly, as Vlassopoulos has demonstrated, many enslaved people did not in fact have ethnic or foreign names: in Athens, for example, a majority (albeit a small majority) had names that were shared by citizens. This is a different pattern than we find in fiction, where the majority of slaves do have ethnic or foreign names.[6]

Regardless of the usefulness of names in determining origins, it is generally thought that most enslaved people in Greece were foreign — that is to say, non-Greek.[7] But clearly not all of them were: based on their listed ethnicities, the ratio of foreign to Greek slaves in the Attic Stelai is 7:3, which means that a not-insignificant 30% of these enslaved people must have been Greek.[8] It was *ideologically* important, however, for the Greeks to consider their slaves "other," regardless of their actual origins.[9] After all, this was one of the ways they were able to justify the institution (see further ch. 8.1).

The particular origins of enslaved people did not remain static over time. In an overview of the Greek slave supply, David Braund has argued that enslaved people came mainly from interactions between Greeks and non-Greeks at the periphery of Greek settlement. Sometimes these were peaceful interactions, like trading, but other times they were considerably less so, like raids.[10] Starting in the archaic period, it appears that slaves were acquired primarily from areas northeast of Greece around the Black Sea (e.g. Scythia, Thrace), and in the classical period, more began to be imported from Asia Minor (e.g. Caria, Lydia,

---

4 Braund 2011, 129.
5 See Lewis 2011 and 2018b; see also Wrenhaven 2013a, 9–13.
6 Vlassopoulos 2010; see also Vlassopoulos 2015. Robertson 2008, by contrast, stresses the difference between free and slave names, arguing that the latter both reflect and contribute to the ideology of slavery at Athens; for criticism of Robertson's approach, see Vlassopoulos 2010.
7 See Finley 1981, 167–175; Garlan 1987; Klees 1998, 52–56.
8 Pritchett 1956, 105.
9 Rosivach 1999; see also Harrison 2019.
10 On raiding and trading: Braund 2011; Forsdyke 2021, 53–59. On the importance of trading over raiding: Lewis 2016.

Phrygia). In the Hellenistic period, some individuals were imported from Africa, but they represented a minority of all slaves.[11]

One of our best ancient accounts on the slave supply is Dio Chrysostom, writing in the first century CE. He lists three main ways of acquiring slaves:

> ...of those who from time to time acquire slaves, as they acquire all other pieces of property, some get them from others either as a free gift from someone or by inheritance or by purchase, whereas some few from the very beginning have possession of those who were born under their roof, 'home-bred' slaves (*oikogeneis*) as they call them. A third method of acquiring possession is when a man takes a prisoner in war or even in brigandage and in this way holds the man after enslaving him, the oldest method of all, I presume. (15.25; trans. Cohoon)

Of Dio's "third way," capturing slaves either in warfare or by banditry, the former was indeed an old practice — we find it, for instance, in Homer — and it continued into the classical period and beyond.[12] From the earliest times, "the things conquered in war are said to belong to the conquerors" (Arist. *Pol.* 1255a 6–7), and as a result, it was up to the victor whether to enslave, kill, or release (with or without ransom) any prisoners of war. As such, we might expect that some slaves were acquired in this way, and in fact, it has recently been suggested that a desire for slaves may have driven some warfare.[13] However, while warfare was in fact a source of slaves, it was not nearly as significant as we might expect, for a couple of reasons. For one, it was generally the case that whereas women and children were enslaved, men captured in war were usually killed. Moreover, the Greeks were often engaged in civil war (i.e., one Greek polis against another), and despite their readiness to fight each other, they were nonetheless averse, in principle, to the enslavement of their fellow Greeks, especially Greek men.[14] Moreover, there were, in Yvon Garlan's words, "antidotes to the enslavement of Greeks": friends, family, or prominent fellow citizens could ransom these prisoners or purchase their freedom if they had already

---

11 For a brief synopsis of the shift in slave origins, see Garlan 1988 [1982], 46–47; Hunt 2018, 31–32. On the supply of enslaved people from the Black Sea region, see Tsetskhladze 2008 (specifically in Athens); Fischer 2014; Parmenter 2020, 59–65. On the supply of enslaved people from the "Near East," see Lewis 2011 (specifically in Athens), 2016.
12 On the acquisition of enslaved people through warfare, see Klees 1998, 20–50; Braund 2011, 115–123; Forsdyke 2021, 59–65; Ducrey 2022 (on Greece and Rome).
13 Braund 2011, 119; that it was one among many motivations, see Forsdyke 2021, 63–65.
14 On this aversion, see Rosivach 1999.

been sold into slavery, and sometimes a captive's polis might even intervene, releasing them by treaty or by other means.[15]

As Dio says, another way one might become enslaved was through capture by bandits.[16] Greek sources speak frequently about piracy and banditry, primarily because it makes for a good story, but we should not overestimate the importance of this high rate of attestation. The ultimate fate of most captives was infrequently possession by the bandits themselves; captives were normally either sold on the slave market or ransomed, especially if ransom was more profitable than sale. And just as with war captives, there was generally an effort made by both private individuals and home cities to recover captives ransomed by bandits.[17] A further source of slaves, according to Dio, was reproduction, whether natural or forced, though only recently have scholars begun taking seriously the role of reproduction in the Greek slave supply.[18] True, it played a relatively small role compared to other slave societies (e.g. the antebellum American South): for instance, only 7.5% of the slaves listed on the Attic Stelai are specified as *oikogeneis*.[19] However, we do find greater numbers of homeborn slaves elsewhere in the Greek world, presumably at times and in places where slaves were less cheap to purchase than they were in classical Athens. For example, in the manumission inscriptions from Hellenistic Delphi (dating from 201 BCE to c. 100 CE, on which see ch. 7), 29% of all the manumitted slaves are labeled as homeborn. Moreover, the rates of slave reproduction increased over time: 44% of the slaves manumitted at Delphi from 153 to 100 BCE are designated as homeborn, and Keith Hopkins estimates that for 153 BCE to 47 CE, the percentage (including *oikogeneis* not labeled as such) might be closer to 50%.[20]

There were also ways, not mentioned by Dio, in which free people might become enslaved. In Athens, whoever found an exposed child could decide whether to raise them as an enslaved or a free person, and generally chose the former option.[21] In Thebes, infant exposure was forbidden, but if someone were too poor to raise a child, they could bring the baby to the appropriate magis-

---

15 On ransoming war captives, see Braund 2011, 116–118; Forsdyke 2021, 59–61.
16 On piracy and banditry, see Klees 1998, 50–52; de Souza 1999, 60–65; Gabrielsen 2003; Lewis 2019; Forsdyke 2021, 53–55; Ducrey 2022.
17 On ransoming those captured by pirates: de Souza 1999, 65–69; Gabrielsen 2003, 392–395; Lewis 2019, 93–99.
18 Braund 2011, 125–126; Forsdyke 2021, 65–68.
19 Pritchett 1956, 280–281.
20 Hopkins 1978, 141.
21 The classic work on infant exposure in Greece is Patterson 1985; on infant exposure in late antiquity (through the Renaissance), see Boswell 1990.

trates, who would then sell the child into slavery (Ael. *VH* 2.7). Other means of enslavement included free people falling into slavery because of debt, a practice that was abolished in Athens but continued elsewhere in the Greek world (see ch. 2.2); free people being ransomed and then failing to repay their ransomers; metics (Greek or otherwise) in Athens being enslaved for committing particular crimes; and even Athenian citizens being enslaved for marrying foreigners, at least in the fourth century BCE.[22] None of these would have been large sources of slaves, however.

A relatively new approach to the subject of the Greek slave supply, pioneered by Braund, has been to try to access the *experiences* that individuals had during the process of enslavement and sale.[23] Thus, for example, following Braund's lead, Christopher Stedman Parmenter has tracked the travels of individuals on the Black Sea slave trade on the basis of merchant letters and literary sources, and Forsdyke has reconstructed the experiences of capture, enslavement, and sale using comparative evidence as well as the representations of such experiences in the writings of elite Greek authors.[24] This kind of work has been successful in providing a rich, visceral sense of what becoming enslaved and being on the slave trade might have actually felt like, providing a good counterpoint to our usual perspective: namely, that of the enslavers.

3.2 Numbers of enslaved people

Also of interest to scholars has been the question of how many enslaved people there were in the Greek world. It is, however, difficult to access reliable numbers for any given place or time.[25] Estimates have been attempted for numbers in classical Athens, but even here there is no direct evidence.[26] The closest we come is Athenaeus' (third-century CE) account of the census taken at the end of the fourth century BCE:

---

[22] Klees 1998, 58–59.
[23] Braund 2011, 127–132.
[24] Parmenter 2020; Forsdyke 2021, ch. 2, esp. 70–89. Lewis 2016 also captures well the experiences of being on the slave trade. Very useful for comparative purposes is scholarship exploring the experiences of individuals on the Atlantic slave trade: see Hartman 2007 (esp. ch. 7), Smallwood 2008.
[25] For a recent discussion of slave numbers in Greece, see Forsdyke 2021, 89–92.
[26] The earliest comprehensive attempt to ascertain numbers in classical Athens is Sargent 1924; the most recent exploration of this topic is Akrigg 2019, 90–120.

> Ctesicles, in the third book of the *Chronicles*, says that in the 117th Olympiad [312–308 BCE], there was a census taken by Demetrius of Phaleron of those residing in Athens, and 21,000 Athenians, 10,000 metics, and 400,000 slaves (*oiketai*) were found. (6.272c)

This passage is quoted nearly every time scholars hazard a guess as to the number of enslaved people in classical Athens, but both its meaning and validity are contested.[27] Two other passages are also often cited: Thucydides' report that after the Spartan occupation of Deceleia in 413 BCE, 20,000 enslaved people (*andrapoda*) deserted from Attica (7.27.5), and a fragment of Hyperides suggesting that more than 150,000 enslaved people "from the mines and the countryside" be enlisted to fight (Hyp. fr. 29 Jensen).[28] As limited as our evidence is for Athens, however, it is even poorer for other poleis. Essentially all we have is Athenaeus' report that there were 460,000 enslaved people in Corinth (according to Epitimaeus in the third book of his *Histories*) and 470,000 in Aegina (according to Aristotle's *Constitution of the Aeginetans*) (6.272bd). But scholars have doubted both of these numbers, just as they have Athenaeus' numbers for Athens.

Drawing cautiously from these ancient accounts, coupled with modern estimates both of the total population of Athens and of rates of slave ownership, scholars have proposed a range of estimates for classical Athens, spanning from a low of 20,000 slaves to a high of more than 150,000, with most estimates falling somewhere in the middle.[29] Moreover, these numbers could not have remained constant throughout the classical period: most likely, the number of enslaved people was at its highest immediately before the Peloponnesian War, fell dramatically during the War (as did the population as a whole), and began to increase again after the War. We may never know the precise number of enslaved people in classical Athens (or anywhere else in Greece), and Finley famously refused to play what he called "the numbers game"; more significant than arriving at an exact number, he said, was that we try to understand the role these people played in society.[30]

---

27 See e.g. Akrigg 2019, 90–91.
28 Akrigg 2019, 91–92.
29 For brief summaries of the debate on slave numbers in Athens, see Garlan 1988 [1982], 55–60; Fisher 2001 [1993], 34–36; Akrigg 2019, 92–94. Estimates continue to vary: Van Wees 2011, 107 posits 323,000 enslaved people in Athens in 317 BCE, whereas Pritchard 2020, 130 has suggested that there were only 50,000 in Athens in the late 430s.
30 Finley 1998 [1980], 147.

3.3 Roles in the economy

Thus, in "Was Greek Civilisation Based on Slave Labour?" (1959) — an old but still cited article — Finley surveyed the roles that enslaved people played in various sectors of the Greek economy, including agriculture, mining and quarrying, manufacturing, commerce and banking, and domestic service, concluding that "slavery was a basic element in Greek civilisation."[31] But he also thought that the article's title question should not be the endpoint of our analysis: more significant for increasing our understanding of ancient societies, he said, is a study of how slavery functioned, not whether (or at least, not solely whether) it was the economic base of society.

Nonetheless, following Finley, this question persisted for many years, with most of the debate centering on the extent to which enslaved people were involved in agriculture (since the Greek economy was primarily agricultural).[32] N.R.E. Fisher uses the helpful terms "minimalist" and "maximalist" to describe the two main camps of scholars on this question, with a focus on Athens.[33] To put it somewhat reductively, those espousing a "minimalist" view hold that slavery was little used on farms in Attica, whereas "maximalists" argue that slaveholding was widespread.

It would be hard to argue that elite landowners did not have slaves, a fact that is simply taken for granted in texts like Xenophon's *Oikonomikos* and pseudo-Aristotle's *Oikonomika* (see ch. 4.1).[34] The question, rather, is how widespread

---

[31] Finley 1981, 111. For broad overviews of the role of enslaved labor in the Greek (and Roman) economy, see Andreau and Descat 2011 [2006], ch. 4; Hunt 2018a; Rihll 2022; in the Hellenistic economy (focused on Asia Minor), Descat 2011. For detailed surveys of the various types of labor performed by enslaved people in Greece, see Kyrtatas 2011; Forsdyke 2021, ch. 3. Rihll 2022 helpfully divides the productive activities of enslaved people in Greece and Rome (which she describes in great detail) into primary, secondary, and tertiary sectors; the first deals with "the acquisition or production of raw materials" (e.g. farming, fishing, forestry, mining, quarrying), the second "the conversion of raw materials into products" (e.g. manufacturing and construction), the third "the provision of services" (e.g. cooking, entertainment, hairdressing, prostitution, secretarial work).
[32] For recent discussions of the role of enslaved people in agriculture in Greece, see Rihll 2011, 62–64; Akrigg 2019, 105–120; Forsdyke 2021, 103–109. On the archaeological evidence for their role in Greek agriculture, see Thompson 2003, ch. 2.
[33] For these terms, see Fisher 2001 [1993], 37–47. Fisher himself tentatively adopts a "less extreme version of the 'maximalist' view, with the important qualification that the extent of slave-owning probably varied considerably over time" (46).
[34] On the role of enslaved people in elite agriculture, see, e.g., Lewis 2018: 173–76; on slavery in the *Oikonomikos*, see, e.g., Porter 2021a.

slavery was beyond the farms of the elites. A.H.M. Jones, an early minimalist, asserted that, given the seasonal nature of agriculture, it would not have been economic for enslaved people to be used on a large scale. He concluded, then, that citizens must have farmed their own land, with only the richest citizens owning slaves to help with this labor.[35] This argument was expanded by Ellen M. Wood in her book *Peasant-Citizen and Slave*, who claimed that "there is simply no direct evidence to indicate the importance of agricultural slavery," and that what textual evidence there is "is seldom unambiguous." For this reason, and because she agreed with Jones that enslaved labor would have been an unprofitable way of working the land, Wood asserted that it was the laboring peasant-citizen, rather than the slave, who formed the base of the Athenian economy.[36] Wood's argument has been chipped away at over the years, and it has finally been thoroughly debunked by Lewis, who points out a number of errors and false assumptions underlying her work. In particular, he criticizes her complete dismissal of evidence from Athenian comedy (a reliable source of social-historical information and full of sub-elite slaveholders); her division of the Athenian citizenry into "rich landowners" and undifferentiated "peasant farmers" (whereas in fact wealth ownership varied considerably within the sub-elite class); and her assumption that small farmers aimed only at subsistence, leading her to believe that slaveholding and the intensification of cultivation would not have made economic sense for them. As Lewis points out, Wood does not take into account that small farmers might have sold their surplus food for profit on the market, nor does she factor in the *non-economic* benefits that enslaved labor granted slaveowners (see further below).[37]

The maximalist position, by contrast, was well established roughly fifty years ago by Michael Jameson, who based his argument on the specific nature of agricultural work in Attica, which entailed "intensification, diversification, and specialization." All of these methods would have required many hours and many workers, thus justifying the purchase of an enslaved worker (or workers) to supplement the family work force. Jameson also argued for the profitability of this practice on a number of grounds, including, most significantly, the "social gain" for the Athenian citizen, who with slaves working his land could engage

---

[35] Jones 1952.
[36] Wood 1988, esp. ch. 2, with quotations on p. 47. See also Sallares 1991 for another maximalist perspective.
[37] See Lewis 2018a, 180–194; he also criticizes her insistence that the *oiketai* mentioned working in agriculture were free workers (rather than enslaved), as well as her ignoring of the low prices of slaves in Attica, which would have made enslaved labor affordable to a large swath of the population.

in civic life and enact his role as a participant in the democracy.[38] G.E.M. de Ste. Croix, in turn, argued for the prominence of agricultural slavery both in Greece and in Rome and consequently the "essential" contribution of slavery to the ancient economy. Conceding that the evidence for agricultural slavery in Greece is sparse, he nonetheless collected a handful of pertinent references in classical literature and asserted further that we should not deny the existence and extent of agricultural slavery simply because of the paucity of evidence; after all, this should not be a surprise given the nature of our (elite) sources.[39]

The minimalist-maximalist debate has in recent years abated, with the majority of scholars now favoring some version of the maximalist position.[40] Indeed, in *Ökonomik und Hauswirtschaft im klassischen Griechenland* (2021), a massive study of household economics in classical Greece, Moritz Hinsch demonstrates that the exploitation of enslaved labor was in fact economically rational. That is, it was a deliberate and effective strategy, one among others, for generating wealth.[41] Most contemporary scholars, then, deem slavery, whatever the precise number of chattel slaves, inextricable not only from the economy but also from Greek society as a whole — including, but not limited to, seemingly admirable facets of "Greek civilization" like Athenian democracy.[42] Cartledge has pointed out that the benefits of slavery from the Greek perspective were not simply (or even primarily) economic, but rather social and political.[43] While Cartledge focuses on the benefits of slavery to the Athenian elite in this respect, Jameson and others have shown that slavery also benefited those who had only small slaveholdings.[44]

In addition to their important role in agriculture, enslaved people also contributed to nearly every other sector of the Greek economy. For instance, a large number of enslaved people were engaged in domestic service. In most households (apart from the very wealthy), each domestic slave served a variety of

---

[38] Jameson 1977/78. See also Osborne 1995, who argues that there was a "structural necessity" for agricultural slavery: it not only allowed citizens to participate in civic life but was also economically justifiable.

[39] de Ste. Croix 1957 and 1981. For his collection of literary evidence, see de Ste. Croix 1981, Appendix II.

[40] This view is not universal, however: Lenski 2018a, 130–131, e.g., asserts that slavery played a small role in agriculture in classical Athens.

[41] Hinsch 2021, esp. ch. 12.

[42] On the interconnections between slavery and democracy: Cartledge 2002b; Jameson 2002; Hunt 2018b, 68–75; Ismard 2017a [2015] and 2019.

[43] Cartledge 2002b.

[44] Jameson 2002.

roles.⁴⁵ Most often, enslaved men would attend to their male owners' needs, enslaved women to their female owners', with both also doing gender-specific productive work (on gendered labor, see ch. 5.1). In larger households, there would have been more specialization of slave occupations, with individuals serving as butlers, housekeepers, maids, hairdressers, etc. The highest-up position for an enslaved person within the household was the manager of other slaves: in Xenophon's *Oikonomikos*, the wealthy landowner Ischomachus notes that his especially trusted male slaves serve as supervisors (*epitropoi*) of work in the fields (12.3–15.1), and his especially trusted female slaves as housekeepers/overseers (*tamiai*) of the domestic work (9.11–13).

Another area in which enslaved people worked was mining and quarrying.⁴⁶ The most important mines in Athens were at Laurion in eastern Attica. These mines were owned by the city of Athens, which leased out rights to bidders to mine for a period of time. Successful bidders would then either buy or rent slaves to work their part of the mine. (The practice of enslaved people being rented out by their owners for income [*misthos*] is something we find not only in this industry but in others as well, including prostitution, building projects, and rowing in the navy.)⁴⁷ Among the archaeological evidence found at Laurion are slave accommodations and shackles, as well as lamps still containing olive oil, from which it has been estimated that work shifts lasted roughly 10 hours.⁴⁸ The conditions in these mines were, needless to say, terrible: mining was (and still is) extremely dangerous work.⁴⁹

---

45 On domestic service, see Forsdyke 2021, 125–133.
46 Rihll 2011, 68–69; Forsdyke 2021, 119–125. On the archaeological evidence for enslaved people in quarrying and mining in both Greece and Rome, see Thompson 2003, ch. 5.
47 On enslaved people who were rented out (*andrapoda misthophorounta*), see Kazakévich 2008; Ismard 2019, 80–95.
48 The classic work on enslaved people working in mines at Laurion is Lauffer 1979 [1956].
49 For a vivid description of this kind of work, see D. S. 5.38.1: "To continue with the mines, the slaves who are engaged in the working of them produce for their masters revenues in sums defying belief, but they themselves wear out their bodies both by day and by night in the diggings under the earth, dying in large numbers because of the exceptional hardships they endure. For no respite or pause is granted them in their labours, but compelled beneath blows of the overseers to endure the severity of their plight, they throw away their lives in this wretched manner, although certain of them who can endure it, by virtue of their bodily strength and their persevering souls, suffer such hardships over a long period; indeed death in their eyes is more to be desired than life, because of the magnitude of the hardships they must bear" (trans. Oldfather).

Enslaved people also worked in skilled trades, including the manufacturing of goods.[50] Manufacturing in Greece was generally done by small family-owned businesses, with enslaved people working in small factories or workshops, each of which produced a specific product (e.g. weapons, pots, statues, knives, lamps, clothes, furniture). For example, Demosthenes says that his father owned two factories: one factory manufactured swords, with 32–33 slaves, from which his father received an income of 30 mnas a year; the other manufactured sofas, with 20 slaves, bringing in an income of 12 mnas a year (27.9).

Some enslaved people, moreover, were engaged in commerce and banking.[51] These are among the types I have elsewhere called "privileged slaves," since they had considerably more agency and independence than the average chattel slave.[52] In many cases, privileged slaves would "live apart" from their owner and hand over some portion of their earnings (the *apophora*), reserving the rest for themselves as a sort of allowance.[53] Jason Porter has recently argued that these individuals were thought of as leasing property from their owners, with the *apophora* a sort of rent, in an arrangement that was beneficial to both parties.[54] Many of these individuals were trusted to conduct financial transactions on their own, although there is debate about their degree of liability. On one side stands Alberto Maffi, who points out, first of all, that the rules underlying Greek commerce would have been similar to what we find in Rome, where enslaved people were not liable. Moreover, he says, Solon's law stating that the enslaver was responsible for any "wrongs" (*adikēmata*) committed by the person he held as a slave (cited in Hyp. 3.22) suggests that the former would also have been responsible for any debts the latter incurred.[55] Cohen, by contrast, argues that the very speech that Maffi cites (Hyp. 3) suggests that the enslaved person in question personally owed debts, and that the cited law of Solon does not apply to slaveowners' liability for contractual obligations incurred by their

---

50 Rihll 2011, 64–68; Forsdyke 2021, 110–119; on manufacturing in Athens more broadly, see Acton 2014.
51 Cohen 1992, ch. 5; Forsdyke 2021, 141–150.
52 Kamen 2013a, ch. 2. On these "privileged" or "independent" slaves, see also Klees 1998, 142–154; Cohen 2003 [2000], ch. 5; Fisher 2008; Ismard 2017b, 30–40 and 2019, 96–105.
53 On the *apophora*, see Kazakévich 2008; Kamen 2016; Porter 2021/22.
54 Porter 2021/22.
55 Maffi 2008. This interpretation has gained the support of most scholars: see Dimopoulou-Piliouni 2012; Ismard 2019, 109–110; Porter 2021/22. As Porter 2021/22, 196–198 points out, this had the benefit of preserving the ideology of slavery by not granting any slaves, even "privileged" ones, the right to be fully independent.

slaves.⁵⁶ Either way, it is possible that, at least as of the middle of the fourth century in Athens, enslaved individuals who were engaged in commerce could try or be tried in a particular type of legal suit dealing with imports and exports (the *dikē emporikē*) – which might imply they held a degree of liability – but our evidence for their involvement in these suits is admittedly slim.⁵⁷

Public slaves, in turn, performed different tasks, from menial jobs to those requiring intellectual skills.⁵⁸ Some were paid regular (if small) salaries, which allowed them to save up money and potentially buy their freedom (see ch. 7). At least at Athens, the work of public slaves included filing, archiving, and sometimes even composing public documents; guaranteeing the authenticity of coins and protecting the standards for weights and measures; serving as police officers, assistants to the Eleven (the board in charge of prisons), and executioners; working as artisans and laborers in the city's construction sites; and managing sanctuaries and occasionally serving as priests.⁵⁹ Ismard has compellingly argued that in addition to providing the labor that allowed the city to run smoothly, public slaves were also crucial for the development of Athenian democracy. Rather than running the risk of any given citizen-politician gaining too much knowledge (and therefore too much power), the city decided instead to entrust its public slaves with the expertise required to run the government. This scheme also allowed for the preservation of institutional knowledge, since citizens' terms of office were generally only a year, whereas public slaves might hold their post for life.⁶⁰

Finally, some enslaved people worked in milling (both in commercial mills and in domestic contexts) as well as in the making and selling of bread.⁶¹ Milling was a particularly onerous and unpleasant job, and for that reason it could be used as a punishment for disobedient slaves (e.g. Lys. 1.18). As noted above,

---

56 Cohen 2012 and 2018. However, regardless of whether the owner was *technically* liable for his slaves, in many cases he might in fact have been held liable, a point Cohen himself concedes.
57 See Lanni 2006, 149–74, but cf. Ismard 2019, 101–103 who thinks there is insufficient evidence to prove that enslaved people used these suits.
58 The most comprehensive recent work on public slaves is Ismard 2017a [2015], who estimates that at any given time in classical Athens, there were between 1,000–2,000 public slaves (p. 50); see also Ismard 2014b. See further Hunter 2006 and Forsdyke 2021, 134–141 on public slavery.
59 For a survey of these jobs, see Ismard 2017a [2015], ch. 2.
60 Ismard 2017a [2015].
61 On enslaved labor in mills, see Porter 2019, 37–44; in milling, baking, and cooking, Forsdyke 2021, 155–156.

other enslaved people worked as prostitutes, rented out by their owners or pimps/madams.⁶² As far as we can tell, prostitutes in Greece, both male and female, were most often enslaved or formerly enslaved. Their labor ranged from higher-status "escorts" to lower-status streetwalkers or brothel prostitutes (see further ch. 5.2).

3.4 Prevalence of slave labor

One issue that has preoccupied scholars of Greek (and Roman) slavery in recent years is how to account for the relative prevalence of slave labor in different societies at different times.⁶³ These questions are not new, per se, though they have received renewed interest lately. Scheidel, for example, has formulated a model to help answer them.⁶⁴ He uses as his starting point a model developed by the economic historian Stefano Fenoaltea, which sees a key division between two types of labor — "effort-intensive activities" (e.g. mining, quarrying, construction work) and "care-intensive activities" (e.g. domestic service, artisanal and commercial work) — the latter of which, Fenoaltea argues, are particularly suited to slave labor.⁶⁵ While Scheidel sees much value in this model, he finds that it does not account for the pervasiveness of slave labor in certain care-intensive activities in the ancient world, including large-scale viticulture. He therefore supplements Fenoaltea's model by drawing on the work of the economic historian Christopher Hanes on the benefits of guaranteed long-term labor obligations (primarily, lower turnover costs) as well as the anthropologist James L. Watson's distinction between "open" slave systems, where enslaved people can be freed and assimilated into society, and "closed" systems, where they remain a separate group even after being freed.⁶⁶ Combining these three approaches, Scheidel has developed a composite model accounting for the range of variables that determine whether slave labor was used on a wide scale: namely, the specific economic activities pursued, the incentive systems used,

---

62 On enslaved prostitutes, see Forsdyke 2021, 150–154.
63 For an earlier discussion of the emergence and prevalence of slavery in Greece, see Finley 1998 [1980], ch. 2.
64 Scheidel 2008; see also Scheidel 2005.
65 Fenolatea 1984. "Effort-intensive activities" are usually done under close supervision, use "pain incentives" as motivation, and offer little to no chance of manumission; "care-intensive activities," on the other hand, do not require close supervision, use rewards as motivation, and usually provide some chance of manumission.
66 Hanes 1996; Watson 1980.

the norms and values of a society (including but not limited to whether it was "open" or "closed"), and the nature of free people's commitments (e.g. to politics, warfare, etc.). Scheidel also emphasizes that the relationship between free wages and slave prices is instrumental in determining the prevalence of slave labor.[67] Deriving slave prices from the Attic Stelai and scattered references in Greek texts, he estimates that the average price of an adult slave in classical Athens was 200–500 drachmas. From this, he concludes that it was at least twice as expensive to pay a free laborer over a period of, say, ten years than to buy an unskilled slave and feed them for ten years. This combination of low slave prices and expensive free labor, then, was a key factor in the flourishing of slavery in Athens.[68]

More recently, Lewis has expanded on Scheidel's model, as well as a newer one developed by the late antique historian Kyle Harper, to explain the regional variations in the magnitude of slaveholding throughout the eastern Mediterranean.[69] In addition to the factors noted by other scholars to explain the choice of enslaved versus free labor — e.g. the monetary costs of slavery versus other forms of labor, the institutional advantages of differing labor forms, cultural variables like ideology and honor, and the "dynamics of labor use" (i.e., the particular ways individual landowners choose to manage their estates) — Lewis adds to the mix two more factors: namely, political geography (who could be enslaved where) and economic geography (how much it costs to transport enslaved people, given geographic features like distance, travel by land vs. sea, etc.). He derives these latter two variables from the work of the economic historian Jeffrey Fynn-Paul, who distinguishes between "slaving zones" (areas affected by a society's demand for slaves) and "no-slaving zones" (areas considered off limits by a given society for slave raiding).[70] We might conclude, as Lewis does, that there is no one explanation for regional variation in the use of slave labor, but instead a matrix of economic, social, geographic, and other factors.[71]

---

[67] Scheidel 2008.
[68] Scheidel 2005. He argues, moreover, that this combination was probably also found in Roman Republican Italy, but not the Roman Empire.
[69] Lewis 2018a, ch. 4. Among other scholars, he draws on Scheidel 2008 (discussed above) and Harper 2011, 149–162, who argues that the four determinants of the prevalence of slavery are "supply, demand, formal institutions, and the dynamics of estate management" (p. 152).
[70] Fynn-Paul 2009.
[71] Lewis argues that the ideal environment for slavery has the following features: "(i) strong state institutions guaranteeing citizen rights, law and order, and market infrastructure; (ii) capital formation, especially if it is distributed relatively equitably across the citizen body;

3.5 Conclusion

Apart from these developments in determining why some societies were more or less inclined to use enslaved labor, one of the biggest advances in understanding the slave supply in recent years has been the consideration not just of *where* enslaved people came from, but also the experiences of those who were captured, transported, and sold on the market. And while it remains difficult to derive slave numbers from our surviving sources, recent work in Greek demography, coupled with the employment of methodologies used in the study of Roman demography, may pave the way for better-informed estimates in the future. Finally, consensus has yet to be reached on the degree to which enslaved labor was fundamental to Greek farming, but most scholars now acknowledge that it played at least some role, and the study of enslaved labor in other (comparatively less-explored) sectors of the Greek economy is a trend that will likely continue to develop.

(iii) high levels of commitment to civic activities and strong disinclination among citizens to work for one another; (iv) markets for slave-produced goods; (v) geographic proximity to a slavery zone; (vi) commercial networks linking buyers and sellers, ideally by sea; (vii) high demographic density within the slaving zone (i.e. strong potential supply)" (Lewis 2018a, 287).

4 Treatment of Enslaved People

This chapter explores how Greeks treated their slaves. Well into the twentieth century, there existed a romanticizing strain in scholarship on ancient slavery, perhaps best exemplified by the work of Joseph Vogt, who argued that slaves in antiquity were treated relatively well and that slavery was simply "part of the sacrifice which had to be paid for [the] achievement" of Greek civilization.[1] Nearly no one holds these views anymore, and scholarship has moved away from what Vlassopoulos calls the "humanitarian debate" toward investigations into slaveowners' strategies for "managing" their slaves, the types of violence faced by enslaved people and the effects of this violence, and the degree to which enslaved people were (or were not) protected from the worst kinds of abuse.

4.1 "Slaving strategies" and household management

Before turning to specific strategies in the treatment of enslaved people, I begin with a useful distinction formulated by William Thalmann in the context of Greek and Roman slavery: namely, between what he calls a "benevolent" model of slavery and a "suspicious" one, two simultaneous (if seemingly contradictory) ideas of slavery that the ancients held in their minds.[2] On the one hand, the Greeks (and Romans) held a paternalistic view of the institution, telling themselves — and presumably their slaves too — that slavery was in their slaves' best interest and that the latter were like members of the family.[3] What is sometimes called "fictive kinship" is in fact a common phenomenon across slave societies, a way of making the enslaver-enslaved relationship appear mutually beneficial while masking its inherent inequalities.[4] This benevolent model of slavery is exemplified, in turn, by the figure of the "good slave," who is obedient and happy with their lot in life: a good example is Eurycleia, the kindly wet-nurse in Odysseus' household.[5] On the other hand, Thalmann argues, the ancients also

---

1 Vogt 1975 [1965]. For a discussion of the humanitarian approach to ancient slavery, see Vlassopoulos 2016a and 2020, ch. 2.
2 Thalmann 1998; he first presents these ideas in Thalmann 1996 in the context of Plautus.
3 On the paternalism of Greek slavery going back to Homer, see Porter 2021a.
4 On fictive kinship in the context of slavery, see Patterson 1982, 62–65.
5 See the portrait of Eurycleia in Hom. *Od.* 1.427–435: "A loyal slave went with him [Telemachus], Eurycleia, / daughter of Ops; she brought the burning torches. / Laertes bought her

viewed their slaves with fear and suspicion. This suspicious model of slavery offers as its paradigm the "bad slave," who seeks to advance their own interests and betrays their owner whenever they get a chance. We might think, for instance, of the *Odyssey*'s Melantho, who, despite being treated well by Penelope, treats her owner (and her owner's husband) insultingly — and as a result is hanged as punishment.[6] Both models, then, were ways for enslavers to naturalize the institution of slavery and legitimize their treatment of slaves: the benevolent model for the benefits it allegedly brought the enslaved person, the suspicious model as justification for treating harshly those who were "naturally" inferior.

There was, in practice, great variation in the treatment of enslaved people. As recent work by Porter and Vlassopoulos has shown, this differing treatment was part of a broader system of "slaving strategies," with slaveowners' actions driven less by concerns about their slaves' well-being than about their own ability to most effectively manage their households.[7] Indeed, in Plato's *Laws*, in a discussion of slave management in a hypothetical utopia, the unnamed Athenian character recommends that enslavers maintain their slaves well, "not only for [the slaves'] sakes but even more for our own." The Athenian clarifies that this means that one should not treat slaves insultingly (*hubrizein*, "act with *hubris* toward," on which see ch. 4.4, below): indeed, if possible, one should try to harm (*adikein*) them less than one does one's equals (777d)! However, this does not mean avoiding punishment when it is warranted; rather, one should punish slaves "fairly" (*en dikēi*). The Athenian also suggests that one avoid rebuking one's slaves the way one would a free person, since doing so runs the risk of making them conceited. It is best, he says, to issue direct orders and not joke around, since going too easy on one's slaves makes life harder for both owner and slave (777e–778a).

---

many years before / when she was very young, for twenty oxen. / He gave her status in the household, equal / to his own wife, but never slept with her, / avoiding bitter feelings in his marriage. / She brought the torches now; she was the slave / who loved him most, since she had cared for him / when he was tiny" (trans. Wilson).

[6] See the portrait of Melantho in Hom. *Od.* 18.320–326: "Pretty Melantho, child of Dolius, / had been brought up by Queen Penelope, / who gave her toys and treated her just like / a daughter. But Melantho, unconcerned / about Penelope, was sleeping with / Eurymachus [one of Penelope's suitors]. She started to insult / Odysseus, and taunt him" (trans. Wilson).

[7] For the term "slaving strategies," see Miller 2008. See Porter forthcoming a on the methods of coercion and other "slaving strategies" used by enslavers in Athens to get what they want from their slaves. On "slaving strategies" in antiquity more broadly, see Vlassopoulos 2021, ch. 4. See also Forsdyke 2021, 235–238 on the sticks and carrots used by enslavers in Greece.

Other advice is found in texts dealing more explicitly with household management.[8] Porter has shown that in these works, we find a hierarchy of treatment that corresponds to a hierarchy of enslaved members of the household, with those higher up receiving praise and even honor in exchange for good work.[9] Thus, in Xenophon's *Oikonomikos*, Ischomachus describes how he runs his own household, explaining that it is necessary to train one's slaves the way one would wild beasts in order to get them to obey; as with animals, the most effective reward is food. Ischomachus does, however, draw a distinction in how he treats different types of enslaved people, saying that for especially ambitious (*philotimoi*) slaves, praise can also work as a motivator, just as food does for other slaves. He also ensures that better workers get better clothing and shoes, inferior ones inferior, since slaves have to see that rewards (and punishments) are proportional to work done (13.9–12). Finally, Ischomachus says that he treats "like free men" (*hōsper eleutherois*) — "making them rich" (*ploutizōn*) and "honoring" (*timōn*) them "like gentlemen" (*hōs kalous te kagathous*) — any of his slaves who are righteous not for any advantages it brings them but out of a desire to be praised (*epaineisthai*) by him (14.9). This description of slave treatment should probably not be taken at face value, but it does speak to the wide range of ways a slaveowner might think of his slaves — from wild beasts to gentlemen — and how he might treat them accordingly.[10]

In another household-management text, Pseudo-Aristotle's *Oikonomika*, the author advises slaveowners not to let slaves be hubristic (*hubrizein*) in their interactions with them, nor to treat their slaves grievously (*anian*). Instead, they should give a share of honor (*timēs*) to those who are "freer" (*eleutheriōterois*) — presumably, he means enslaved managers — and reward laborers with extra food (1344a29–31).[11] As with Xenophon, we see here too a distinction between higher-up, nearly-free individuals who warrant treatment in the form of honor or praise, and lower-down ones who receive more traditionally servile rewards. Pseudo-Aristotle explains further that all slaves must be given an appropriate

---

8 On these household management texts in the context of a study of the domestic economy, see Hinsch 2021, esp. Part II. Most of these are fourth-century BCE philosophical texts, but the roots run deeper: see Hunnings 2011, who reads Homer's *Odyssey* as a proto-slave-management manual, and Porter 2021a, who demonstrates the continuity in slave-management advice from the *Odyssey* to Xenophon's *Oikonomikos* and beyond.
9 Porter forthcoming b.
10 On the rewards and punishments for enslaved people in Xenophon's *Oikonomikos*, see also Porter 2021a.
11 A few lines earlier, pseudo-Aristotle draws a distinction between two types of slaves: the *epitropos* (manager) and the *ergatēs* (laborer) (1344a25–26).

ratio of work, punishment, and food, since food without punishment or work makes them hubristic, and work with punishment and no food is violent (*biaion*) (not to mention impractical, since it deprives them of strength). The best compromise, then, is to give slaves work and sufficient food, and to dole out rewards and punishments (as regards food, clothes, free time, etc.) in accordance with what they deserve (*kat' axian*) (1344a35–b11).

Lest one get the impression from these texts that enslaved people were treated mildly, other genres of evidence make clear that they were subject to all sorts of violent treatment.[12] This violence, like other forms of treatment, could serve various purposes, from punishment to intimidation to social control more broadly. As Hunt has shown, even the *threat* of violence served to keep enslaved people in check (or so enslavers hoped), since it reminded them both of their vulnerability and of their enslavers' power.[13] Violence against slaves also had an ideological component: important work by duBois and by Virginia Hunter has shown how corporal punishment — and in particular the use of the whip — drew an ideological line between free and slave.[14] Indeed, as Demosthenes says in an oft-quoted passage, the difference between a free man and a slave is that slaves' bodies are liable to punishment for all offenses, whereas free men's bodies are not (22.55). And not only was the enslaved person's susceptibility to violence taken as a sign of their innate slavishness, but the particular violence they endured, and their reactions to it, had the potential to bolster negative stereotypes about slaves as cowering and animal-like.[15]

4.2 Types of violence and its effects

For many people who ended up in slavery, the violence they faced began at the moment of their capture. Kathy Gaca has written extensively about the violence that was inflicted on captives in warfare, part of a process she calls "andrapodizing" (after the Greek verb *andrapodizesthai*). She argues that this practice refers not, as some scholars take it, to the sale of captives, but to a violent process that involves subduing a population through aggressive armed assault, rounding up the remaining inhabitants, sorting the captives, and forcibly re-

---

12 As Hunt puts it, "Violence against slaves was ubiquitous in and crucial to the institution of slavery in ancient Greece" (2016, 136). For overviews of violence against enslaved people in Greece, see Hunter 1994, ch. 6; Klees 1998, ch. 6; duBois 2003, ch. 4; Hunt 2016.
13 On violence against slaves as a means of social control, see Hunt 2016, 138–143.
14 duBois 1991, 62–64; Hunter 1992 and 1994, ch. 6.
15 For violence as a "symbolic system," see Hunt 2016, 143–150.

moving the most desirable ones (primarily young women and children).[16] As she puts it, andrapodizing is "a systematic procedure for liquidating an overthrown populace that involves intense dehumanizing violence every step of the way."[17]

Once an enslaved person entered a household or a workplace, they continued to face a range of forms of violence. The intensity and frequency of this violence likely depended on several factors, including the personality of their owner, their owner's "slaving strategies" (ch. 4.1), and the type of labor they were compelled to do (ch. 3.3): that is, an enslaved person laboring in the mines would have been more likely to experience physical violence than a beloved wet-nurse. The various types of violence they risked encountering is illuminated by an early-fourth-century BCE lead letter found in the Athenian Agora (Ag. Inv. IL 1702), written by a boy named Lesis, which reads:

> Lesis is sending (a letter) to Xenocles and his mother by no means to overlook | that he is perishing in the foundry but to come to his masters (*despotas*) | and to find something better for him. For I have been handed over to a man thoroughly wicked; | I am perishing from being whipped; I am tied up; I am treated like dirt — more and more.[18]

Although David Jordan interprets Lesis as a metic on an apprenticeship, Harris has to my mind persuasively argued that Lesis was in fact a slave — a case substantiated by Lesis' mention of *despotai*, "masters."[19] If Harris is correct, this lead letter may be our only first-hand testimony from Greece of an enslaved person writing about their treatment.

Lesis mentions, albeit hyperbolically, "perishing" from being whipped, and indeed, whipping was the most common form of violence against enslaved people in Greece. It could be used either as punishment or as part of judicial torture (*basanos*; see further below). The use of whips on enslaved people was in fact so widespread that a pejorative term for "slave" was *mastigias* (related to the Greek word *mastix*, "whip"), meaning "whipping post" or "someone who needs a whipping." It was also the standard punishment by the polis for enslaved people who had committed particular offenses. For example, the public slaves in Athens who worked as coin testers were subject to 50 lashes with the public

---

16 See especially Gaca 2010.
17 Gaca 2010, 142.
18 Trans. Jordan 2000, 95.
19 That Lesis is free, see Jordan 2000; see also Maffi 2014, 202–203. Jordan concedes, however, that we have little to no evidence for apprenticeship in classical Athens. That Lesis is enslaved, see Harris 2004, with whom Harvey 2007 and Forsdyke 2021, 1 agree. Jordan 2000, 98 thinks *despotai* must have a "looser sense" than masters here; Maffi 2014, 202–203 suggests that the sense is "owners of the foundry."

whip if they did not sit at their post or test coins according to the law (Ag. Inv. I 7180, lines 13–16). But whipping was not the only form of corporal punishment enslaved people faced: they could be struck with sticks, bare hands, or any other implement an owner had available. For example, in Aristophanes' *Wasps*, the enslaved character Xanthias says: "Ah tortoises, I envy you your shells! It was good and brainy of you to roof your backs with tile and so cover your sides. Me, I've been bruised (*stizomenos*) within an inch of my life by a walking stick" (1291–1295; trans. Henderson). The word here translated as "bruised" is the same word used for "tattooed" or "branded" — i.e., it refers to an indelible mark (*stigma*; see further below). Although this example comes from comedy, it confirms what we know from other sources and from comparative evidence about corporal punishment, namely, that at its most brutal it could cause welts and eventually scars to form.[20]

Another form of violence directed against enslaved people was shackles, chains, and fetters, the use of which is attested in both literary sources and archaeological evidence.[21] In some rural households, all or most of the enslaved people were shackled, and sometimes locked in towers, in order to prevent their running away (if not always their attempts to run away) (Xen. *Oik.* 3.4).[22] Fetters were also used as a punishment for enslaved people who were deemed disobedient (Ar. *Vesp.* 435), and enslaved people forced to work in the mills were also generally shackled (Men. *Her.* 2–3).[23] All of these forms of constraint would have been painful, digging into the enslaved person's flesh, and again sometimes leaving scars.[24]

As alluded to above, enslaved people were also subject to tattooing and branding, generally referred to in Greek with forms of the verb *stizein* or the noun *stigma*.[25] These marks were used for a variety of purposes, including humiliating war captives, labeling slaves as property, and marking enslaved people who had tried to escape. Some runaways in Greece apparently had phrases along the lines of "Catch me, I'm escaping" tattooed or branded on their fore-

---

[20] On the marks left by violence against the enslaved body, as well as the attempts made by enslaved people to remove the marks of their slavery, see Kamen 2010.
[21] On shackling, see Klees 1998, 185–189. On archaeological evidence for shackles and other forms of restraint, see Thompson 2003, ch. 7; Morris 2018. On archaeological evidence for Greek slavery more broadly, see Morris 2011.
[22] On slave towers in Greece, see Morris and Papadopoulos 2005; cf. Descat 2011.
[23] On the brutal nature of work in the mills, see Porter 2019, 37–44.
[24] Cf. Trimble 2016 on the physical experience of wearing a slave collar in the Roman world.
[25] On tattooing and branding, see Jones 1987; specifically of enslaved people, Klees 1998, 193–197 and Kamen 2010.

heads (Schol. Aeschin. 2.79), whereas others may have been marked with an equivalent symbol (e.g. a possible deer tattoo in Lys. 13.19). Thus, in all of the forms of violence mentioned thus far — whipping, beating, chains, tattooing, and branding — the enslaved person's body was "inscribed" with marks of their enslavement, as duBois has demonstrated.[26]

Finally, enslaved women and children were also susceptible to sexual violence, at the hands of both their owners and sometimes others (see ch. 5.3).[27] Recent scholarship by Allison Glazebrook and Konstantinos Kapparis, among others, has illuminated the vulnerability of enslaved prostitutes in particular to such violence, a risk that Cohen has to my mind understated.[28] The sexual abuse faced by many enslaved people — not only prostitutes — presumably traumatized at least some of them, leading to psychological scars in addition to physical ones.

4.3 Institutionalized violence

Violence could be used institutionally as a way to elicit testimony from enslaved people. At least in Athens, the practice of judicial torture (*basanos*) was thought to be an effective way to pry the truth from enslaved people and introduce it into the courts.[29] *Basanos* always resulted from a challenge: if a litigant wanted to introduce into court the testimony of an enslaved person, he issued a challenge before the trial, either offering up his own slave or requesting his opponent's slave for interrogation. The other party would then either accept or reject

---

26 duBois 2003, ch. 4; see also Kamen 2010 on the enslaved body as metaphorically inscribed.
27 On the sexual violence faced by enslaved women in classical Athens, Breitenfeld 2022.
28 On violence against prostitutes, see Kapparis 2018, 209–241. See also Glazebrook 2015b on the hierarchy of violence in Menander's *Epitrepontes* (with prostitutes most susceptible) and Glazebrook 2021a on violence inflicted upon the Olynthian captive woman in Dem. 19.196–198 (who, though not a prostitute, is treated as one; see also Breitenfeld 2022, ch. 1). Contrast Cohen 2015, ch. 5, who argues that measures were in place to protect violence against prostitutes.
29 The classic work on slave torture is duBois 1991; see also, more recently, Ismard 2019, 140–155. For an explanation of why the Greeks use *basanos*, see Dem. 30.37: "Now, you all consider interrogation under torture to be the most reliable of all methods of proof in both private and public affairs, and whenever slaves and free men are present and the facts need to be ascertained, you don't make use of the free men's testimonies, but you seek to discover the truth by interrogating the slaves. That's quite reasonable, men of the jury: some of those who have testified before now have been found to have given untrue testimony, but it has never proved that any of those interrogated under torture have made untrue statements in consequence of the interrogation" (trans. MacDowell); see similarly Is. 8.12.

the challenge; alternatively, he could issue a counter-challenge offering up different slaves or different conditions. If the two parties agreed to have a particular person interrogated, that individual was tortured in the presence of their owner by the litigant who was not their owner, and if testimony was successfully elicited, it could then be introduced into court. A proposed interrogation in Aristophanes' *Frogs* gives us a sense for what *basanos* might have entailed, comic exaggeration notwithstanding: "Bind him to the ladder. Hang him up. Bristle-whip him. Flay him. Rack him. Pour vinegar up his nose too. Put bricks on him. Anything at all, except don't beat him with a stalk of leek or onion" (616–622, trans. Henderson).

Although we have references in Athenian lawsuits to *basanos* challenges, there is no clear evidence for *basanos* actually being carried out. For this reason, some scholars have concluded that *basanos* rarely, if ever, occurred. Gagarin has suggested that it was essentially a legal fiction: its purpose, at least by the classical period, was no longer (if it had ever been) to elicit truth from enslaved people, but was instead a way of making one's opponent look bad by issuing a challenge he would have to reject (out of fear of what the slave might say). This is not a universal view, however. David Mirhady, for example, has argued that *basanos* did take place, but that it functioned as a dispute-resolving alternative to going to court, which is why our existing court cases do not mention it having happened.[30] duBois, in turn, has stressed the *ideological* function of *basanos*, arguing that it was, like other violence against enslaved people, a way of drawing a clear line between slave and free: that is, it marked the enslaved person as distinctly "other."[31] Even if *basanos* was never or rarely used, its very existence may have reinforced the idea that enslaved people — unlike free men — had bodies that were vulnerable to routine abuse.

Of all the forms of institutionalized violence we find attested, that directed against the Helots was especially harsh.[32] As Theopompus, a historian writing in the late fourth/early third century BCE, writes, "The Helot population is in an altogether cruel and bitter condition" (BNJ 115 F 13), and Plutarch adds that "it was considered best to keep [the Helots] constantly employed so as to crush

---

[30] Gagarin 1996; Mirhady 1996. Cf. Ismard 2019, 144–148, who argues that *basanos* is not a fiction, but that *basanos* challenges were generally rejected because slave testimony, believed always to be true, was considered definitive proof and therefore impossible to challenge.
[31] duBois 1991.
[32] For a brief overview of the treatment of Helots, see Cartledge 2011, 84–86; see also Ducat 1990, 107–127. Aristotle points out, however, that Spartiates have to strike the proper balance: if they treat the Helots too badly, they will hate their masters and plot against them; if they treat them too well, the Helots will become insolent (*Pol.* 1269b7–12).

their spirit by perpetual toil and hardship" (*Sol.* 22.2). More specifically, we learn from the third-century BCE historian Myron that the Helots were forced to wear dog-skin caps and wrap themselves in animal skins, and that they received a set number of beatings per year; all of this was explicitly done, Myron says, in order to shame the Helots and remind them that they were slaves. In addition, enslavers were required, under pain of penalty, to rebuke any of their Helots who grew fat (BNJ 106 F 2). According to Plutarch, the Spartans would force the Helots to drink copious amounts of unmixed wine and bring them before the young Spartan men in the common mess halls to demonstrate what drunkenness looked like; they also forced the Helots to perform shameful songs and dances (*Lyc.* 28.4). Plutarch then quotes approvingly the saying that in Sparta, "the free man is the freest in the world, the slave the most slave" (*Lyc.* 28.5), clarifying that he believes that "such cruelties" (he does not specify which in particular) were imposed only after the Helots revolted following the earthquake in 464 (*Lyc.* 28.6) (on Helot revolts, see ch. 6.3).

While no one disputes that Helots were poorly treated, a few specific features of their treatment are debated. One is the nature of the *krypteia* (often translated, not uncontroversially, as "secret police force"), on which our sources provide differing accounts as to its nature, origin, and purpose.[33] So, for example, Megillus, the Spartan character in Plato's *Laws*, makes no mention of violence against Helots in his description of the *krypteia*: he calls it "wonderfully severe training in hardiness," in which Spartan men go barefoot and sleep without bedding in winter, have no servants to attend them, and wander the countryside day and night (633bc). These are presumably young men, although this is not specified; the word *neos* ("young") is, however, supplied in the scholion on this passage. We get a different account in Plutarch, who reports that violence against Helots played a key role in the *krypteia*. After noting that Aristotle claimed the *krypteia* was invented by the legendary lawgiver Lycurgus (*Lyc.* 28.1) — an account Plutarch himself doubts (28.6) — he explains that the *kypteia* involved sending the most intelligent young men out to the countryside, armed only with daggers and necessary rations. They were supposed to disperse and hide quietly in out-of-the-way places during the daytime, and at night come down onto the roads and cut the throat of any Helot they caught. They also, Plutarch says, "often" went into the fields where the Helots were working and killed the strongest of them (28.2-3).[34] Scholars have struggled to account for

---

[33] For an overview of these inconsistencies in our sources, see Ducat 2006, ch. 9.
[34] As Welwei 2004, 37 notes, Plutarch does not explicitly cite Aristotle for this description of what the *krypteia* entailed, so his source may be someone else.

the differences between Plato's and Plutarch's/Aristotle's account regarding the place of violence against Helots in the *krypteia*, arguing variously that Helot-hunting was always part of the *krypteia* but simply omitted by Plato; that it was a complete fiction; or that it was a late addition to the *krypteia*, dating either to after the Battle of Leuctra (371 BCE) or to Theban liberation of the Messenians in 369 BCE.[35] This is a question that is unlikely to be resolved.

Plutarch also reports that Aristotle said that the Spartan ephors, upon entering office each year, formally declared war on the Helots so that it would not be unholy to kill them (28.4).[36] This measure is likely connected to the *krypteia* in some way, though Plutarch does not make this explicit. The purpose of the constant attacks, however, is clear: whether part of the *krypteia* or not, it must have served to terrorize the Helots, as well as being a brutal reminder to them of their subordinate status. The same can likely also be said about the other degrading (if less violent) ways they were treated, like wearing dog-skin caps.

Yet another debate about the treatment of Helots centers on the credibility of the account in Thucydides that the Spartans once massacred 2,000 Helots (4.80.2–4; cf. Plut. *Lyc.* 28.3). Apparently, on one occasion during the Peloponnesian War, the Spartans were worried about the Helots revolting, so they hatched a plan. They asked the Helots to choose among their number those who were the best fighters, implying that those individuals would be given their freedom. This offer would not necessarily have surprised the Helots, since participation in the military was in fact one of the ways they could gain their freedom.[37] But in this case, the offer was a trick: the Spartans were simply trying to target Helots most likely to revolt (on Helot revolts, see ch. 6.3). The Helots who were selected put garlands on their heads and made the rounds of sanctuaries as if they had been freed, only to be killed (literally, "made to disappear") shortly afterwards by the Spartans. Cartledge not only finds this account believable but deems it the paradigmatic case of how the Spartans mistreated the Helots.[38] Annalisa Paradiso, however, doubts the historical reality of this massacre, especially the enormous number of Helots who were allegedly killed. Arguing, then, that the story must be propaganda, perhaps concocted by the Spartans to send a

---

35 That Helot-hunting was always a part of the *krypteia*: see Ducat 2006, 304–307. That it was a fiction invented after 369 BCE, see Welwei 2004. That it was added to the *krypteia* after Leuctra, see Link 2006; that it was added after the liberation of the Messenians, see Nafissi 2015; see also Couvenhes 2014, who argues that the *krypteia* only emerged as a militarized force after 369 BCE.
36 Nafissi 2015, 222 argues that this practice began only after 369 BCE.
37 On the politics of Helot manumission in Thucydides, see Paradiso 2008.
38 Cartledge 2003, 20–23; see also Harvey 2004 and Lewis 2018a, 135–136.

message to the Messenians and to runaway Helots, she concludes that this episode cannot add much to our understanding of the treatment of Helots.³⁹

4.4 Protection from (extreme) violence?

Despite enslaved people's susceptibility to abuse (demonstrated above), there were some limitations to this violence. As Hunt has shown, there were reasons an enslaver might refrain from inflicting excessive violence on his slave, even if it was his right to do so. For one, a whipping might make a "disobedient" slave even more obstinate, or, if sufficiently injured, unable to perform work (either temporarily or permanently). And extreme violence of course runs the risk of death, resulting in the loss of valuable property. Moreover, at least in Athens, an enslaver was not allowed to kill his own slaves (Antiph. 5.47). Although it is unlikely that he would be prosecuted for it, if he did kill his slave, even unintentionally, he would have to purify himself from the ritual pollution (*miasma*) caused by the bloodshed (Antiph. 6.4). Finally, abuse of one's subordinates could also reflect poorly on one's character. As the Athenian character in Plato's *Laws* explains, "it is his way of dealing with men whom it is easy for him to wrong that shows most clearly whether a man is genuine or hypocritical in his reverence for justice and hatred of injustice" (776d). Similarly, an enslaver might avoid striking his slaves out of anger, since impulsive violence, regardless of its target, ran counter to Greek ideals of moderation and self-control.⁴⁰

An enslaved person, however, could not rely upon their enslaver (or other free people) to restrain themselves. Fortunately, there were other avenues open to enslaved people who faced abuse, whether at the hands of their enslavers or others. One option was running away to an asylum like the Theseion (the temple of the hero Theseus) or the altar of the Eumenides in Athens (Ar. *Eq.* 1311–1312; see also ch. 6.2).⁴¹ Another strategy was seeking help from friends or other connections who might offer protection; this seems to be what Lesis was hoping for in the lead letter discussed above. A related tactic may have involved exploiting the practice of noxal surrender (i.e., handing over to a victim an enslaved person who committed an act of damage or wounding against them). Forsdyke suggests, based on passages of Plato's *Laws* (936ce, 879ab), that en-

---

39 Paradiso 2004.
40 For all of these reasons an owner might avoid violence, see Hunt 2016, 150–155.
41 On slave asylum, see Gottesman 2014, ch. 6; Ismard 2019, ch. 4; Forsdyke 2021, 227–235 and forthcoming.

slaved people seeking a new owner might collude with a third party to bring a charge of damage or wounding against their owner, precisely in order to be handed over.[42]

And if an enslaved person faced violence at the hands of someone who was not their owner, there were steps the owner could take to redress the wrong (if more in the service of recouping his own losses than in seeking justice for the enslaved person). At least in classical Athens, in the case of injury to his slave, the owner could bring a suit against the offender for property damage (*dikē blabēs*), and in the case of his slave being killed, a suit for killing (*dikē phonou*).[43] A *dikē phonou* on behalf of an enslaved person would have been brought to the Palladion, a court that heard cases of unintentional homicide of citizens as well the killing of enslaved people and metics (Arist. *Ath. Pol.* 57.3; Dem. 23.71), thus reinforcing the lesser status of non-citizens even in death.[44] Given that the *dikē blabēs* was a frequently used suit encompassing a broad range of damage, and also given that we have no attestations of owners bringing *dikai phonou* on behalf of a slave (only a reference to an owner unable to bring one on behalf of his freed slave: Dem. 47.68–73), it is possible that a plaintiff might choose to bring a *dikē blabēs* rather than a *dike phonou* even in the event of his slave's death.

One final protection that enslaved people were granted, at least in classical Athens, was from a form of violence called *hubris*. *Hubris* has been variously defined by scholars: Fisher takes it as a deliberate insult to another's honor, whereas Douglas Cairns and Mirko Canevaro have stressed the disposition of exuberant arrogance as the most salient feature of *hubris*.[45] The reason that enslaved people were protected from *hubris* continues to be a source of heated debate. Some scholars, following the explanations provided by Demosthenes (21.46) and Aeschines (1.17), assert that the purpose of this protection was to demonstrate how unacceptable any and all *hubris* was.[46] The aim, then, was to

---

[42] On enslaved people using third parties to achieve their ends, see Forsdyke 2021, 223–227 and forthcoming.
[43] On the *dikē blabēs*, see Todd 1995, 279–282; on trials for homicide, including the *dikē phonou*, see Todd 1995, 271–276.
[44] On the killing of enslaved people, see Ismard 2019, 193–198.
[45] Deliberate insult: Fisher 1992, 1; disposition: Cairns 1996 and Canavero 2018 (= 2019), building on MacDowell 1990.
[46] See Fisher 2001 [1993], 141–142. Dem. 21.46: "[the lawgiver] went to such extreme lengths that even if a slave was assaulted [lit. if someone committed *hubris* against him], he granted him the same right of bringing a public action. He thought that he ought to look, not at the rank of the sufferer, but at the nature of the act, and when he found the act unjustifiable, he would not give it his sanction either in regard to a slave or in any other case. For nothing, men

prevent behavior that was thought damaging to the polis as a whole: as Canevaro puts it, committing *hubris* against anyone, including enslaved people, entailed overestimating one's own claims to honor (*timē*), thereby violating community standards.[47] Other scholars have suggested that the law protected enslaved people from *hubris* in their capacity as part of their owner's household, or as human beings who possessed some (albeit small) share of honor that warranted protection.[48] The explanation is most likely some combination of the above. There is some question, however, about the degree to which enslaved people might actually have been able to make use of the *graphē hubreōs*, the suit prosecuting *hubris*. Cohen contends that they could and did use this *graphē*, with free Athenians bringing the suit on their behalf, but we have no evidence for this happening.[49] I have argued, by contrast, that the costs and other risks of bringing such a lawsuit would have made it unlikely for an Athenian to bring a *graphē hubreōs* on behalf of an enslaved person (though the likelihood may have increased slightly in the case of "privileged" slaves).[50] It may be, then, that this protection was more nominal than actually attainable.

4.5 Conclusion

While the treatment of enslaved people depended in part on the personalities and whims of individual slaveowners, recent scholarship has shown that it was also dictated by their particular slaving strategies. Violence against enslaved bodies was, if not universal, at least very common: it could be inflicted by owners or (in certain circumstances) by the polis, serving as a form of punishment, a mode of control, and a way of reinforcing the ideological line between slave and free. Committing violence against one's own slave was more or less permissible

---

of Athens, nothing in the world is more intolerable than a personal outrage (*hubris*), nor is there anything that more deserves your resentment" (trans. Murray). See also Aeschin. 1.17: "Now perhaps some one, on first hearing this law, may wonder for what possible reason this word 'slaves' was added in the law against outrage (*hubris*). But if you reflect on the matter, fellow citizens, you will find this to be the best provision of all. For it was not for the slaves that the lawgiver was concerned, but he wished to accustom you to keep a long distance away from the crime of outraging free men, and so he added the prohibition against the outraging even of slaves. In a word, he was convinced that in a democracy that man is unfit for citizenship who outrages any person whatsoever" (trans. Adams).

47 Canevaro 2018 (= 2019); Ismard 2019, 201–202 and Vlassopoulos 2021, 132–133 agree.
48 Part of the owner's household: Dmitriev 2016; residual honor: Fisher 1995, 48–62.
49 Cohen 2000, 160–166; 2014, 185–190; 2015, 126–129.
50 Kamen forthcoming.

(though impractical if it affected the slave's productivity), but doing so against another's slave was legally actionable. And although scholars continue to debate why enslaved people, at least in Athens, were protected from *hubris*, there is near consensus that it had more to do with regulating the behavior and interests of citizens than protecting enslaved people themselves.

5 Sex and Gender

Some of the most important developments in the study of Greek (and Roman) slavery the past twenty-five years have been in the areas of sex and gender. A pioneer in this field was the volume *Women and Slaves in Greco-Roman Culture: Differential Equations* (1998), co-edited by Sandra Joshel and Sheila Murnaghan.[1] Exploring many facets of the interactions between women and enslaved people in Greco-Roman literature and material culture, this volume has had a profound influence on subsequent scholarship on gender and slavery. This work has included, among other things, investigations into the ways that free people defined their (gender) identities in relation to enslaved people, the gendered nature of enslaved labor, the relationship between gender (and sex) in manumission, the sexual use of enslaved people by their owners and other free people (including but not limited to prostitution), and the sexual lives of enslaved people apart from their use by free people. I address each of these areas in turn.

5.1 Gender

Free people in the Greek world defined themselves, in general, in opposition to unfree people, and these oppositions were often gendered. As Joshel and Murnaghan observe, "the honor of the free woman was frequently established and fortified through her pointed differentiation from the female slave."[2] Harper has further developed this point, arguing that from classical Greece through late antiquity, the word *eleuthera* (literally, "free [woman]") often had the specific sense of "sexually respectable woman," ideologically constructed in opposition to (sexually dishonored) slaves and prostitutes.[3] Free men in antiquity were also defined in opposition to enslaved males, if perhaps to a lesser extent. Wrenhaven, for example, has written about how the (notionally ugly) bodies of enslaved men in Greek art sometimes serve to illuminate by contrast, and define in turn, the ideals of beauty for free men.[4]

---

[1] Joshel and Murnaghan 1998a.
[2] Joshel and Murnaghan 1998b, 4.
[3] Harper 2017a.
[4] Wrenhaven 2021, 76–83. See also Weiler 2002, who argues that the depictions of enslaved men as unattractive or deformed represent an inversion of the nobility or goodness (*kalokagathia*) characteristic of citizen men, which was also manifested in their external appearance.

Another topic of interest has been the gendered division of labor in the Greek world. As Glazebrook points out, certain jobs performed by enslaved people were considered "male," others "female," though she provides the important qualification that in non-elite households, the division between these tasks may have been less strict.[5] One of our best sources for the division of labor, discussed by Glazebrook, is Xenophon's *Oikonomikos*, in which Ischomachus describes the distinct chores done by women and by men in the household. Ischomachus justifies the gendered division of labor by explaining that men's bodies are suited for outdoor jobs: plowing, sowing, planting, and herding (7.20). Women's bodies, by contrast, are less capable of endurance and therefore are more suited for indoor jobs: nursing newborns, making bread, spinning wool and making clothing, and guarding the things brought into the house (7.21–25). The patterns we find in the *Oikonomikos* are the same we see, for example, in Homer's *Odyssey*, which suggests a fairly consistent picture of gendered slave labor in the Greek world.[6]

Two types of such labor are of particular note here: that of the (male) *paidagōgos* or child-minder and the (female) *titthē* or wet-nurse/nanny.[7] The closeness between these individuals and their charges, even after the child was grown, is a common motif in Greek literature of all genres.[8] One has only to think of Odysseus' wet-nurse Eurycleia, who knew his body so intimately that she immediately recognized the scar he had incurred as a child (Hom. *Od.* 19.392–393), and when she realized that he was still alive, she cried tears both of joy for his return and of grief over his imagined loss (19.471–472). Similarly, the nurse Cilissa in Aeschylus' *Libation Bearers* is distraught when she thinks Orestes is dead, saying that she wore out her soul toiling for her beloved (*philon*) charge, nursing him from his birth, waking to his cries during the night, tending to his every need[9] — and of course Cilissa is far from being the only nurse who

---

[5] On the gendered division of labor in Greece, see Glazebrook 2017.
[6] On the gendered division of labor in Homer, see Lewis 2018a, 114–117. On continuities in slave management from Homer to Xenophon, see Porter 2021a.
[7] On child-minders and wet-nurses, see Forsdyke 2021, 131–133. On breastfeeding (including wet-nursing) in Greek literature and thought, see Marshall 2017.
[8] Mark Golden explains the prominence of these figures in our sources by the intimate nature of their services: "answering cries at night, carrying the child around to ease pressure on its tender limbs, steadying its first steps, singing lullabies, storytelling, wiping noses, changing and cleaning swaddling clothes, toilet training, pre-chewing food, accompanying older children on trips outside the home" (2011, 141).
[9] See Aesch. *Cho.* 747–764: "...I have never yet had to endure a sorrow like this. Under the other troubles I patiently bore up. But dear Orestes, who wore away my life with toil, whom I

plays a prominent role in Greek tragedy. Moreover, the affection between these nurses and their charges tends to be represented as reciprocal: the speaker of the lawsuit *Against Evergus and Mnesibulus* (Dem. 47) talks about his elderly childhood nurse, whom his father had freed and whom the speaker welcomed back into the household after her husband died (47.55); as he says, "I could not allow my *titthē* or my *paidagōgos* to be in need" (47.56). But it is also important that we not take at face value the rosy picture presented by our elite authors about the intimacy between the *paidagōgos* or *titthē* and their charges — after all, the emotional labor the latter provided was a required component of their enslavement.[10]

A final subject that scholars have explored in this context is the relationship between gender, sex, and manumission in the Greek world (on manumission, see further ch. 7). In nearly all slaveholding societies, including those of Greece, enslaved women are manumitted more often than enslaved men.[11] As Ingomar Weiler has pointed out, this gender discrepancy is due in large part to sex: that is, because enslaved women were often the sexual objects of free men (whether their own enslavers or other individuals), these men were more likely to help them become free.[12] These women included, but were by no means limited to, enslaved prostitutes (on whom see further below, ch. 5.2). So, for example, an enslaver might free one of his own slaves whom he has been using sexually, either in order to make her his free concubine or in order to acknowledge his paternity of her children, or both.[13] Alternatively, a free person might pay for the freedom of someone else's slave, either to obtain exclusive sexual access to that individual (e.g. in the case of enslaved prostitutes; see ch. 5.2) or sexual access

---

reared after receiving him straight from his mother's womb! <Over and over again I heard> his shrill, imperative cries, which forced me to wander around at night <and perform> many disagreeable tasks which I had to endure and which did me no good. A child without intelligence must needs be reared like an animal — how could it be otherwise? — by the intelligence of his nurse; when he's still an infant in swaddling clothes he can't speak at all if he's in the grip of hunger or thirst, say, or of an urge to make water — and the immature bowel of small children is its own master. I had to divine these things in advance, and often, I fancy, I was mistaken, and as cleaner of the baby's wrappings — well, a launderer and a caterer were holding the same post. Practising both these two crafts, I reared up Orestes for his father; and now, to my misery, I learn that he is dead!" (trans. Sommerstein).

10 On the emotional labor performed by enslaved people, see Levin-Richardson forthcoming, which focuses on the emotional labor of prostitutes in Greece and Rome.
11 Patterson 1982, 263. See also Tucker 1982, who demonstrates this same trend in the Delphic manumission inscriptions.
12 Weiler 2001.
13 Tucker 1982; Klees 1998, 310–314; Weiler 2001; Zelnick-Abramovitz 2005, 167–169.

at all (since it was not generally permitted to use someone else's slave sexually; see ch. 5.3).[14] And it was not only enslaved women who were freed for these reasons: we sometimes hear, albeit less frequently, of enslaved boys manumitted for sexual purposes (e.g., Hyp. 3 where the speaker is attracted to another man's slave and tries to purchase the boy's freedom; see further below, ch. 5.3). Another connection between sex and manumission has to do with reproduction; in a number of cases, enslavers require that enslaved women, in exchange for their manumission, bear a child and hand it over as their replacement.[15] Finally, in addition to sex, Glazebrook has shown that another important factor in the manumission of women was the *non-sexual* relations of intimacy that some had with their enslaver and their enslaver's wife and children, often by virtue of the types of labor they performed.[16] We might think again, for example, of the wet-nurses mentioned above.

5.2 Prostitution

Until recently, much of the work that had been done on sex and slavery in Greece focused on prostitution. Greek prostitution in particular has seen a relative explosion of scholarly interest in the past twenty-five years, since the publication in the late 1990's of James Davidson's book *Courtesans and Fishcakes* and Leslie Kurke's work on the *hetaira* (conventionally understood as a higher-status prostitute, as compared to the lower-status *pornē*, though this distinction is contested; see below).[17] Since that time, a handful of edited volumes and a few monographs have been published on the topic.[18] The focus of this work, however, has not always been on the enslaved status, per se, of these prostitutes.[19] Instead, much (excellent) work has been done on the distinction between the

---

[14] Glazebrook 2014; Kamen 2014b.
[15] Tucker 1982, 233–235; Zelnick-Abramovitz 2005, 229–230.
[16] Glazebrook 2017.
[17] Davidson 1997; Kurke 1997 and 1999, ch. 5.
[18] Edited volumes on prostitution in both Greece and Rome: Faraone and McClure 2006; Glazebrook and Henry 2011a; Glazebrook and Tsakirgis 2016; see also Glazebrook 2015a, a special issue of the journal *Helios* on this topic. Monographs on prostitution in Athens: Cohen 2015; as represented in the Athenian courts: Glazebrook 2021b; in the Greek world more broadly: Kapparis 2018.
[19] One recent book on Greek prostitution (Kapparis 2018) does not list "slaves" or "slavery" in the index. Scholars often simply assume that prostitutes in Greece were enslaved or manumitted, though Cohen 2015 argues that prostitutes (especially *hetairai*) could be free, and Kennedy 2015 suggests that the term *hetaira* was originally used of aristocratic women.

pornē and the *hetaira*; the representation of prostitutes and sexual labor in Greek literature, especially Attic oratory; and spaces of prostitution in the Greek world.[20]

When the enslaved status of prostitutes is explicitly addressed by scholars, it is often in the context of discussions of manumission (on which see further ch. 7). One of the earliest attested examples of a manumitted prostitute comes from Herodotus, who says that the *hetaira* Rhodopis had her freedom purchased at great expense by Charaxus of Mytilene (Sappho's brother, who allegedly railed at her brother for doing so) (2.135). The bulk of our textual evidence, however, comes from Attic oratory, from which we learn of prostitutes being freed through a practice that scholars sometimes call *prasis ep' eleutheriai* ("sale for the purpose of freedom"). As Glazebrook points out, *prasis ep' eleutheriai* is usually mentioned in court as part of an attempt to tar one's opponent — namely, by accusing them of spending vast sums of money on prostitutes.[21] Though it was not only prostitutes who were freed in this way, it is possible that these sales were of particular use to *hetairai*, who could be relatively well paid and who had access to men (past and present clients) who could put up the money for their freedom.[22] One of our best such examples is the manumission of a prostitute named Neaira, described in detail in Apollodorus' *Against Neaira* ([Dem.] 59). In this speech, we learn that Neaira collected money from past and present clients, adding some of her own savings to the mix, in order to pay her owners for her freedom (59.31–32).

Other (albeit more speculative) evidence for the manumission of prostitutes comes from epigraphy. For example, a few of the manumission inscriptions from Hellenistic Delphi (see further ch. 7) use the word *ergasia* ("work") or the

---

20 On the distinction between *pornē* and *hetaira*: it has been argued that the distinction between the two is an ideological one, with the *pornē* symbolizing commodity exchange, the *hetaira* aristocratic gift exchange (Davidson 1997, 73–210; Kurke 1997); that *pornai* worked under another's control (and thus were or were regarded as servile), whereas *hetairai* worked independently (and were not looked down upon) (Cohen 2003; 2006; 2015, ch. 1); that the *hetaira* was a subtype of *pornē* (Kapparis 2018); and that the terms are fluid and the distinction not always clear-cut (Glazebrook and Henry 2011b, 4–8 and many of the essays in Glazebrook and Henry 2011a). On the representation of prostitutes in literature, see McClure 2003; in Attic oratory specifically, see Miner 2003; Glazebrook 2006, 2021b. On spaces of prostitution, see Glazebrook 2011; Glazebrook and Tsakirgis 2016.
21 Glazebrook 2014; see also Kamen 2014a, which also argues that *prasis ep' eleutheriai* is a secular parallel to the later-attested sacral sales of enslaved people to gods for the purpose of freedom (see ch. 7).
22 On the well-paid status of many *hetairai*, see Cohen 2015, ch. 7. On the usefulness of *prasis ep' eleutheriai* to prostitutes, see Kamen 2014a.

verb *ergazomai* ("to work"), which in Greek literary texts often refers to sexual labor (including in [Dem.] 59, mentioned above). If that holds in this context as well, these inscriptions may attest to the manumission of enslaved prostitutes.[23] We may also have epigraphic evidence for manumitted prostitutes in classical Athens. More than 80% of the women listed on the late-fourth-century BCE inscriptions recording dedications of silver *phialai* ("bowls") — conventionally thought to represent the verdicts of trials in which acquitted freed slaves attain their full freedom (see ch. 7.1)[24] — are referred to as *talasiourgoi*, "wool workers." Drawing out the various links between wool-working and prostitutes in literary, artistic, and archaeological sources, Wrenhaven has suggested that the term is used here as a euphemism for prostitute.[25] If this interpretation is correct, it has the potential to add to our (admittedly small) body of epigraphic evidence for the manumission of prostitutes.

5.3 The sexual use of non-prostituted enslaved people

The sexual use of enslaved people *outside* the context of prostitution has only recently become a dedicated area of scholarly interest, as attested by the publication in 2021 of the first edited volume on the subject.[26] Admittedly, evidence for the sexual use of non-prostituted slaves is less plentiful than that for prostitutes, but conventional wisdom nonetheless holds that enslaved women and boys in Greece were, as a rule, routinely subject to sexual exploitation.[27] This exploitation took different forms. As Gaca has shown, girls and women (and sometimes boys) who were captured in war were routinely subject to rape.[28] The sexual abuse, moreover, continued long after their initial capture.[29] For in-

---

23 Kamen 2014b; this interpretation is adopted in turn by Mulliez 2021a, 148–150.
24 Cf. Meyer 2010 who has a radically different interpretation of these inscriptions; on this, see ch. 7.1.
25 Wrenhaven 2009. That the *talasiourgoi* were prostitutes was suggested earlier by Cohen 2006, 105–108 (see also Cohen 2015, 53–59), but he does not argue that the term is euphemistic. Cf. earlier interpretations of the *talasiourgoi*: e.g. Rosivach 1989, 366–367 (generic term for housewives); Labarre 1998, 794–795 (actual wool-workers).
26 Kamen and Marshall 2021.
27 On the routine sexual use of enslaved people: Klees 1998, 161–166; Paradiso 1999; Fischer 2010b; Golden 2011, 146–151; Walin 2012, ch. 4; Glazebrook 2017; Breitenfeld 2022 (focusing on the vulnerability of enslaved women to sexual assault). Cf. Cohen 2014, discussed below.
28 See Gaca 2011, 2014, 2015.
29 But cf. Gaca 2021, who argues that men did not have the same free rein in their households as they did on the battlefield.

stance, in Lysias' speech *On the Murder of Eratosthenes*, the defendant narrates that when he told his wife to tend to their crying baby, the wife responded that he just wanted to "have a go at" (*peirais*) their female slave, which he had done before when he was drunk (1.12). Taking advantage of a wife's temporary absence is seen also in Aristophanes' *Peace*, when the Chorus of men sings that one of the joys of peacetime is kissing one's pretty Thracian slave girl when one's wife is in the bath (1138–1139). Ischomachus acknowledges that the sexual use of one's slaves was both routine and not consensual when he says that wives are more sexually appealing than slaves, since the former can give willingly whereas slaves are forced to submit (Xen. *Oik.* 10.12). Sexual relations between enslaver and enslaved are also suggested in those manumission inscriptions where the woman being manumitted appears to be the sexual partner of the manumittor; this is clearest when she is said (implicitly or explicitly) to be the mother of his child or children.[30] Sometimes, albeit rarely, we hear of free men having sex with enslaved individuals who were not their own: this is something that was not generally permitted, except in certain contexts, including prostitution (see above, ch. 5.2) and apparently occasionally as a punishment for committing some sort of offense. For example, in Aristophanes' *Acharnians*, Dikaiopolis sings about wanting to catch an enslaved girl named Thraitta (or perhaps "an enslaved Thracian girl") stealing wood from his property so he can catch her, throw her down, and "de-pit" her (271–275). Presumably the fact that she was stealing would have exempted Dikaiopolis from charges of harming her owner's property (on such charges, see ch. 4.4).

Enslaved boys, too, were subject to sexual advances and sexual assaults. Rafał Matuszewski has recently explored the sexual use of enslaved boys in classical Athens, drawing primarily on vases with sympotic scenes, in which symposiasts make overtures toward enslaved boys, from flirting to touching.[31] We find similar practices in our literary sources as well.[32] In Xenophon's *Symposium*, the Syracusan character says that he sleeps with his slave boy "all night every night" and is worried that other men will try to persuade the boy to sleep with them, too (4.53–54). In another instance, the tragedian Sophocles, seeing an attractive slave boy at a symposium try to fish a piece of straw out of a cup

---

30 See Mulliez forthcoming a, which tracks these and other relationships in the Delphic manumission inscriptions.
31 Matuszewski 2021.
32 Old Comedy also contains references to the sexual use of enslaved males: e.g. the Sausage Seller gives Demos a folding stool along with a well-endowed enslaved boy to carry it, saying that if Demos wants, he can use the boy as his "stool" (Ar. *Eq.* 1384–1386).

with his finger, tells the boy to blow it off instead, prompting the boy to put his face close enough for Sophocles to kiss (Athen. 13.604c). Sometimes a man's lust for an enslaved boy provides the background for a lawsuit. One of the most involved instances comes from Hyperides' speech *Against Athenogenes* (3). The plaintiff, a man named Epikrates, claims he fell in love with the enslaved boy of a certain Athenogenes and wanted to purchase the boy's freedom. According to Epikrates, Athenogenes swindled him by selling him the boy (along with the boy's brother and father) without disclosing that the slaves were saddled with debt – a debt that then redounded to Epikrates. In another lawsuit, the speaker, defending himself on a charge of wounding a man named Simon with intent to kill, describes his rivalry with Simon over a Plataean boy named Theodotus (likely but not definitely a slave), with whom they were both in love (Lys. 3).[33]

Despite these numerous examples, Cohen has argued against overstating the degree to which enslaved people, both male and female, were subject to sexual use. He claims that the evidence we have is "sparse and equivocal," and that such abuse would have been mitigated by measures designed to prevent men from being excessively predatory.[34] This is true, up to a point. Enslaved people were technically protected from *hubris*, including sexual assault (though it is unclear how real this protection was in practice: see ch. 4.4).[35] Moreover, Greek men were encouraged, in general, to control their desires, and there seem to have been unspoken rules about which emotions were appropriate for a free man to feel for an enslaved person.[36] Drawing on Lysias 4, Marshall demonstrates that an owner who felt excessive love for his female slave might be considered *duserōs* ("love-sick"), which was not only frowned upon but thought damaging to the city of Athens.[37] Matuszewski similarly shows that while *epithumia* ("desire") for enslaved boys was completely acceptable by Athenian standards, *erōs* ("love") was ideally meant to be directed only toward free boys.[38] These various factors may have made men somewhat less inclined to indulge all of their sexual urges, but our evidence suggests that it was not enough to stop them altogether.

---

[33] Matuszewski 2021, 112–114 considers Theodotus to be enslaved.
[34] Cohen 2014, 185–192, quotation at p. 186.
[35] See Kamen forthcoming.
[36] On controlling desires, see Ormand 2018 [2008].
[37] Marshall 2021.
[38] Matuszewski 2021.

In comparison with free men using enslaved people for sex, we have considerably fewer attestations of free *women* doing the same, apart from a handful of examples in literature.[39] For example, a man in Aristophanes' *Women at the Thesmophoria*, in disguise as a woman, says that Euripides never mentions the fact that women have sex with slaves and muleteers when they have no one else to sleep with (490–492).[40] In an episode of the anonymous *Life of Aesop*, Aesop's owner's wife lusts after Aesop after seeing him masturbate, promising him a new shirt if he has sex with her ten times (*Vita* W 75). And in Herondas' *Mime* 5, one of the most frequently cited examples of a woman using a male slave sexually, Bitinna is jealous that Gastron (the slave she is having sex with) has slept with another woman, and so has one of her other slaves strip and bind him, threatening him with two thousand lashes and tattooing.[41] In a survey of such episodes from various genres of Greek literature, Stephen Todd concludes that men did not generally consider male slave sexuality a threat to their (freeborn) women.[42] They may have been more concerned about the safety of their sons, if this is how we are to interpret the law from Athens stating that an enslaved person cannot be the lover of (*eran*) or follow a free boy; if caught, he was to receive fifty lashes from the public whip (Aeschin. 1.139).

At least some men, however, may have worried that enslaved men were having sex with their wives, and this anxiety may have been more pronounced when they were away at war and could not keep an eye on what was going on back home.[43] In fact, the Greeks tell stories of precisely this kind of thing happening. In a famous example, Herodotus reports that when the Scythian men were away at war for twenty-eight years, they returned home to find that their wives had been having sex with their slaves. Not only that, but the children they bore from these unions tried to fight the Scythian soldiers upon their return (4.1–4)! According to Herodotus, the Scythians managed to scare them into backing down by brandishing whips, thus (in the logic of the story) revealing

---

39 Klees 1998, 166 thinks these relations, at least in the classical period, were probably rare.
40 Walin 2012, ch. 1 has argued that sexual relationships between free women and enslaved men in Greek literature often serve ideological purposes: in Old Comedy, he suggests that they blur the line between slave and free in order to uphold a more rigid distinction between wealthy and lower-class Athenians.
41 Fountoulakis 2004 argues that the tensions in the relationship between Bittina and Gastron — namely, his fear of punishment and her fear of losing power — stem from their relationship being built on fear and authority, as well as the male being the subordinate one in their relationship (thus reversing normative sex/gender hierarchies).
42 Todd 2013.
43 See Golden 2011, 149–150 on anxieties about women having sex with male slaves.

the "natural" slavishness of their wives' bastard sons. The story's outcome, along with the fact that it was not Greek men but Scythians who were cuckolded by slaves, may have made the story less anxiety-producing for Herodotus' Greek readers — but this does not mean they did not have concerns about their own wives' behavior.

5.4 Enslaved people as sexual subjects

Another area that scholars have explored, especially recently, is the sexual lives of slaves apart from their use by their owners or other free people. In Old Comedy, for instance, we find slaves talking about visiting prostitutes (Ar. *Vesp.* 500–502) and masturbating (Ar. *Eq.* 24–29; cf. Ar. *Ran.* 542–548) — and presumably these are things that were known to happen in real life as well.[44] At least on the stage, Daniel Walin has argued that licentious slaves would have given the audience members a vicarious thrill, since they could temporarily put themselves in the enslaved person's shoes and shed the constraints of appropriate citizen behavior.[45]

Although enslavers could not always control what happened outside their households, they did try to manage what happened with their slaves' sex lives under their own roofs. Of particular interest in this context are the works on household management mentioned above (ch. 4.1).[46] For example, in Xenophon's *Oikonomikos*, Ischomachus says that he separates the men's quarters of his house from the women's quarters with a bolted door so that the slaves cannot breed without his permission. He also notes that because honest slaves become more loyal when they have children, whereas bad ones become worse when they mate, reproduction should be allowed as an incentive only to the former (9.5). Pseudo-Aristotle, in turn, advises letting one's slaves bear children, since this was thought to make them less likely to run away (*Oik.* 1344b17–18). After all, they would have wanted to keep their families together as best they could.

---

44 See also Porter 2021b, 98–99 on enslaved men having sex with prostitutes.
45 Walin 2012. On the stereotype of the sexually boundless slave in Old Comedy, see also Walin 2009 and Todd 2013, 37–41.
46 See Klees 1998, 156–157; Fischer 2010b; Porter 2021b, 90–93.

While marriages per se between slaves were not recognized, nor were kin relations in general, marriage-like and family-like groupings did exist.[47] And it is likely that enslaved people who lived and worked semi-independently — either because of the nature of their labor or because they belonged to the city — had greater opportunity to pursue sexual relationships of their choosing.[48] In Menander's *Epitrepontes*, for example, the relatively privileged charcoal-burner slave Syros has a "wife" (*gunaika*) (267). Evidence for family units also exists in epigraphic sources, including the Delphic manumission inscriptions, as Dominique Mulliez has shown. In addition to identifying such groupings, Mulliez also finds evidence for family solidarity akin to what we find among the free, including parents helping their children, children supporting their parents, and even adoptive (or quasi-adoptive) relationships.[49] But "marriages" and "families" among slaves were of course different in many ways from legally recognized ones: members of an enslaved couple might live in separate households if they had different owners, and enslaved people had no right to protect their spouses or their children (Pl. *Grg.* 483b) or to prevent them from being sold off. However, we do find an interesting statement in a recently discovered fragment of Hyperides' *Against Timandrus*, in which the speaker, accusing Timandrus of separating a (free) orphan girl from her siblings, claims that even slave-dealers keep families together. As Christopher Jones points out, it is hard to know how representative this statement is of Athenian or Greek views more broadly. Nonetheless, it does seem to indicate at least some degree of recognition of slave families, even if it is not *legal* recognition.[50]

5.5 Conclusion

Recent scholarship has demonstrated the importance of taking into account an enslaved person's gender in fully understanding their status and life experiences. After all, gender affected many aspects of an enslaved person's existence, including the types of labor they performed and the likelihood they might attain manumission. The sexual experiences of enslaved people have also begun to be taken seriously as an area of inquiry. Investigation into slave-prostitution began in earnest about twenty-five years ago and has continued to yield fruitful re-

---

47 On the marriages/families of enslaved people, see Klees 1998, 155–161; Fischer 2010b; Golden 2011, 143–146; Lewis 2013; Porter 2021b, 93–97; Mulliez forthcoming a.
48 See Cohen 2014, 189–190.
49 Mulliez forthcoming a.
50 Jones 2008.

sults. In addition, scholars have turned in recent years to the study of the vulnerability of *non-prostituted* enslaved people to sexual assault, as well as the capacity of enslaved people to be sexual subjects or agents in their own right. Both are still relatively new areas of inquiry and have potential to be explored in much greater detail, with one promising approach being a study of these topics through the lenses of gender studies, queer theory, or comparative material.

6 Agency, Resistance, and Revolt

As previous chapters have shown, the condition of being enslaved was in general one of subordination and violence. With this systemic oppression having been demonstrated, scholars in recent years have turned their attention to the ways that at least some enslaved people, despite their subjugated status, were able to carve out an existence of their own. Whether or not we call this "agency" (see further below in ch. 6.1), we can and should look for traces of the personhood officially denied to enslaved people by their enslavers. After discussing the question of slave agency more broadly, I turn to one important area in which this agency has been detected: namely, in the resistance of enslaved individuals to their enslavers. In the Greek world, this usually came in the form of small-scale resistance, with actual revolts being considerably less common (the Helots being a notable exception).

6.1 Agency

Vlassopoulos has argued over the course of much of his scholarship that we ought to recognize the agency of enslaved people in Greece, as well as fleshing out what this agency looked like.[1] Part of what drives this work is a (multi-part) challenge to Patterson's articulation of slavery as social death (see ch. 1.4). First, Vlassopoulos argues that this conception of slavery reflects the enslaver's perspective rather than that of the enslaved person. "Slave" is, after all, an imposed identity: it is how other people categorized those they enslaved, not necessarily how enslaved people understood or identified themselves. This is not to say, of course, that enslaved people were unaware of their status, just that the ways they thought of themselves were not restricted to this facet of their condition.[2]

---

[1] See most recently Vlassopoulos 2021 *passim*, especially 189–199 on slave agency as a force in historical change. See also Forsdyke 2021, a theme of which is slave agency.

[2] See Vlassopoulos 2021, ch. 5, which draws on identity studies from other disciplines to explore the complex and contradictory aspects of slave identity. Vlassopoulos notes that there are two modes of identification that enslaved people partake in: a categorical mode (i.e., belonging to the same category as others based on certain shared features) and a relational one (i.e., based on relationships between people, e.g. kinship). He also draws a distinction between direct relationships (i.e., those based on personal encounters) and indirect relationships (i.e., those lacking personal encounters); primary relationships (i.e., those between persons as a whole) and secondary relationships (i.e., those between persons as enactors of specific roles);

Secondly, Vlassopoulos demonstrates that many enslaved people were parts of communities and networks — ones that may have been invisible to their owners — thus making them less alienated than Patterson's social death definition might have us believe. Moreover, these networks, formed on the basis of, for example, shared household, profession, ethnicity, or religious practices, were an important way for enslaved people to exercise agency and at least sometimes overcome some of the barriers they normally faced based on their legal status.[3] Indeed, McKeown considers the building of communities, and especially groups that included both enslaved and free people, one of the "collective strategies" used by enslaved people as "active subjects."[4] The networks built between enslaved and free people is a topic also addressed by Forsdyke in her work on slave agency. More specifically, she argues that the bonds that enslaved and formerly enslaved people formed with citizens, coupled with their own knowledge and navigation of Athenian law, could help them attain their freedom and even "pass" as citizens.[5]

Another of Vlassopoulos' objections to Patterson's definition of slavery is that, to Vlassopoulos' mind, it does not leave any room for the hopes and dreams that enslaved people might have had. Even if these hopes were unacknowledged or deliberately squelched by their owners, the fact that enslaved people had aspirations — and acted to try to accomplish these aspirations — is worth recognizing.[6] Thus, through his study of Artemidorus' second-century BCE *Dream Book* as well as oracular questions and votive dedications of enslaved people, Vlassopoulos finds that their most commonly expressed hope

---

and definitional categories (i.e., those strictly defined by certain criteria) and prototypical categories (i.e., those that are more fuzzily defined). In addition, he explains that identity itself has three aspects: categorization (i.e., how others categorize you), self-understanding (i.e., how you categorize yourself), and "groupness" (i.e., a combination of categorization, self-understanding, and networking). He also calls attention to the different arenas or orders of social life: the "interaction order" of everyday life and the "institutional order" of life within formal institutions or organizations (e.g. the legal system). Finally, he distinguishes between nominal identities (i.e., being categorized with a certain label) and actual identities (i.e., how a particular categorization is applied in reality and how it affects you).

3 See Vlassopoulos 2021, 134–146 on relationships within slave communities. See Hunt 2015b, who argues that enslaved people who were able to form communities with others from their homelands (e.g. Phrygian mining slaves) were more likely to retain their ethnic identities.
4 McKeown 2019. See also Taylor 2015 on interlocking "social networks" that cut across divisions of status and class in Athens.
5 Forsdyke 2018; on enslaved people "passing" as free, see also Forsdyke 2021, 38–39, 190–193.
6 Vlassopoulos 2018 and 2021, ch 7 on the hopes of enslaved people.

was (perhaps unsurprisingly) to gain their freedom or otherwise enhance their condition. He also extracts the fears of enslaved people from these texts, including that of facing an unknown fate under a new owner or after acquiring freedom, and of losing their communities and networks if they were sold or manumitted. He builds here on the work of Esther Eidinow, who has demonstrated persuasively that the oracular tablets from fifth- to fourth-century BCE Dodona, especially those that seem to have been authored by enslaved people, can give us a glimpse into specific hopes and fears.[7] For instance, an oracular tablet from 350 BCE reading "Will Kittos get the freedom from Dionysius that Dionysius promised him?" provides a first-hand attestation of a particular enslaved person's desire for manumission.[8]

The consultation of oracles points to a broader area where scholars have looked for traces of slave agency, namely, religious practice.[9] Work on this topic was begun in earnest by Franz Bömer, who in the middle of the twentieth century published a four-volume investigation into the role of enslaved people in Greek and Roman religion. Bömer argued that there was no such thing as "slave religion," by which he meant that enslaved people participated in the religious practices of their owners rather than having their own cults with special resonances for them as enslaved people.[10] Given the work's pessimistic tone, it is perhaps unsurprising that for about fifty years after its publication, the role of enslaved people in Greek religion was relatively neglected as a field of research. But this has begun to change over time, and in 2012, Hodkinson and Geary co-edited a volume on various aspects of enslaved people's involvement in religion; the work covers both Greco-Roman antiquity and modern Brazil, with many pieces explicitly or implicitly calling Bömer's thesis into question.[11] More recently, John North has written a handbook piece on the involvement of en-

---

7 Eidinow 2012; for more on the oracular questions from Dodona, see Eidinow 2007, ch. 5.
8 Eidinow 2012, 260, text no. 14. McArthur 2019 has argued that this is the same Kittos who appears in an Athenian manumission inscription (*IG* II^2 1554, ll. 10–13; on these inscriptions, see ch. 7.1). If this is correct, these inscriptions provide unique insight into the life of an enslaved man who sought freedom and then apparently received it.
9 Falling under this category are curse tablets inscribed or commissioned by enslaved people; while authorship of curse tablets is often hard to determine, Dickie 2000 has argued that many erotic curses were authored by prostitutes (at least some of whom were likely to be enslaved or formerly enslaved); see further Eidinow 2007, ch. 11 on this category of curses, and Breitenfeld 2022, ch. 3, who argues that curse tablets are a particularly good way of accessing the agency of enslaved women.
10 Bömer 1958–63.
11 Hokinson and Geary 2012.

slaved people in both Greek and Roman religion, arguing that the "privileged" slaves of Athens and Rome were more likely than the average enslaved person to engage in their own religious activity (e.g. performing rituals and vows, paying for monuments, etc.).[12]

While the shift toward exploring slave agency, whether in religion or in other areas, is a welcome one, some cautions should be noted. Vlassopoulos has stressed that we need to recognize that enslaved people's agency was always constrained by the conditions of their enslavement.[13] In fact, given these constraints, some scholars hesitate to use the term "agency" of enslaved people at all. Walter Johnson, a historian of American slavery, has problematized historians' use of — and especially their over-reliance on — the concept of agency in this context. He points out that the term connotes a liberal notion of selfhood that arose in the nineteenth century, in direct opposition to slavery, and is therefore inapplicable to enslaved individuals, who lacked such autonomy. A better term, he suggests, might be something like "enslaved humanity," which acknowledges the ways that the lives of enslaved people are conditioned by but not reducible to their enslavement.[14] We should take Johnson's cautions seriously, but much value nonetheless remains in speaking of enslaved people's agency, provided that we recognize, with Vlassopoulos, its limited nature.

6.2 Resistance

A significant facet of enslaved people's agency is resistance, both to their enslavers and to their condition more broadly.[15] However, scholars face many challenges in trying to find traces of this resistance in ancient Greece.[16] Primary among these is the fact that our sources are for the most part authored by elites who held other people as slaves, not by enslaved people themselves. A solution proposed by McKeown is to hunt for "footprints" of this resistance in the consciousness of enslavers. Reading several Greek texts in this way, McKeown finds evidence for enslaved people fleeing, committing violence against their owners, stealing or otherwise acting against their owners' interests, using their sexuality

---

12 North 2020.
13 See Vlassopoulos 2021, 191.
14 Johnson 2003.
15 But see again Johnson 2003, who cautions against conflating the concepts of agency, humanity, and resistance, a mistake he says scholars of slavery often make.
16 Challenges are of course also encountered by scholars investigating slave resistance in the Roman world; for a successful attempt to access this resistance, see Joshel and Petersen 2014.

to their advantage, using their owners' secrets to their advantage, and deliberately working poorly.[17] Hunt, in turn, has explored acts of slave resistance in both Greece and Rome. He distinguishes "contrary strategies," that is, strategies that involve working *against* one's enslaver to achieve some aim, from "collaborative strategies," which entail working *with* one's enslaver (or in some cases, another free person) in order to gain something (e.g. clothing, food, praise, money, a new position, freedom, etc.).[18] Both types of strategies, of course, were a way for enslaved people to cope with their situation, even if the latter strategy looks less obviously like resistance.

Also helpful for scholars seeking traces of slave resistance has been the work of the political scientist James C. Scott, who studies modern-day peasant communities.[19] In his book *Weapons of the Weak: Everyday Forms of Peasant Resistance*, Scott identifies what he calls "everyday forms of resistance," namely, acts like "foot dragging, dissimulation, desertion, false compliance, pilfering, feigned ignorance, slander, arson, sabotage, and so on."[20] These are precisely the kinds of things we find attested about enslaved people in Greece, even if these behaviors are framed by ancient authors not in terms of resistance but instead as misbehavior. Scott's book *Domination and the Arts of Resistance: Hidden Transcripts*, in turn, draws an important distinction between what he calls the "public transcript" (i.e., what subordinated people say in the presence of their dominators) and the "hidden transcript" (i.e., what they say amongst one another, which includes resistance to their oppressors).[21]

In the Greek context, one notable example of a "hidden transcript" might be the stories about the famous fabulist Aesop, who was said to be a Thracian or Phrygian slave living in 6th century BCE Greece, and who was ultimately manumitted (Hdt. 2.134, *Vita* W 1). His famous fables, moreover, often feature lower-status animals who are cleverer than, and even "win" in their contests with, higher-status animals.[22] Regardless of whether Aesop really existed, it is possi-

---

17 McKeown 2011.
18 Hunt 2017a; see also Hunt 2018b, 141–144 on the everyday resistance of enslaved people in Greece and Rome. On accommodation as a strategy, see Forsdyke 2021, 202–203.
19 See Forsdyke 2012, ch. 2; 2021, 203–207 ("weapons of the weak") and 207–210 ("hidden transcripts").
20 Scott 1985, at xvi. An excellent study of the everyday resistance of enslaved people (specifically, women) in the American South is Camp 2004; this work has inspired recent work on slave resistance in the Roman world (e.g. Joshel 2013, Joshel and Petersen 2014).
21 Scott 1990.
22 A good translation of Aesop's fables is Gibbs 2002. On visual representations of Aesop and his fables, see Lissarague 2000.

ble that at least some of the stories and fables that arose surrounding him may have originated with enslaved people, or if not, at least resonated with them: we might imagine enslaved people telling each other fables as a coded way of expressing resistance or otherwise managing their condition. At the same time, some scholars have observed that many of these fables implicitly warn enslaved people and other low-status individuals that they should know their place; in this way, they have an essentializing force that ultimately serves the interests of the elites.[23]

Of the various modes of resistance attested in our sources, flight is a particularly common one.[24] Fugitives from slavery appear primarily in one of two contexts. One is during times of crisis, especially war, when enslavers were otherwise occupied and things were generally in turmoil. For instance, during the latter part of the Peloponnesian War (413–403 BCE), when the Spartans were occupying a fort at Deceleia in Attica, more than 20,000 Athenian slaves (*andrapoda*) fled from the Attic countryside to seek refuge at Deceleia (Thuc. 7.27.5; see above, ch. 3.2). They did so presumably for freedom, but at least for most of them, this did not happen: the *Hellenica Oxyrhynchia* (17.4) reports that they were sold into slavery to the Thebans. Also, during the Peloponnesian War, in 411 BCE, after Athens attacked the Greek island of Chios (until recently their ally), many of the enslaved people (*oiketai*) on Chios deserted, using their knowledge of their owners' land to help the Athenians destroy it (Thuc. 8.40.2).

Another context in which we hear about runaways is the practice of enslaved individuals seeking asylum at temples, including, perhaps most famously, the Theseion, the slave sanctuary at Athens (Philoch. BNJ 328 F 177).[25] As Alex Gottesman has demonstrated, enslaved people in Attica who were particularly desperate escaped to the Theseion in the hope that someone would come by to assert their freedom. In most cases, however, the ultimate outcome was not that they became free: rather, what happened was a transfer of ownership to their "vindicator," someone who was ideally preferable to the owner they fled. Gottesman reads these actions, which he calls "stunts" and "performances," as a way for enslaved people to exercise agency and take control of their lives. He suggests, furthermore, that the repeated nature of these performances may have

---

23 See duBois 2003, ch. 8; Kurke 2010 (esp. pp. 11–12); Forsdyke 2012, ch. 2.
24 On flight in Greece, see Forsdyke 2021, 211–216; in both Greece and Rome, see Andreau and Descat 2011, 138–141; Hunt 2018b, 147–152.
25 The classic discussion of the Theseion as slave sanctuary is Christensen 1984.

checked enslavers' excessive abuse, since they did not want to lose their slaves in this way.[26]

A more radical form of resistance comes in the form of violence against one's enslaver. In an imagined conversation between King Hiero of Syracuse and the poet Simonides of Ceos, Simonides says: "many masters (*polloi kai despotai*) have died with force [i.e., been murdered] by their slaves" (Xen. *Hier.* 10.4). Whether or not this is true, we do hear of a (failed) attempt at murder in a speech of Antiphon. Euxitheus, the defendant in the case, mentions an enslaved boy, not yet twelve years old, who recently tried to stab and kill his owner. But upon hearing his owner's cries, he fled, leaving the knife in the wound; ultimately, he was caught and confessed (5.69). Regardless of how often such violence happened – probably not often – it was clearly something that at least some slaveowners feared, since they knew that their slaves could potentially poison their food or kill them while they were sleeping.[27] Indeed, in Plato's *Republic*, Socrates posits a hypothetical scenario in which a god picks up a rich man, one with fifty or more slaves, and wafts him, his wife and children, and his slaves to an isolated place with no free men around to assist him. Socrates asks Glaucon, his interlocutor, how great this man's fear would be that he and his family would be killed by the slaves, to which Glaucon replies "the greatest in the world" (578e).

6.3 Revolt

Even more extreme than any individual act of resistance were large-scale revolts. These are not attested often in the Greek world, however, especially as compared to Rome.[28] One of the more interesting slave revolts, if "revolt" is the appropriate word for it, involves the possibly apocryphal story of an enslaved man named Drimacus and most likely dates to the third century BCE (Athen.

---

26 See Gottesman 2014, ch. 6, who also provides evidence for slave refuges elsewhere in the Greek world. On slave asylum at temples, see also Ismard 2019, 202–221 and Forsdyke 2021, 227–234.
27 For free people's fears of enslaved people in antiquity, see the edited volume Serghidou 2007.
28 On slave revolts in Greece and Rome, see Urbainczyk 2008; Hunt 2018b, ch. 10. On slave revolts in Greece, see Forsdyke 2021, 216–222. The classic work on slave revolts in the Roman world is Bradley 1989.

6.265d–266e).²⁹ At the time, enslaved people on Chios had been running away in large numbers, gathering in the woods and mountains and pillaging the country houses of their owners. They crowned as "king" a fellow enslaved man named Drimacus, who helped them fight off their owners' attempts to recapture them. Eventually, Drimacus persuaded the Chians to sign a peace treaty stipulating that the runaways would not steal more than a fixed amount and that Drimacus would accept into his community only those who had been "intolerably treated" by their owners. Years later, after the Chians put a bounty on Drimacus' head (redeemed by Drimacus' boyfriend at Drimacus' request), the runaways began stealing again at the levels they had before the treaty. Somewhat surprisingly (at least for a modern reader), not only enslaved people but also free Chians apparently honored Drimacus as a hero after his death. This may be, as Forsdyke suggests, because the story of Drimacus resonated with both groups, albeit for different reasons: whereas the former might have read it as an inspiring tale of successful reversal (with enslaved people gaining the upper hand), for slaveowners the story ultimately reinforced the normative social order, since Drimacus never sought the abolition of slavery, just accommodation within it.³⁰

Apart from the Drimacus story, the majority of our evidence for Greek slave revolts deals with the Helots, who revolted with some degree of frequency, at least relatively speaking.³¹ The most famous instance took place in 465 BCE, following a huge earthquake. Many Spartans were killed in this natural disaster, and then the Messenian Helots staged a huge revolt, with some fleeing to Mt Ithome (in Messenia) and setting up something resembling a maroon community. The Spartans were in such a bad way that they appealed to Athens for aid, but fearing that the Athenians might actually help the Helots against them, they ended up rejecting the Athenians' assistance (Thuc. 1.101–102; Paus. 1.29.8).

---

29 Another slave revolt, or at least an attempted one, allegedly took place in Syracuse in 414 BCE, led by an enslaved man named Sosistratus, during the Athenians' siege of the city. The Syracusan general Hermocrates sent an envoy to tell Sosistratus that the generals wanted to reward the insurrectionists for their bravery by giving them freedom, arms, and military rations, and by making Sosistratus general. But when Sosistratus went to meet the generals with twenty of his strongest men, they were immediately seized and put in chains. Hermocrates' men then captured the other insurgents and promised them they would not face any punishment if they went back to their owners; all but three hundred, who deserted to the Athenians, complied (Polyaen. 1.43.1).
30 Forsdyke 2012, ch. 2. For a comparison of Athenaeus' account of Drimacus to the twentieth-century Trinidadian radical C.L.R. James' portrayal of Haitian revolutionary Toussaint L'Ouverture, see Langerwerf 2012.
31 On the Helots' revolts, see Urbaincyzk 2008, ch. 7; Hunt 2018b, 157–161.

The reasons that Helots revolted, whereas other enslaved people in Greece for the most part did not, has long been a subject of scholarly inquiry. In an important and still oft-cited article from 1985, Cartledge tried to answer precisely this question, using as his guide the American historian Eugene Genovese's list of conditions leading to slave revolts, as laid out in *From Rebellion to Revolution: Afro-American Slave Revolts in the Making of the Modern World* (1979). In this book, Genovese presented eight factors that, if present in some combination, would suggest a higher probability of slave revolt.[32] Certainly, applying Genovese's criteria to the ancient world requires adjustments (especially when it comes to race), but even after these, it quickly becomes clear that these criteria do not hold for most enslaved people in Greece.[33] By contrast, as Cartledge shows, at least half of Genovese's criteria do apply to the Helots, especially the Messenian Helots. Of particular significance in this context are the Helots' shared ethnicity and language, their physical distance from their Spartan owners, their large numbers, and their geographical environment (including mountainous areas like Mt Ithome, mentioned above).[34] The especially brutal treatment of Helots (discussed in ch. 4.3) — and their desire to escape this violence — probably also contributed to the Helots' tendency to revolt.

---

32 Genovese 1979, 11–12: "(1) the master-slave relationship had developed in the context of absenteeism and depersonalization as well as greater cultural estrangement of whites and blacks; (2) economic distress and famine occurred; (3) slaveholding units approached the average size of one hundred to two hundred slaves, as in the sugar colonies, rather than twenty or so, as in the Old South; (4) the ruling class frequently split either in warfare between slaveholding countries or in bitter struggles within a particular slaveholding country; (5) blacks heavily outnumbered whites; (6) African-born slaves outnumbered those born into American slavery (creoles); (7) the social structure of the slaveholding regime permitted the emergence of an autonomous black leadership; and (8) the geographical, social, and political environment provided terrain and opportunity for the formation of colonies of runaway slaves strong enough to threaten the plantation regime." Genovese's list of criteria is cited by Cartledge 1985; Urbanicyzk 2008, 4–5; Hunt 2018b, 169–171; Forsdyke 2021, 216–217. Hunt focuses on four of these criteria: "the proportion of slaves in the population, their organization, their alienation from their masters, and disunity among the free" (2018b, 169).
33 The only exceptions might be Genovese's (4) and (6), but Cartledge 1985, 24–39 explains that in the case of Greece, these factors, while present, were not in fact conducive to revolts.
34 Cartledge 1985, 40–46. See also Hunt 2018b, 157–161 on Helots' revolts.

6.4 Conclusion

A fairly recent turn in ancient slavery studies has been to search for evidence of slave agency, drawing inspiration, whether directly or indirectly, from years of work on slavery in the Americas. Remaining cognizant that the agency of enslaved people was by necessity always constrained, scholars have made considerable progress in teasing out the ways that enslaved people formed communities and networks, negotiated relations with their owners and other free people, and expressed — and sometimes even realized — their hopes and dreams. Of particular interest has been the subject of slave resistance, instances of which have been accessed by reading ancient texts (both literary and epigraphic) against the grain. In some cases, this has entailed positing slave authorship of texts where authorship is uncertain, in others reframing enslavers' complaints about their slaves shirking work, stealing food, running away, or even revolting as testimonials of enslaved people asserting their personhood, reclaiming their identities, or simply surviving. It is stories like these that I hope scholars continue to tell.

7 Manumission

The last chapter looked at ways that enslaved people might resist their owners or their condition of enslavement (or both). Sometimes, however, they emerged from enslavement through manumission, that is, by being set free by their owner or by the state. As I will show in this chapter, the study of Greek manumission in the past twenty or so years has been concerned above all with three key issues: the classification and explanation of various modes of manumission; the implications of *paramonē* (i.e., the obligation to remain by one's manumittor and perform continued services); and the status of formerly enslaved people.[1]

7.1 Modes of manumission

The modes of Greek manumission are many, varying by polis and by time period.[2] One constant, however, is that enslaved people in the Greek world could not purchase their freedom directly from their owners, since they were, in general, unable to enter into contracts, including contracts of sale.[3] This meant that an enslaved person seeking freedom had to hope that their owner was motivated to manumit them for free (whether out of generosity, because the enslaved person was too old or sick to be useful, or out of love or lust for them); that the state would intervene to facilitate their manumission; or that they could have a third party pay for their freedom (a practice that sometimes seems to have involved elaborate legal fictions; see further below).

I begin my discussion of manumission modes with classical Athens, the evidence for which is primarily literary, drawn especially from Attic oratory. These sources attest to how an enslaved person could be freed. The most straightforward methods were through verbal manumission by an owner (e.g. Dem. 29.25–26) or through the owner's will, a practice for which the so-called "wills of the

---

[1] The best scholarly overview of Greek manumission is Zelnick-Abramovitz 2005; see also Klees 1998, ch. 8; Zanovello 2017 (=2021). For Greek and Roman manumission, see Andreau and Descat 2011 [2006], ch. 6 and Hunt 2018b, ch. 8. For encyclopedia/handbook entries on Greek manumission: Lewis and Zanovello 2017 and Vlassopoulos 2019. For an edited volume on various aspects of Greek (and Roman) manumission, see Gonzales 2008.
[2] Scholars used to categorize manumission modes as either "sacral" and "secular/civic" (see e.g. Calderini 1908 and Rädle 1969), but on the lack of "radical separation of sacred and secular" in ancient Greece, see Connor 1988.
[3] This is the conventional wisdom, but cf. Cohen 2015: ch. 4, who argues that enslaved people could enter into contracts (here, in the context of prostitution).

philosophers," recorded by the second-century CE biographer Diogenes Laertius, are our best evidence.⁴ We also hear about declarations of manumissions in the Theater of Dionysus in Athens, at least until the practice was halted by law sometime in the fourth century (Aeschin. 3.41–42); it is unclear whether these declarations were speech acts releasing the enslaved person or announcements of manumissions that had been conducted earlier.⁵ Another practice is referred to by some scholars as *prasis ep' eleutheriai* ("sale for the purpose of freedom"; see ch. 5.2), that is, the (fictive) sale of the enslaved person from one owner to another, with the express purpose of setting the enslaved person free.⁶ Other scholars, however, have argued that these transactions were conceived of not as sales, fictive or otherwise, but as a third party paying for the freedom of someone else's slave.⁷ Either way we classify it, the phenomenon is something we find attested quite a few times in our sources, especially in the case of *hetairai* (e.g. [Dem.] 59.29–31) and others found sexually attractive by free men (see the enslaved boy in Hyp. 3).⁸ An enslaved person working independently, like a banker and other skilled laborers, could also sometimes save up enough money to pay for their freedom through the help of a third party.⁹

In exceptional circumstances, enslaved people could also be freed by the Athenian polis.¹⁰ One of the best-known examples is the "emancipation" of 406 BCE, the year of the large naval battle between Athenian and Spartan fleets at Arginousai during the Peloponnesian War.¹¹ The Athenians, whose fleet was numerically weaker in this endeavor, had to take desperate measures. This seems to have involved not only drafting enslaved men but also freeing them

---

4 See Canevaro and Lewis 2014, 103–110, who argue for the validity of these wills.
5 Mactoux 2008 argues that the proclamation served both as a performative utterance facilitating the enslaved person's transition into freedom and as a way of communicating to the theater's audience the fundamental difference between free and slave. Velissaropoulos-Karakostas 2016 connects the passing of the law against these announcements with the emergence of the process underlying the *phialai exeleutherikai* inscriptions, on which see further below.
6 See Kamen 2014a and Glazebrook 2014. Zelnick-Abramovitz 2005, 81–82, 96, 218 describes this practice using the similar term *prasis epi lusei*, "sale for the purpose of release."
7 Sosin 2015, 358–372; Lewis and Zanovello 2017; Zanovello 2017, 139–143 (=2021, 127–131).
8 Both Kamen 2014a and Glazebrook 2014 look at prostitutes' use of the *prasis ep' eleutheriai*. On prostitutes and manumission in Athens, see also Wrenhaven 2009.
9 See Kamen 2016 on the slave-allowance in Athens, which allowed at least some enslaved people to save up money towards their freedom; see also Porter 2021/22.
10 See Zanovello 2017 (=2021), ch. 5; Forsdyke 2021, 243–245. This practice was not limited to Athens: for discussion of the Helots, who could be freed only by polis, see Zanovello 2017, 210–221 (=2021, 190–199).
11 See Hunt 2001; Tamiolaki 2008.

and granting them citizenship, along with the other foreigners who took part (Xen. *Hell*. 1.6.24; Ar. *Ran*. 33, 190–192, 693–695). Enslaved people could also be freed, at least in Athens, if they acted as informers in lawsuits that were of particular concern to the city. As Robin Osborne has suggested, this may have been especially so for cases involving religious offenses, like the mutilation of the Herms and the defamation of the Mysteries in 415 BCE (Thuc. 6.27.2, Andoc. 1.12–18, 27–28).[12]

One of the main epigraphic sources for Athenian manumission — although its status as such has been contested by Elizabeth Meyer (see further below) — is what are referred to as the *phialai exeleutherikai* ("freedman bowls") inscriptions, dated to ca. 330–320 BCE and recording the outcome of trials and (in nearly all instances) the dedication of 100-drachma *phialai*.[13] These inscriptions exhibit three distinct formulas, the first two of which mention a *phialē*.[14] Most have the name of the defendant in the nominative (along with their deme of residence and often with their occupation), the participle *apophugōn/ousa* (literally, "fleeing," with the sense "having been acquitted"), and the name of the prosecutor (along with their demotic) in the accusative. Some, however, leave out the participle *apophugōn/ousa* entirely and appear to reverse both the order and the grammatical case of the defendant and prosecutor.[15] Finally, a few use the aorist indicative of *apopheugō* rather than a participle and do not mention *phialai* at all.[16]

For many years, these inscriptions have been interpreted as referring to acquittals in a lawsuit called a *dikē apostasiou*, "lawsuit for desertion," which fell under the jurisdiction of the polemarch, the magistrate in charge of foreigners'

---

12 Osborne 2000.
13 *IG* II² 1553–1578; Ag. Inv. I 1580 (possibly), 3183, 4665, 4763, 5656, 5774. The most up-to-date edition of these inscriptions, with photographs and commentary, is Meyer 2010, who contends that they are not in fact manumission inscriptions (see further below). For the argument that they are inventories of dedications rather than records of trials, see Meyer 2010, 59–69 and Harris forthcoming; cf. McArthur 2019, who reasserts that they are records of trials.
14 For a survey of interpretations of this variation, including that it indicates who won the case or who paid for the *phialē*, see Klees 1998, 348–351 and more recently Velissaropoulos-Karakostas 2016. Most scholars now believe that there is no significant difference in meaning between the two most common formulas (see Meyer 2010, 66–68).
15 Cf. Harris forthcoming, who thinks the formula is not reversed and that the nominative in all instances represents the successful defendant.
16 The lack of *phialai* in these inscriptions is either because these records are the earliest of the set (perhaps dating to a time before the dedication of *phialai* became necessary) or because the *phialai* were dedicated *prior to* the trial being recorded (Velissaropoulos-Karakostas 2016).

affairs in Athens (Arist. *Ath. Pol.* 58.3).[17] The *dikē apostasiou* could be used by slaveowners against their former slaves "if [the latter] stand apart from them, or enroll another as *prostatēs* (patron), or fail to do the other things required by the laws." Acquittal entailed full freedom from one's manumittor, whereas conviction entailed being re-enslaved (Harp. s.v. *apostasiou*).[18] This interpretation of the inscriptions is bolstered by Wilamowitz's restorations [*dikai apo*]*stasiou* and [*polemarchoun*]*tos* ("being polemarch") in one inscription (*IG* II² 1578) and by the reference to *phialai exeleutherikai* melted down to make *hydriai* (water jugs) in an inscription from 321/0 (*IG* II² 1469).[19] The (apparently required) *phialē* dedication is usually explained as being part of the Athenian statesman Lycurgus' measures to increase state revenues, whereby formerly enslaved people who were victorious in *dikai apostasiou* paid a fee to the state in order to get a record of their acquittal.[20]

There has also been some discussion about whether these trials were simply a legal fiction — a way of rubber-stamping the release of these individuals from their former owners — or whether trials were actually held. Many scholars lean toward the former interpretation, since it is hard to imagine so many of these trials coming to court in a relatively short period of time.[21] But genuine trials may also have been procedurally possible: Zelnick-Abramovitz has suggested that the *dikē apostasiou* belonged to the category of trials called "monthly trials" (the *dikai emmēnoi*), and because *dikai emmēnoi* could be speedy and per-

---

17 Acquittals in *dikai apostasiou*: Zelnick-Abramovitz 2005, 274–292, recently upheld by McArthur 2019. But cf. Meyer 2010, discussed below, who takes them as records of *graphai aprostasiou*. Cf. Velissaropoulos-Karakostas 2016, who thinks they record the result of trials but does not specify which type(s); and Scafuro 2016 and Harris forthcoming, who assert they could be all kinds of cases.
18 Full freedom as the result of acquittal is, to my mind, the most logical way to understand Harpocration's use of the adverb *teleōs* in the phrase *teleōs ēdē eleutherous* ("now completely free"): see also Kamen 2013, 39; Canevaro and Lewis 2014, 99–100; Lewis and Zanovello 2017; cf. Sosin 2015, 361 who renders *teleōs* as "finally." Scholars generally assume that the re-enslavement after conviction meant re-enslavement to the original owner, but Klees 1998, 334–338 argues those who were convicted were sold off by the state to a new owner.
19 For a challenge to both of Wilamowitz's restorations, see Harris forthcoming.
20 Klees 1998, 353; Zelnick-Abramovitz 2005, 290; Meyer 2010, 59–69; McArthur 2019. On manumission taxes and fees to ensure the publication of one's manumission elsewhere in the Greek world, see Zelnick-Abramovitz 2013. Velissaropoulos-Karakostas 2016 suggests a (not mutually exclusive) interpretation for the requirement of the *phialē* dedication, namely, that it offered concrete, demos-approved proof of manumission.
21 For a survey of scholarship calling the trials fictive (a view with which she disagrees), see Zelnick-Abramovitz 2005, 283–285.

functory, many such (real) trials could in fact be held on one day.²² Even if the trials did actually take place in court, they were likely to have been formalities. That is, acquittal would have been a foregone conclusion, at least in most instances — a way to release formerly enslaved individuals from any remaining obligations they owed to their former owners.

As mentioned above, however, Meyer has proposed a radically different interpretation of these inscriptions. She argues that the *phialai* inscriptions have nothing to do with manumission, but are instead records of dedications by metics acquitted on charges of not having a patron (*graphai aprostasiou*), with the *phialai* paid for by their unsuccessful accusers. This view has garnered some support, but it has also faced criticism from scholars, including most compellingly from Vlassopoulos.²³ Given that a more convincing restoration of [*dikai apo*]*stasiou* in *IG* II² 1578 has not been proposed, I am inclined to stand by the traditional interpretation of these inscriptions. And if we accept these inscriptions as attesting not to manumission per se but to a second stage of manumission — the release of formerly enslaved people from continuing obligations — they yield a great deal of information about the role of the courts in facilitating this transition. They also tell us about the occupations of formerly enslaved people, since professions are more often than not listed alongside the names in these records.²⁴

Even more informative than this Athenian material are the copious manumission inscriptions from central Greece, most of which are Hellenistic in date

---

22 Zelnick-Abramovitz 2005, 285–288. That the trials were real, see also Andreau and Descat 2011, 150–151.
23 Vlassopoulos 2011c makes the following objections to her argument: he finds improbable her explanation that the *phialai exeleutherikai* were so called because of a connection to the cult of Zeus Eleutherios, with acquitted metics calling themselves *exeleutheroi*; he thinks it unlikely that one party (in her reading, the victorious metics) dedicated *phialai* that another party (the prosecutors) paid for; and he argues that her interpretation does not account for the nature of the prosecutor in a few cases (namely, minors and a public slave), individuals who would be unlikely to be bringing *graphai* against metics, or the nature of the defendant in others (namely, children), who would be unlikely targets of prosecution (as opposed to their parent or guardian). For further criticism, see Zelnick-Abramovitz 2013, ch. 4; Harris forthcoming. For support of Meyer's argument, see Glazebrook 2014, 63–65; Zanovello 2017, 134–139 (=2021, 123–127); Lewis and Zanovello 2017.
24 Scholars have long been interested in the occupations listed in the *phialai* inscriptions; see Wrenhaven 2009 on the *talasiourgoi* ("wool-workers"). See also Mulliez 2021a on the occupations listed in the Delphic manumission inscriptions.

and involve the gods in some way or another.²⁵ These inscriptions attest to three (possibly overlapping) types of manumission: 1) manumission involving the gods as witnesses and protectors; 2) manumission through consecration of an enslaved person to a god; and 3) manumission through sale of an enslaved person to a god. Scholars generally believe that the inscriptions were a way to maximize publicity for the formerly enslaved person and to guarantee the protection of their new status.²⁶

The first of these modes of manumission is the most straightforward. From a relatively early date (possibly as early as the fifth century BCE), we find inscribed records of enslaved people being manumitted along with an invocation or mention of a god or gods.²⁷ For example, a second-century BCE stele from Thespiae (in Boeotia) reads: "With Eurymeilus as archon, Saon set free (*aphieiti* ... *eleutheron*) Ateas, facing (*enantia*) Asclepius and Apollo. Witnesses (*histores*): Antimenon, Asius, Athanodorus, Euphrastus" (*IG* VII 1779 = Darmezin 1999, #136). In this case, the gods Asclepius and Apollo might be thought of as offering a sacral bonus, an additional, more authoritative form of protection than that provided by the named human witnesses. While these gods are not explicitly called witnesses, they might have been thought of as such, especially given that Asclepius is listed as a witness in another inscription from Thespiae (Darmezin 1999, #139). In yet other inscriptions, gods are explicitly invoked as "defenders," and in some instances, their priests are ordered to collect fines from whoever tries to re-enslave the manumitted individual.²⁸

The second mode of manumission mentioned above involved the dedication (usually using the verb *anatithēmi*) of an enslaved person to a god as *hieros* ("sacred").²⁹ In general, consecration was not for the purpose of manumission

---

25 For collections of these inscriptions with text, translation, and commentary: Darmezin 1999 (manumissions through consecration); Mulliez 2019 and forthcoming b (Delphic manumission inscriptions). For a catalogue of Thessalian manumissions, see Zelnick-Abramovitz 2013, 151–156.
26 See Lewis and Zanovello 2017. But Vlassopoulos 2019 questions this interpretation, asking why, if this is the case, we find these inscriptions almost entirely in central and northern Greece, in small communities rather than urban areas (the latter of which would be an obvious location for maximum publicity), and none in Athens, which had a highly developed epigraphic habit.
27 One of the earliest manumission inscriptions, a bronze tablet from Arcadia (*IG* V 2.429), has been dated to either the fifth century (*SEG* XI 1164) or the fourth century BCE (Darmezin 1999, 22).
28 For examples, see Zelnick-Abramovitz 2005, 87–91.
29 For a collection of relevant inscriptions, see Darmezin 1999. That *hieros* refers to a free person in this context, see Caneva and Delli Pizzi 2015; cf. Zanovello 2018.

but was instead a way to provide a sanctuary with an enslaved workforce — we might think, for example, of Ion in Euripides' play of the same name, who was dedicated to Apollo's sanctuary to serve as a temple slave. Sometimes, however, consecrations were clearly performed with the intention of setting an enslaved person free, in a process scholars call "fictive consecration" or "consecration manumission."[30] One place this practice is commonly attested is Chaeronea, in inscriptions from the end of the third to the end of the second century BCE.[31] At Chaeronea, as in many poleis, the intention to manumit is usually not explicit, but in at least one inscription the formulation "set free" (*aphiēmi eleutheron*) is substituted for the verb "dedicate" (*anatithēmi*) (*IG* VII 3321), implying that the two were thought equivalent.[32] A similar equivalence is found elsewhere, as for example in consecration inscriptions from Bouthrotos where we find both *aphiēmi eleutheron* and *anatithēmi* attested, sometimes individually in separate inscriptions and sometimes both in one inscription.[33]

Recently, however, Zanovello has argued that all consecrations of enslaved people should be considered *real* consecrations, that is, that the dedicated were in all cases considered the property of the god.[34] Focusing on the consecration inscriptions from Chaeronea, she asserts, correctly, that there is nothing in the language to indicate the fictionality of these consecrations, nor is there (unlike with manumission through sale, discussed below) any need to resort to fiction.[35] She argues, then, that the language of dedication and the designation of the dedicated slave as *hieros* can best be understood through comparison to the practices of *consecratio* and *dedicatio* under Roman law, which involve the resignation of the dedicant's property in the first instance and the transfer of

---

30 See Darmezin 1999 ("affranchissements par consécration"); Zelnick-Abramovitz 2005 *passim* ("consecration-manumission"); Kamen 2012, 178–180 ("fictive consecration"); Vlassopoulos 2019 ("consecration manumission"). Cf. Zanovello 2018 (also Zanovello 2017 (=2021), ch. 3, Lewis and Zanovello 2017), who argues that they should be viewed as real consecrations and not as manumissions; see further below.
31 For a collection of consecration manumissions from Chaeronea, see Darmezin 1999, 31–76.
32 The lack of explicit mention of manumission sometimes makes it difficult to know whether a given consecration was or was not designed for that purpose. See the mid-second- to early fourth-century CE dedications to the Indigenous Mother of the Gods, primarily of enslaved children, at Leucopetra in Macedonia: although some scholars think these children were manumitted through this process (Petsas et al. 2000), others argue that they became temple servants (Ricl 2001) or that they resided somewhere between slave and free (Meyer 2002).
33 For the consecration manumissions from Bouthrotos, see Darmezin 1999, 127–154.
34 See especially Zanovello 2017 (=2021), ch. 3 and 2018.
35 Legal fictions do not generally flag themselves as such, however, so we should not necessarily expect to see the language of fictionality.

said property to the god in the second as sacred property (*res sacra*). Analogously, she says, the *hieros* should be understood as the *res sacra* of the god.

Zanovello also tackles some of the arguments that others have made in favor of considering these consecrations to be records of manumission. For instance, she argues that the frequent phrase *mē prosēkonta mētheni mēthen* ("not belonging to anyone at all") — and the less frequent adjective *anephaptos* ("untouchable") — indicate not (as others have supposed) that the *hieros* is free, but rather that, since they belong to the god, they cannot be re-claimed by the dedicator or seized by anyone else. She also contends that the elements that other scholars have taken as proof of dedicated individuals' freedom — e.g. their (occasionally) recognized family relationships, their (apparent) ownership in some cases of other slaves, their ability to dispose of their enslaved property — do not preclude their being slaves of a god. And although a number of these inscriptions have *paramonē* clauses mandating that the individual remain by their former owner to provide further services (on *paramonē*, see ch. 7.2), she argues that this too is not an indication that the individual is necessarily free; rather, they could owe continued obligations to a former owner while now having a new (divine) owner, and this might be an arrangement agreed upon by all parties. She also points out that the occasional consecration of formerly enslaved people (*apeleutheroi*) to the gods suggests that consecration, per se, was not designed to make one free, since *apeleutheroi* are already free.[36] Finally, although she concedes that *hieroi* are sometimes described as *eleutheroi* in these inscriptions, she contends that this does not mean that they are *legally* free: rather, she argues, *eleutheros* describes not their legal status but their *de facto* situation, since without an actual (human) owner to exercise power over them, they were in many ways more like free people than slaves. This seems to me the hardest claim to substantiate: *eleutheros* can and often does of course have a figurative sense (see ch. 8.3), but in a legal document like a manumission record one would expect words to be used in their literal sense.

Ultimately, despite Zanovello's challenges to the status quo, her argument is not substantively different from the argument that these consecrations are fictive; rather, it is differently framed. When we conceive of this practice as fictive consecration, we assume that the owner dedicates the slave to the god with the understanding that the god will not exercise his right of ownership, and so the slave in effect is free. By Zanovello's interpretation, the consecration

---

[36] This does not mean that consecration could *not* make one free: rather, there might be many reasons to consecrate someone. In the case of a freed slave, it might offer them more protection from being re-enslaved.

is *real*, since the dedicated individual does in fact become a slave of the god; that is, they are technically still enslaved, but they are in effect free because they lack a human owner. The outcome in both cases is the same: regardless of whether one adopts the language of fictionality, the idea is that the dedicated slave becomes (at least in most cases) more or less free.

A similar mode of manumission to that involving consecration entailed the sale of an enslaved person to a god by their owner. This practice is attested primarily at Delphi from 201 BCE to c. 100 CE, where inscriptions detail the sale of around 1400 enslaved people to Apollo.[37] It is possible that the money for the purchase actually came from the person being sold, who is said to "entrust the sale" to the god (see below); Apollo (or his priests), as the notional buyer, presumably then handed this money to the enslaved person's original owner/seller.[38] This elaborate scheme of routing the purchase money through the god seems to have been designed, at least in part, as a way of allowing enslaved people to buy their own freedom.

These inscriptions are heavily formulaic, with some small variations. Here is one representative example, which helps to give a sense for the genre:

> When Patreas son of Andronicus was archon, during the month of Busius, Sosias son of Sosias sold (*apedoto*) to Pythian Apollo a female slave (*sōma*, lit. "body") named Nicaia, from Argithea by origin, and her own son Isthmus, for a price of five minas of silver, and [Sosias] holds the whole price, since Nicaia and Isthmus entrusted the sale (*episteuse…tan ōnan*) to the god, on the terms that they be they be free (*eph' hōite eleutheroi eimen*) and untouchable (*anephaptoi*) by anyone for their whole lives. Let Nicaia and Isthmus remain by (*parameinatō*) Sosias as long as Sosias lives, doing everything ordered by Sosias as blamelessly as possible. If Nicaia and Isthmus do not do this, let the sale be not guaranteed for them but let it be invalid. If Sosias brings any charge against Nicaia or Isthmus, let it be judged by three men, and whatever these men decide, let that be authoritative. If Sosias suffers something (i.e. dies), let Nicaia and Isthmus do all the customary rites pertaining to his funeral. The guarantor in accordance with the law of the city is Timocritus son of Eucleidas. If anyone seizes Nicaia or Isthmus for re-enslavement after Sosias has suffered something, let the guarantor present the sale to the god as guaranteed, and likewise let passersby be authorized to carry them off on the grounds that they are free and not liable to any fines or penalties. Witnesses: the priests of Apollo, Amyntas, Andronicus; and among the magistrates, Polycrates, Pasion; and as private individuals, Patreas, Euagoras, Timocritus (*GDI* II 1689 = *CID* V 1.388)

Scholars disagree about whether to consider the practice attested here and in the other similar inscriptions a fictive sale or a genuine one. However, regard-

---

37 See Mulliez 2019 and forthcoming b for a corpus of these inscriptions.
38 See Zanovello 2017, 46–57 (=2021, 42–51), who takes *ōnan* as "purchase money."

less of their interpretation, all agree that the outcome of the transaction is that the enslaved person became free.[39] There is usually a clause explicitly detailing the purpose of the sale (e.g. "on the condition of freedom" or "so that the slave become free"), and the freed individual is frequently designated as unseizable (*anephaptos* or similar periphrastic expressions) and sometimes explicitly as *eleutheros* ("free"). The impression one gets is that the enslaved person, like any bought and sold commodity, was thought to pass into the possession of the buyer — namely, the god — but in this case with the understanding that the latter would make no use of his right of ownership. As a result, the enslaved person, without the supervision of any owner, was in effect free.

More controversial is the question of how soon the enslaved person who was sold to the god became free. Most scholars believe that the sale made the enslaved person free, but Joshua Sosin, who considers these real sales, argues that there were in fact two stages: 1) the sale to the god, and 2) the manumission of the enslaved person by the god in his capacity as their new owner. Sosin bases this argument in part on the fact that an enslaved person (as above) is often said to be sold "on the terms that (*eph' hōite*) they be free," which he claims means that their freedom was a *future* condition of the sale, not something that came *along with* the sale.[40] However, *eph' hōite* can just as easily mean "for the purpose of" (Smyth 2279), in which case freedom might indeed be the intended (and immediate) aim of the sale. Also, we have no evidence in our inscriptions for there being two distinct steps (i.e., sale and then manumission). On balance, then, I am inclined to think that the sale itself effected freedom.

---

39 For the argument that the sale is fictive, see Hopkins 1978, 133–171 ("fictional sale," 142); Zelnick-Abramovitz 2005 *passim* ("the fictitious nature of manumissions by sale to a god," 97); Kamen 2012, 180–182 and 2014a, 285–289 ("fictive sale"); Forsdyke 2021, 243 ("fictive sale"). For the argument that the sale is genuine, see Sosin 2015; Mulliez 2016. Cf. Zanovello 2017 (=2021), ch. 2 (see also Zanovello and Lewis 2017), who argues that it is not a sale at all — fictive *or* genuine — since manumission and sale have opposite purposes (i.e., cessation vs. transfer of ownership, respectively). Instead, she contends, it is a "bilateral legal transaction," whereby the enslaved person entrusted money to the god, and the god transferred the money to the owner. She is correct that we need to take seriously the language of "entrusting," but the explicit use of language of sale (*apedoto*) indicates that this was conceived of as some type of sale.
40 Sosin 2015, 329–331.

7.2 *Paramonē* and its implications

Complicating matters is the fact that in manumissions by consecration and especially in manumissions by sale, it is sometimes (as in our example above) stipulated that the individual being manumitted "remain" by their manumittor for some specified period of time (usually until the latter's death, though early release, *apolusis*, is sometimes stipulated as a possibility). This obligation is generally referred to as *paramonē*, expressed in the inscriptions either with the noun itself or (more often) with a verbal form (as above, *parameinatō*). Such obligations are never referred to as such in classical Athens, but many scholars, including most recently Lewis and Canevaro, think that something roughly equivalent may have existed there as well.[41]

There has been much debate, however, about whether *paramonē* service was provided *after* the individual became free or whether it was a condition that *preceded* the individual becoming free.[42] Zelnick-Abramovitz has classified manumission with *paramonē* as "deferred manumission," meaning that during the period of *paramonē*, individuals were not yet free; more recently, she has clarified that they continued to be slaves vis-à-vis their manumittors, while being free vis-à-vis others.[43] Vlassopoulos likewise thinks that those under *paramonē* were free vis-à-vis other people, but has declared them "in a state between freedom and slavery" vis-à-vis their manumittors.[44] Zanovello and Lewis, by contrast, have argued that those under *paramonē* were essentially free, albeit with continuing obligations, since they were no longer the property of their former owner.[45] And Sosin has classified them as slaves, pure and simple.[46]

This last interpretation is, to my mind, flawed. First, Sosin takes as a given that there was no grey area between slavery and freedom in Greece, which causes him to read the evidence in a particular way. For example, he argues that the use of the aorist participle of *paramenein* in many of the inscriptions indi-

---

41 The wills of Diogenes Laertius are often cited in this context, sometimes along with the implicit evidence of Pl. *Leg.* 915a and Athen. 6.267b. On *paramonē*-like obligations in Athens, see Kamen 2013, ch. 3; Canevaro and Lewis 2014; Zanovello 2017, 164–176 (=2021, 149–160); Zelnick-Abramovitz 2018, 381; Todd 2018. Cf. Meyer 2010, 27n.69; Glazebrook 2014, 63–65.
42 For a good review of this debate, see Zelnick-Abramovitz 2018, 390–397.
43 Zelnick-Abramovitz 2005, 222–223 and more recently Zelnick-Abramovitz 2018. See similarly Dimopoulou-Piliouni 2008. Cf. Canevaro and Lewis 2014, who argue the manumission is not deferred.
44 Vlassopoulos 2019.
45 Canevaro and Lewis 2014; Lewis 2015; Lewis 2017; Lewis and Zanovello 2017.
46 Sosin 2015. For a convincing rebuttal, see Zelnick-Abramovitz 2018.

cates that the individual under *paramonē* was still enslaved: that is, that *paramonē* must be *prior to* their freedom.⁴⁷ Although he is correct that some inscriptions do use an aorist participle, most often we find an aorist imperative, and in some manumissions from other poleis, we find the future indicative, neither of which indicates anterior time.⁴⁸ The frequent use of the aorist imperative suggests, rather, that what is meant by the aorist participle is likewise aspect, not time, implying the simpleness of the action rather than its priority.⁴⁹

Second, Sosin overlooks some of the ways that an individual under *paramonē* does not neatly fit into the categories of "slave" or "free." Some inscriptions stipulate, for example, that such individuals can pay for their release from *paramonē*, or that they can enter into arbitration, both of which stipulations presuppose free (or at least semi-free) status.⁵⁰ And while Sosin argues that certain features of those under *paramonē* suggest servile status — e.g. the susceptibility of at least some to corporal punishment — one could alternatively argue that this reflects only the degraded, non-citizen status of these individuals, rather than their servility per se.⁵¹

The status of those under *paramonē* can best be understood in light of similar statuses in other slave societies. The closest comparison seems to be Roman *statuliberi*, individuals who had been bequeathed by their owner to an heir, with the promise that they would acquire freedom at some point in the future: for example, after fulfilling a particular obligation, or paying a sum of money, or after some period of time had elapsed (*Dig.* 40.7.1.pr.). Until the specified terms had been met, these individuals were still technically the slaves of their owner's heir (*Dig.* 40.7.9.pr.), meaning that the heir could exercise any and all rights of ownership over them. However, the fact that these people possessed a distinct legal status — namely, as *statuliberi* — meant that they were conceptualized as slaves with a difference: as the jurists put it, they were unique in possessing the "hope of freedom" (*Dig.* 40.7 *passim*). This important difference was not only

---

47 Sosin 2015, 334–335.
48 Zelnick-Abramovitz 2018, 396 n. 39.
49 Canevaro and Lewis 2014, 209; Lewis and Zanovello 2017; Zanovello 2017, 64 n. 192 (=2021, 57 n. 72).
50 Being able to pay for release as a sign of freedom: Lewis 2015; Zanovello 2017, 76 (=2021, 67–68); Lewis and Zanovello 2017. Arbitration in the Delphic manumission inscriptions as evidence of freedom: Lewis 2015; cf. Sosin 2015, 346. On arbitration between individuals in the Delphic manumissions more broadly, see Mulliez 2021b.
51 Physical punishment as evidence of continued enslaved status: Sosin 2015, 346–347; Zelnick-Abramovitz 2018, 391, 396; but cf. Lewis and Zanovello 2017.

psychological, though it surely was that as well; it also had ramifications for them in law.

This kind of in-between status is, moreover, not unique to Rome. We also find it, for example, under Islamic law, where two different types of conditional manumission existed. Those who were freed under a "resolutive" type of manumission were given their freedom immediately, with the understanding that they would fulfill certain duties *after* their manumission; those granted "suspensive" or "deferred" manumission, by contrast, obtained their freedom only after they had fulfilled certain stipulated conditions. The latter type of manumission, the suspensive/deferred type, yields a status that is in many respects akin to the Roman *statuliber*.[52] We also find similar in-between statuses in the Americas. In eighteenth-century colonial Brazil, slaves could be freed either conditionally or unconditionally, with those given conditional freedom receiving the deferred type of manumission: that is, they had to perform additional labor before their freedom was recognized.[53] The historian Emily A. Owens' recent work on manumission in Louisiana under both Spanish and American rule has lent a new perspective to the status of enslaved people who were freed conditionally, and in particular to the psychological dimension of conditional freedom. Under Spanish rule (roughly the second half of the eighteenth century), enslaved people in Louisiana could purchase their future freedom, but before this freedom was realized, they inhabited a "liminal form of existence." And after Louisiana came under American rule, the status of *statu liber*, borrowed from Roman law, was introduced to designate those who had been promised their freedom at some future point. In Owens' words, this status entailed "enslavement that was tempered by imminent freedom."[54]

In all of these historical contexts — from Rome to the Middle East to North and South America — we find individuals occupying a kind of recognized limbo status until they fulfilled the specified terms of their manumission. This status was not identical in all of these societies, but a recognition of something between slave and free existed in all of them. This of course is not proof that something like this existed in the Greek world, but there is also no *a priori* reason that a similar in-between status could not have existed there. Even if this status was not defined by law (as it was, for example, in Rome and in the other societies mentioned here), it may well have been recognized in practice.

---

52 Crone 1987, 64–76.
53 Higgins 1999, 154–156.
54 Owens 2017; quotations at pp. 182, 201.

7.3 The status of formerly enslaved people

Related to the understanding of *paramonē* are scholarly debates about the status of formerly enslaved people more broadly in the Greek world. Those who believe that a person who was manumitted with *paramonē* or *paramonē*-like obligations was free — or somewhere between free and enslaved — sometimes draw a distinction between two categories of formerly enslaved people: those with continuing obligations and those who were fully freed.[55] Zelnick-Abramovitz has argued that *apeleutheros* is the term the Greeks used for the former category, *exeleutheros* for the latter, but there is limited evidence to support this terminological distinction.[56]

Scholars also discuss whether formerly enslaved people were considered metics, focusing in particular on classical Athens. Technically they do appear to have been metics, in the broad sense of the word, but there were also ways in which they differed from freeborn metics.[57] For instance, whereas both groups had to pay the *metoikion* (metic tax), formerly enslaved people had to pay an additional *triobolon* tax (Harp. s.v. *metoikion*); freeborn metics were able to choose their patron (*prostatēs*), whereas formerly enslaved people had to have their former owner as *prostatēs*; formerly enslaved people had less leeway than freeborn metics in bequeathing their estates, and if they died childless, their estate went to their former owner; and there existed laws (the content of which is unknown) that applied specifically to formerly enslaved people (*exeleutherikoi nomoi*) as a distinct group (Poll. 3.83).[58] It is also the case that in some contexts, a distinction is drawn between metics (in the narrow sense of freeborn metics) and formerly enslaved people, as for example when the Old Oligarch writes that one cannot strike "a slave, or a metic, or a freedman" in Athens ([Xen.] *Ath. Pol.* 1.10).

---

[55] Distinction between formerly enslaved people with continuing obligations and those with full freedom: Klees 2000, 15–17; Kamen 2013a (chs. 3 and 4, respectively); Zanovello 2017 (=2021), ch. 4; Lewis and Zanovello 2017.
[56] Zelnick-Abramovitz 2005, 99–126; cf. Dimopoulou-Piliouni 2008, 36–38, who relies on the scholia to argue that *exeleutheroi* were distinguished from *apeleutheroi* by having been born free.
[57] On the differences between formerly enslaved people and freeborn metics, see Zelnick-Abramovitz 2005, ch. 6; Dimopoulou-Piliouni 2008, 30–36; Kamen 2013, 44–46. Dimopoulou-Piliouni 2008 suggests that most formerly enslaved people had to be scrutinized in order to attain metic status.
[58] On laws and legal actions pertaining specifically to formerly enslaved people, see Zelnick-Abramovitz 2005, ch. 5.

Perhaps relevant to the issue of formerly enslaved status is the phrase *chōris oikountes* (literally, "living apart"), which most scholars simply render in English transliteration. It has been taken to refer variously to (relatively privileged) enslaved people living and working apart from their owners; to a category of free foreigners who were not metics; to formerly enslaved people; to a subgroup of formerly enslaved people who were fully freed (and therefore "lived apart" from their former owners, unlike those who had remaining obligations); and to either formerly enslaved people or (privileged) enslaved people, or both, depending on the context in which the phrase is used.[59] But given that the phrase *chōris oikountes* is used exactly once in our sources (Dem. 4.36–37) — and that it is explained in a variety of different ways even by the ancient scholiasts — I propose that scholars simply abandon the term going forward.[60] Preferable to using an ambiguous phrase is *describing* whatever status group we have in mind, whether that is formerly enslaved people with conditional freedom, formerly enslaved people with unconditional freedom, "privileged" enslaved people, etc.

Harder than determining the legal status of formerly enslaved people is delineating their *social* status, that is, the level of honor or respect they were accorded and the degree to which they were integrated into society.[61] Much, it seems, depended on the particular individual and their circumstances, as well

---

[59] Privileged slaves: see Cohen 1992, 2000, and many others. Free non-metic foreigners: Kazakévich 2008. Formerly enslaved people: Kamen 2011 (cf. Canevaro and Lewis 2014). Formerly enslaved people with full freedom: Klees 2000, 15–17; for an elaboration of Klees' argument, see Canevaro and Lewis 2014 (cf. the unconvincing Silver 2015) and Lewis and Zanovello 2017. Either enslaved or formerly enslaved people: Zelnick-Abramovitz 2005, 215–216; Fisher 2006, 337 and 2008, 126–127.

[60] The lexicographer Harpocration identified *chōris oikountes* in the Demosthenes passage as formerly enslaved people, since "freedmen lived by themselves, apart from their manumittors" (s.v. *tous chōris oikountas*). A Byzantine lexicographer concurred with Harpocration but added a secondary definition: "Or slaves living apart from their masters" (*Anecd. Bekk.* I 316.11).

[61] See Zelnick-Abramovitz 2005, 319–334 on the social position of formerly enslaved people in Greece. On the Greeks' ideas about honor, see especially the work of Douglas Cairns, e.g. Cairns 1993 and his recent European Research Council (ERC) project on Honour in Classical Greece (http://research.shca.ed.ac.uk/honour-in-greece/). On respect, see Darwall 1977 (and more recently Darwall 2013), who makes an important distinction between recognition respect and appraisal respect: the former involves *treating* an individual in a way that gives appropriate consideration to a feature of theirs; the latter involves *estimating* someone's worth based on some outstanding attribute they have. On the concept of "arena of honor," namely, "the practical context within which a person's honorable status is practically relevant and something to be respected," see Rabbås 2015 (quotation at p. 634).

as the arena in which they were operating. The formerly enslaved prostitute Neaira (see ch. 5.2), who was taken to court on a charge of unlawfully posing as a citizen ([Dem.] 59), provides an example of failed assimilation into society — but even she might have been able to "pass" had her partner Stephanus not made an enemy of her prosecutor, Apollodorus. In contrast to Neaira, the formerly enslaved banker Pasion appears to have successfully integrated into Athenian society. Exceptionally, he was even given citizenship in exchange for his financial contributions to the polis ([Dem.] 59.2). Pasion himself had a slave named Phormion whom he manumitted, stipulating in his will that Phormion marry Pasion's widow (Dem. 36.8), and Phormion, like Pasion, was eventually naturalized in exchange for his gifts to the state (Dem. 46.13). Despite his integration into the ranks of Athenian citizenship, however, Phormion was hated by Pasion's son Apollodorus (the same man mentioned above), who repeatedly brought his stepfather to court. And even though Apollodorus' own father had been enslaved, this did not stop him from using invective in court targeting Phormion's formerly enslaved status. Indeed, language that played on such prejudices was quite popular in Athens, so much so that it was adopted even in contexts where its targets had no connection to slavery.[62] The prominence of this invective reveals, in turn, that no matter how prominent or wealthy a formerly enslaved person became — even if they obtained citizenship! — they might still be viewed or treated as servile.[63] Zelnick-Abramovitz captures well this condition of the formerly enslaved person in the title of her 2005 book: "not wholly free."

A final facet of being "not wholly free" was the precarity of these individuals' status. For example, after Neaira obtained her freedom, she quickly found herself trapped in an abusive relationship with her client Phrynion, the man who had handed over the money for her freedom. She fled to Megara, where she resumed working as a prostitute, and eventually put herself under the protection of another client from Athens, the Stephanus mentioned above. When Phrynion learned of this, he removed Neaira by force, essentially claiming her as a slave, and Stephanus in turn successfully "removed her to freedom" ([Dem.] 59.40). He did so through an *aphairesis eis eleutherian*, a legal procedure brought before the polemarch by which any Athenian citizen could assert the freedom of someone improperly held as a slave. (The alleged owner could in turn, if he so desired, bring a lawsuit called a *dikē aphaireseōs*

---

[62] On servile invective in the courtroom, see Kamen 2009 and Kamen 2020, 69–74.
[63] On the difficulties faced by freed naturalized citizens in achieving social mobility (with a case study on Apollodorus), see Deene 2011.

against this person's defender.) The *aphairesis*, then, could be employed to protect formerly enslaved people who were wrongly re-enslaved, but its very use in cases like Neaira's demonstrates the degree to which their newfound freedom was tenuous.[64]

Slightly better protection is provided in the case of "sacral" manumissions (see ch. 7.1), where in many cases the gods were called upon or simply understood to protect the newly freed person. Protection was also implicitly offered by the individuals (and sometimes the polis itself) who consented to, guaranteed, or witnessed the act of manumission.[65] And sometimes provisions for the defense of a formerly enslaved person were made explicit: as we saw in the inscription quoted above (ch. 7.1), if anyone tried to re-enslave Nicaia or Isthmus (as, e.g., Phrynion did Neaira), the guarantor Timocritus would guarantee that the terms of the sale were upheld (i.e., that Nicaia or Isthmus remain free), and anyone who happened to witness the re-enslavement could rescue Nicaia or Isthmus with impunity.[66] Although these safeguards were of course very useful for formerly enslaved people, it is important to note, once again, that underlying and motivating these protections was the reality of their precarious status.

7.4 Conclusion

While the modes of manumission attested in classical Athens have been relatively well established by scholars (albeit with continued debate about the function of the *phialai* inscriptions), there remains a lack of consensus about how "sacral" modes of manumission operated elsewhere in the Greek world. Discussion has been particularly heated about the relationship between consecration and manumission, on the one hand, and sale and manumission, on the other, especially as it relates to the standing of the individual dedicated or sold to a god. Relatedly, scholars have shown keen interest in the question of whether a person manumitted with *paramonē* was free, enslaved, or somewhere in between. And finally, there has been a growing recognition that those freed (both

---

[64] On the *aphairesis eis eleutherian*, see Zelnick-Abramovitz 2005, 292–300; Gottesman 2014, 163–169. On the precarity of Neaira's status, see also Forsdyke 2021, 150–153.

[65] On witnesses and guarantors, see Zelnick-Abramovitz 2005, 196–197 and *passim*. On clauses of consent, see Darmezin 1999, 185–187.

[66] See Darmezin 1999, 187–191 for a useful catalogue of anticipated infractions on freedman status, sanctions for defending freed slaves and punishing offenders, and assurances of protection for "defenders."

with and without *paramonē*) occupied a precarious status; despite gaining new-found legal rights through their manumission, many formerly enslaved people in the Greek world faced social barriers or stigmatization and were subject to having their freedom revoked.

8 Representations, Metaphors, and Legacies

Thus far, this book has for the most part discussed scholarship on the "realia" of enslaved people and slavery. In this chapter, I turn to work that has been done on the *representation* of Greek slavery (i.e., how it is depicted in Greek literature and art), the employment of slavery as a metaphor in Greek texts, and the reception of Greek slavery in later time periods. Of particular concern to scholars in recent years has been the ideological and other purposes served by these various representations, metaphors, and uses of the past.

8.1 Representations in literature

In the past twenty years, two books stand out for their exploration of representations of Greek slavery across multiple genres: duBois' *Slaves and Other Objects*, which offers a series of provocative reflections on the topic, and Wrenhaven's *Reconstructing the Slave,* a study of representations of Greek slavery that looks not only at literature but also at multiple types of material culture (e.g. vase paintings, funerary reliefs, figurines, etc.; see further below).[1] Apart from these two works, most scholarship on representations in Greek literature has focused on slavery in *specific* authors or genres. In what follows I survey a selection of such work.

To start with Homer, Thalmann's *The Swineherd and the Bow: Representations of Class in the* Odyssey reads the epic poem as a representation of class dynamics, including slavery.[2] Other scholarship on slavery in Homer's poems has explored, among other things, the *Odyssey* as a precursor to fourth-century BCE slave-management manuals, Odysseus as a figurative slave, and the sexuality of enslaved people in the *Odyssey*.[3] To a lesser extent, scholars have also looked at the representation of manumission (such as it exists) in Homer.[4]

---

1 duBois 2003; Wrenhaven 2012. For a survey of slavery in Greek literature, see Hunt 2011; in Greek and Roman fiction: Sabnis 2021; in Greek and Roman non-fiction: Urbainczyk 2021.
2 Thalmann 1998.
3 See Hunnings 2011 (and also Porter 2021a), Rankine 2011, Wilson 2021, respectively. See also Hunt 2011, 25–28 for a brief overview of the ways that slavery and enslaved people are represented in Homer. See further Lewis 2018a, ch. 5 and Harris 2020 for discussions of slavery in both Hesiod and Homer.
4 On manumission in Homer, see Bouvier 2008, who argues, through a study of Eumaeus, that the focus in Homer is on adopting an enslaved person into the household rather than manumitting or enfranchising them; N'Doye 2008, who argues that manumission in Homer represents

Unsurprisingly, there has been a good deal of scholarship on slavery in Greek tragedy, with a particular focus on Euripides and the fate of the Trojan women.[5] For instance, scholars have noted a split along gender lines in how the Athenian tragedians treat male and female enslaved characters: whereas the former find escape from slavery, the latter do not.[6] Wrenhaven, moreover, investigates the ways in which the tragedians explore the complex relationship between the "good slave" (see above, ch. 4.1) and her enslaver, revealing the paradox that the more intimate their relationship, the greater the potential the enslaved person has to give bad advice or be disloyal.[7] Wrenhaven also looks specifically at Euripides' Trojan War plays, arguing that by representing both "slaves by convention" and "slaves by nature" — for example, Andromache and her nameless loyal slave, respectively — Euripides demonstrates both that fortune is volatile (i.e., anyone can become a slave) and that a change in status does not necessarily produce a change in one's nature (since the enslaved Andromache remains in a sense noble).[8] Scholars have also explored, albeit to a lesser extent, the representation of slavery and manumission in satyr plays, the comic plays that capped off trilogies of tragedies. Slavery in these plays takes a different form than we find in tragedy, with a typical plot involving the satyrs as the slaves of Dionysus.[9]

Recent years have seen an increased interest in the representation of slavery in Greek comedy, a topic that has historically been well studied on the Rome side but less so for Greece.[10] Akrigg and Tordoff's *Slaves and Slavery in Greek Comic Drama*, the edited volume on slaves in both Old and New Comedy mentioned in ch. 1.3, was a welcome contribution to the field, laying the ground-

---

only partial freedom, since it entails maintaining connections with one's former owner); Zanovello 2017 (=2021), ch. 1 (on the liberation of war captives in the *Iliad* and a possible reference to a promised manumission in the *Odyssey* [21.216]) and 2022 (on the vocabulary of manumission in Homer).

5 See Hunt 2011, 32–35 for a brief overview of slavery in Greek tragedy. On slavery in Euripides, see Synodiou 1997. On enslaved women in Greek tragedy: Patterson 1991, ch. 7; Rabinowitz 1998 (specifically Euripides); McCoskey 1998 (Aeschylus); duBois 2003, 138–152.
6 See Rabinowitz 1998; duBois 2003, 138–152. The temple slave Ion in Euripides' play asserts that his slavery to Apollo is benign (*Ion* 128–140), but he is happy to receive his freedom when his true identity is revealed.
7 Wrenhaven 2012, ch. 3.
8 Wrenhaven 2012, ch. 4.
9 On slavery to Dionysus, especially in the context of satyr plays, see Griffith 2002. For a reading of a satyr play (Euripides' *Cyclops*) as a representation of slavery, see Nikolsky 2011.
10 See Hunt 2011, 30–32 for a brief overview of slavery in Greek comedy. For work on slavery in Roman comedy, see McCarthy 2000; Stewart 2012; Richlin 2017.

work for future studies on the topic.¹¹ As with work on Roman comedy, some of the scholarship on Greek comedy has addressed the ways that representations of enslaved people on stage can mitigate slaveholders' anxieties. For example, Tordoff's piece in the aforementioned volume argues that audiences derived pleasure from watching a comic, topsy-turvy version of the enslaver-enslaved relationship, especially since normative relations of dominance and subordination were restored at the end.¹² Akrigg, in turn, argues that Aristophanes' late plays aimed to relieve Athenians' fears in the wake of the Peloponnesian War, which at this point they were losing, by presenting clever slaves whose power could be kept in check by a good master.¹³

Other scholarship on the representation of slavery in Old Comedy has explored a range of topics, including manumission, sex, politics, and the flexibility of identity.¹⁴ Most work on Old Comedy focuses, unsurprisingly, on Aristophanes, but scholars have also worked, for example, on slavery in non-Aristophanic comic fragments and on the development of the comic slave from Old to New Comedy.¹⁵ Scholarship on slavery in New Comedy has likewise been rich in recent years, exploring topics such as the depiction of violence, the socially constructed nature of civic identity, and the plays as windows into the resistance of real enslaved people to their condition.¹⁶ In a particularly compel-

---

11 Akrigg and Tordoff 2013.
12 Tordoff 2013, 36–52.
13 Akrigg 2013.
14 On manumission, see Tamiolaki 2008 on Ar. *Ran.* 694 ("slaves have become Plataeans"), who argues that the word "Plataean" disassociates these formerly enslaved people, now naturalized, from the citizen body, and Buis 2008, who contends that Xanthias in the *Frogs* is depicted as a sort of freed slave. On sex, see especially Walin 2012, a PhD dissertation on enslaved people and sex in Old Comedy. On politics, see duBois 2003, 119–125, who looks at the metaphorical enslavement of poor citizens to demagogues in the *Wasps*, and Olson 2013, who explores Aristophanes' use of the enslaver-enslaved relationship to talk about the Athenian state. On identity, see Lape 2013, who tackles two simultaneous, yet contradictory, ideas present in Aristophanes' comedy: an essentialist view of slavery and a flexible conception of identity.
15 On non-Aristophanic comic fragments, see Sells 2013, who argues that the non-Aristophanic slave has more limited agency than the Aristophanic slave and is more closely linked with his occupational context. On the development of the comic slave, see Bosher 2013, who examines fourth-century BCE comic vases from Sicily and Southern Italy to see what they can tell us about comic developments between Aristophanes and Menander.
16 On the representation of violence, see Konstan 2013, who explores two coexisting types in Menander, one motivated by mimetic realism and one by dramatic purposes. On identity, see Vester 2013, who demonstrates the ways that Menander's *Epitrepontes* reveals that civic identity is socially constructed and status unstable. On resistance, see Profitt 2011, who argues that we can read Menander as a way of accessing the perspectives of enslaved people (and not just

ling article, Marshall reads Roman New Comedy to reconstruct the missing Greek comedies of which they are adaptations, comparing the texts' representation of sex slavery to similar practices in contemporary Southeast Asia.[17]

Considerably less work has been done on slavery in Greek historiography, but two works in this area are worth special attention. As noted in ch. 1.2, Hunt's *Slaves, Warfare, and Ideology in the Greek Historians* radically changed how scholars think about enslaved people in Greek historiography, calling attention to the ways in which the historians elide slave participation in war for ideological reasons.[18] Melina Tamiolaki's *Liberté et esclavage chez les historiens grecs classiques*, in turn, explores the ideas of freedom and slavery in Herodotus, Thucydides, and Xenophon, shedding light on how the two concepts are intertwined in these authors.[19]

Work has also been done on the portrayal of enslaved people in the Greek medical writers. Nancy Demand has looked at the representations of both women and enslaved people in these texts, and finds that unlike women's bodies (which are treated as fundamentally different than men's), there is no sense that the bodies of the enslaved are inherently different from free people's; they are, however, represented as different *in practice*, made so by the different uses to which they were put.[20] McKeown, by contrast, argues that there is no difference noted between free and enslaved bodies in these texts and no distinction made between the physical illnesses suffered by enslaved and free people.[21]

Another genre where the representation of slavery has been studied is Greek philosophy, a good overview of which can be found in Peter Garnsey's *Ideas of Slavery from Augustine to Aristotle*.[22] In general, scholarship has shown that representations of slavery in philosophical texts either reflect contemporary attitudes or serve as justifications for the institution (or both). Far more work has been done on slavery in Aristotle than Plato, likely because Plato (unlike

---

their enslavers' ideology), and Cox 2013, who aims to uncover the daily concerns of enslaved people as portrayed in Menander, including how they cope with their owners' control over their bodies.

17 Marshall 2013.

18 Hunt 1998; chs. 2–3 focus on Herodotus, chs. 4–7 on Thucydides; and chs. 8–10 on Xenophon. See also Hunt 2011, 28–30 for a brief overview of slavery in the Greek historians.

19 Tamiolaki 2010; chs. 1 and 4 focus on Herodotus, chs. 2 and 5 on Thucydides; and 3, 6–8 on Xenophon. See also Serghidou 2008, who examines the ways that Herodotus evokes the emotional experience of deliverance from captivity to talk about freedom on a community level.

20 Demand 1998.

21 McKeown 2002.

22 Garnsey 1996.

Aristotle; see below) does not offer an extended justification of the institution. Nonetheless, scholars have tried to reconstruct Plato's views on slavery and have investigated the place of enslaved people and slavery in Plato's dialogues, especially in the *Republic*.[23] Fisher, for instance, has argued that we can gather Plato's views on slavery from the fact that in his ideal states (as depicted in the *Republic* and the *Laws*), enslaved people are necessary; that Plato espouses the stereotypes common in his day about environmental determinism and implies that enslaved people are mentally inferior; and that he promotes the "mastery" of the intellect, including the rule of the intellectual elite (the philosopher kings) over their (inferior) subjects.[24] On this basis, it appears that Plato held that for some people (i.e., those who are naturally inferior), it was beneficial and even natural for them to be subject to their superiors. These views, in turn, underlie Plato's use of slavery as a metaphor, another topic scholars have explored (see below, ch. 8.3).

As noted above, Aristotle's representation of slavery has garnered a good deal of interest.[25] In the *Politics*, Aristotle famously argues that there is such a thing a slave "by nature" (i.e., a human being who belongs not to himself but to another), that these individuals are easily identifiable, and that slavery is beneficial both to the enslaver and to the enslaved (1253b1–1255b40).[26] Much commented upon by scholars are the apparent inconsistencies in this account of slavery: for example, that Aristotle concedes that nature does not always give free men free bodies (or slaves slave bodies) (1254d32–34) and further that some people are unjustly enslaved in war and therefore not "naturally" slaves, but only slaves by convention (1255a1–2). Paul Millett explains these contradictions as reflecting the complex ways in which slavery operated in practice in Aristotle's day, while others hold that they are best understood when viewed through

---

23 On the place of slavery in Plato's dialogues, see duBois 2003, ch. 7 (with a focus on Plato's *Meno*). The classic study on slavery in the *Republic* is Vlastos 1981 [1968], who demonstrated that slaves existed in Plato's ideal state; cf. Calvert 1987, who argued the opposite. See also, more recently, Gonda 2016, who contends (cf. other scholars) that Plato in the *Republic* simultaneously suggests that slavery is unjust and, by barring Greeks from enslaving other Greeks, implies that the enslavement of barbarians is acceptable. Less has been written on slavery in Plato's *Laws*, on which see Morrow 1939.
24 Fisher 2001 [1993], 92–94.
25 For a recent overview of Aristotle's discussion of slavery, see Forsdyke 2021, 21–31; see also Garnsey 1996, ch. 8 and Hunt 2011, 41–44.
26 Prompting Aristotle's defense of slavery were criticisms of the institution on various grounds, a point he himself addresses. The best discussion of Aristotle's (anonymous) opponents is still Cambiano 1987; on other ancient criticisms of slavery, see Garnsey 1996, ch. 6 and Hunt 2011, 40–41.

the lens of Greek ideology.²⁷ Emily Greenwood has recently argued that Aristotle's theory has a loose style of argumentation that relies on explanatory conjunctions and particles to do the heavy lifting, and moreover that his use of indefinite pronouns and metaphors reveals his reliance on fictions to make his argument.²⁸ But not everyone thinks that Aristotle's defense of slavery is contradictory or incoherent: indeed, some scholars have tried to show that it displays logical reasoning and internal coherence.²⁹

Other, related topics that scholars have explored include the implications of Aristotle's definition of the slave as "some living property" (*ktēma ti empsuchon*); the meaning of "slave by nature"; the ways that modern racialized slavery affects our reading of Aristotle on slavery; whether the benefit to the enslaved person is part of Aristotle's justification of slavery; whether the benefit to the enslaver is part of the justification; and the degree to which enslaved people had the capacity to reason, according to Aristotle.³⁰ Finally, an excellent article by Ranchana Kamtekar demonstrates the value of thinking *along with* Aristotle, even if one disagrees with him or finds his ideas objectionable.³¹

---

27 See Millett 2007; for a more ideological reading, see Wrenhaven 2012, 141–142.
28 Greenwood 2022.
29 See Simpson 2006, who breaks down Aristotle's argument into each of its steps to show how they work together to form a coherent whole; Heath 2008, who says the inconsistencies we find are only apparent, and typical of Aristotle; and Monoson 2011, who argues that Aristotle's argument is philosophically sound and consistent with his discussion of political constitutions.
30 On the slave as *ktēma ti empsuchon*, see Lewis 2017, 32 and 2108, 25, who cites this definition in support his argument for slavery being defined primarily in terms of ownership (see further ch. 1.4), and Greenwood 2022, 343–346, who points out that the indefinite *ti* gives the lie to the idea that the concept of a human as a thing is natural. On the meaning of "slave by nature," see Simpson 2006, who argues that "by nature" means not "by birth" but having a certain (potentially changeable) condition; see also Wrenhaven 2012, 139–149, who argues that in constructing his ideal "natural slave," Aristotle assimilates Greek ideas about physiognomy, environmental determinism, the "good slave," the "bad slave," the slave as tool, and the slave as animal. On the dangers of misreading Aristotle by assimilating Greek slavery to American racialized slavery, see duBois 2003, ch. 9. On the benefit to the slave as simply incidental in Aristotle, see Kamtekar 2016 (responding to previous scholarship arguing the opposite). On slavery as necessary for the "natural master" to have a good life in Aristotle, see Heath 2008. On the capacity to reason, see Heath 2008, who argues that for Aristotle, slaves lack the autonomous rationality that makes them incapable of *eudaimonia* (roughly, "happiness"), and Monoson 2011, who argues that slaves, according to Aristotle, are capable only of the practical reason needed to master a craft.
31 Kamtekar 2016.

8.2 Representations in art

Let us turn now to representations of enslaved people in Greek art.[32] One strain of scholarship on this topic has explored the identifying features of enslaved people in Greek art. Of course, as the Old Oligarch grumbled, it was difficult (at least in Athens) to identify enslaved people simply on the basis of their appearance ([Xen.] *Ath. Pol.* 1.10), which presents a challenge for the modern scholar trying to determine whether a given figure depicted in Greek art is enslaved.[33] Nonetheless, some features have been categorized as typical representations of servility, including small body size; "barbarian" features (e.g., light-colored or reddish hair, non-Greek ethnic features, dark skin, tattoos); simple clothing or nudity (the latter as a marker primarily when there is a contrast to others who are dressed); short hair on women; twisted or deformed bodies; and the performance of certain kinds of labor.[34] However, not all scholars think that enslaved people can be so easily identified: Osborne, for one, has argued that the most reliable criterion of servility is what an individual is depicted doing or how they are treated, not their physical features.[35] The difficulties of identification have also been discussed by scholars in the context of how representations of (potentially) enslaved people are — and should be — labeled in museums.[36]

Most of the work on the ideology of slave representation in art has been done, once again, by Wrenhaven, whose work I focus on here. In *Reconstructing the Slave*, she demonstrates that both positive and negative artistic representations of enslaved people served in various ways to naturalize and justify slavery.[37] For example, she argues that representations of well-behaved and attractive enslaved people in Greek art served as demonstrations of affection between owners and their "good slaves" — thus justifying slavery as mutually benefi-

---

[32] Early work was done on the representation of slaves in archaic and classical Greek art by Himmelmann 1971.
[33] On the difficulties of identifying enslaved people in antiquity, see duBois 2021.
[34] Oakley 2000; Weiler 2002, esp. 18–20; Thalmann 2011; Wrenhaven 2011 and 2012, ch. 2 and 3.
[35] Osborne 2017; see also Lewis 1998/9, who pointed out that status distinctions on Athenian pottery are not always clear-cut.
[36] See duBois 2003, ch. 2. See also Derbew 2018 on problematic museum labeling of black figures in Greek art, including but not limited to equating blackness and slavery; on blackness in Greek antiquity more broadly, see Derbew 2022.
[37] Wrenhaven 2012; see also Wrenhaven 2011. See also Thalmann 2011, who argues that representations of enslaved people in Greek art reinforce ideologies of slavery, including the alleged inferiority of slaves, and Barthe-Deloizy and Charpentier 2015, who argue that the enslaved person's body as represented in Greek art (and in Aristotle) served ideological purposes.

cial – while also displaying the owner's wealth and prestige.[38] John Oakley, similarly, has argued that positive representations of the relationship between women and their female slaves on Athenian vases and grave stelai served to promote an image of "familial harmony."[39] By contrast, representations of enslaved people as "ugly" or engaged in degrading manual labor naturalized the inferiority of slaves.[40] Such representations do not necessarily reflect reality but instead what Weiler calls "inverted *kalokagathia*," a physiognomic concept associating a negative character (i.e., the opposite of the citizen's *kalokagathia*, goodness/ nobility) with a negative physical appearance.[41]

Another area that Wrenhaven has explored is the artistic representations of enslaved characters on the comic stage, specifically terracotta sculptures and vase paintings. She argues that these depictions reflect real-life costumes, with the specific details – padded bellies and rear ends, oversized phalluses, and masks with exaggerated features – designed to represent slavish traits like lustfulness, lack of self-control, and a tendency to gossip.[42] In yet other work, Wrenhaven looks at how attendants at symposia, war captives, and enslaved laborers are sexualized in classical Greek art, with enslaved women depicted as sexual objects and enslaved men as points of contrast to free male beauty.[43] Other scholarship on the depiction of enslaved individuals at symposia, in particular sexualized wine-pouring boys, has been done by Matuszewski (see ch. 5.3).[44]

All of this scholarship, along with other studies of marginalized or "othered" bodies in Greek art, has shown how representations of slavery in art and literature operate, both individually and together. Representations reflect not only the realities of the institution but also – and likely even more so – the various, sometimes conflicting ideologies of slavery.[45] Enslaved audiences may or may not have read or viewed these representations in the same ways that free people did, and some scholarship has explored the question of how the recep-

---

38 Wrenhaven 2012, 86–89 and ch. 3.
39 Oakley 2000.
40 Wrenhaven 2012, ch. 2.
41 Weiler 2002; Wrenhaven 2012, 52–63 also discusses this idea, which she refers to as "reversed *kalokagathia*."
42 Wrenhaven 2013b.
43 Wrenhaven 2021.
44 Matuszewski 2021. Cf. Topper 2012, ch. 3, who argues Athenian sympotic vases represent not enslaved boys but freeborn wine-pourers in an imagined past.
45 On the construction of "others" in Greek art, see the contributions to B. Cohen 2000.

tion by enslaved people might have differed.[46] Enslaved people's potentially subversive readings of literature and art represents an especially promising field of inquiry for the future, in line with the studies of slave agency and resistance explored above (ch. 6).

8.3 Metaphors

Related to the representation of slavery is the use of slavery as a metaphor. It has long been observed that the Greeks used slave metaphors to think through other issues that preoccupied them, but only fairly recently have scholars taken into account the impact of real-life slavery on this metaphorical language.[47] This is an important development: as duBois has shown, literal and figurative slavery are inextricable from one another, and even when they are not explicitly paired, literal slavery usually lurks behind the use of slave metaphors.[48] For example, in historiographic and oratorical discourse, we find slave metaphors employed to talk about, among other things, the subjection of Greek city-states to an external empire, one Greek polis to another, or the citizens of a given polis to a particular governing body.[49] Given that these phenomena often entailed (at least the threat of) individuals literally losing their freedom, such metaphors (or metonyms) had the potential to be especially evocative.[50]

---

46 For the ways that enslaved people may have read such visual representations differently, see Lewis 1998/9; Thalmann 2011. Another question is how enslaved people might have viewed Greek art that was not explicitly about slavery: see Lee 2015 on the viewership of the Aphrodite of Knidos statue by *hetairai*. More work has been done on the question of enslaved viewers of art and other material culture in the Roman world: see Severy-Hoven 2012; Joshel and Petersen 2014.
47 On the metaphor of slavery in Greek thought, see duBois 2003, ch. 5; Brock 2007; Hunt 2011, 23–25. In linguistic terms, slavery was the "source domain" from which the Greeks drew metaphors to talk about non-servile subjection (the "target domain") (see Lakoff and Johnson 1980).
48 duBois 2003, ch. 5.
49 On the figurative language of slavery/freedom as used to describe relations between and within cities, see Tamiolaki 2010, Parts I and II, respectively.
50 The frequently contiguous nature of real and figurative slavery in these contexts means that metonymy might be a more precise term to use here than metaphor, since metonymy involves the substitution of one term with another term from the same sphere of activity, whereas metaphor (strictly speaking) involves the substitution of one term with another from a different sphere. However, because metonym is a subcategory of metaphor (see Cic. *Orat.* 93–94), "metaphor" can encompass both metaphor (in its narrow sense) and metonymy. On the evocative nature of these metaphors, see Hunt 2011, 25, though he suggests that there are

In his study of the development of freedom in Greece, Kurt Raaflaub argues that while the concept of political (internal, i.e. intra-polis) freedom arose out of the Greeks' fear of (external) subjection to the Persians, the concept or metaphor of political *slavery* can be dated considerably earlier.[51] In fact, the archaic lawgiver Solon is one of our earliest sources for the Greeks' use of slavery as a metaphor.[52] Releasing those Athenians who were in various states of unfreedom, from debt bondage to chattel slavery (see ch. 2.2), Solon describes himself as (figuratively) liberating the land of Attica itself, which had been a "slave" before (Sol. fr. 36 West). Solon also employs slavery as a political metaphor to describe subjection to tyrants, warning that the coming tyranny of Pisistratus will impose "slavery" on the people of Athens (Sol. fr. 9 West; see also Sol. fr. 11 West, lines 3–4).[53] While those living under a tyrant were not (in general) literally enslaved, it was thought that anyone subject to a tyrant was deprived, to some extent, of autonomy, making them figurative slaves. Other Greek writers adopt Solon's metaphor of slavery to Pisistratus, and some extend this motif to tyrants in general: Plato, for example, describes the generic tyrant figure as one who holds his homeland "enslaved" (*Resp.* 575d; see also 577c).

Another context where we find metaphors of slavery is narratives about the Persian Wars, with the Persians cast as metaphorical enslavers.[54] According to Herodotus, the Ionian Greeks were urged to seek their independence from "enslavement" to the Persians (unfortunately for them, their attempts failed), and Greek authors from Herodotus to Plutarch describe many of the battles of the Persian Wars as fights for freedom (implicitly or explicitly from metaphorical slavery): thus, the Greek victory at the Battle of Marathon (490 BCE) is described as a major step in securing freedom for Greece, as is the Battle of Salamis (480 BCE) (with Themistocles, whose leadership was most responsible for the victory at Salamis, referred to as a great liberator), and so too the Battle of Plataea (479 BCE). And in oratorical and historiographical texts from the fourth century, the

---

"some signs that the constant use of the metaphor of slavery did blunt its edge and take its shock value away."

51 Raaflaub 2004; cf. Patterson 1991, who argues that the concept of freedom arose out of the experiences of enslaved people.
52 On Solon and the political metaphor of slavery, see Raaflaub 2004, 45–57. On slave metaphors in Solon more broadly, see Martin 2006.
53 On metaphorical slavery to tyrants, see Raaflaub 2004, 89–102.
54 On the concept of freedom during the Persian Wars, see Raaflaub 2004, 58–89. On slavery and freedom specifically in Herodotus: Serghidou 2004 and 2008; Tamiolaki 2010, ch. 1 and 4.

Athenians continued to portray their ancestors as the liberators of Greece from Persian rule.[55]

The metaphorical language of slavery and freedom escalated in the period after the Persian Wars, and it came to a boiling point during the Peloponnesian War.[56] However, the target of the metaphor had shifted: it was now used to describe the political subjection of one Greek polis to another, most frequently other cities' subjection to Athens. This is particularly common in Spartan propaganda, though the Athenians themselves claimed to be their allies' liberators.[57] After the war, these metaphors evolved yet again: fourth-century writers use the language of freedom to characterize (pejoratively or not, depending on their political leanings) the citizens of democratic Athens,[58] and Attic orators frame the innumerable external conflicts of this time as contests for Greek cities' freedom from "enslavement," whether to other Greek poleis, the Persians, or Philip of Macedon.[59]

Metaphors of slavery and freedom also play an important role in Greek philosophical thought, and while a handful of scholars have taken into account how the institution of slavery informs this figurative language, much work remains to be done.[60] After all, the Greek philosophers, writing for an audience of slaveholders and being members of a society where enslaved people were ubiquitous, had intimate connections with slavery. A number of them owned slaves whom they manumitted in their wills (see ch. 7.1), and some either experienced slavery first-hand (like Plato, allegedly [D. L. 3.19–20]) or were descended from slaves.[61] It is not a stretch, then, to suggest that philosophers' knowledge of

---

55 On these texts, with references, see Marincola 2007.
56 After the Persian Wars: Raaflaub 2004, ch. 4; during the Peloponnesian War: Raaflaub 2004, ch. 5. On slavery specifically in Thucydides, see Tamiolaki 2010, chs. 2 and 5.
57 On Athens' freedom propaganda, see Raaflaub 2004, 166–181; Sparta's freedom propaganda, Raaflaub 2004, 193–202. Since literal enslavement was a real threat faced by Greek cities at this time, perhaps most famously by the Melians at the hands of the Athenians (Thuc. 5.116.4), the metaphorical language underlying all of this propaganda must have had teeth.
58 On democratic freedom, see Raaflaub 2004, ch. 6; Liddel 2007; Hansen 2010; Campa 2018.
59 Once again, these were not dead metaphors: sometimes literal and figurative slavery appear side by side, as when Isocrates says that it is shameful that the Athenians think it right for barbarians to be their (literal) household slaves while simultaneously allowing their allies to be "enslaved" to the Persians (4.181).
60 Those who look at philosophical metaphors of slavery in the context of literal slavery include Just 1985; Patterson 1991; duBois 2003, chs. 7 and 9; and Tamiolaki 2010, Part III (specifically on Xenophon). On the concept of freedom in Greek philosophy, see Patterson 1991, chs. 9–11; Hansen 2010, 9–27.
61 On enslaved philosophers, see duBois 2003, 153–156.

slavery shaped the ways they deployed metaphors. In fact, a similar argument has been made by New Testament scholars regarding Paul's use of slave metaphors. For example, Dale Martin argues that Paul's reference to himself as the (metaphorical) "*oikonomos* of Christ" alludes to the contemporary *oikonomos*, a managerial slave of high standing. By using this term metaphorically, Martin argues, Paul demonstrates that upward mobility is possible through service to Christ.[62] Michael J. Brown, in turn, contends that Paul's use of the metaphor "*doulos* of Christ" called to mind — and helped Paul align himself with — a particular status group, namely enslaved and formerly enslaved members of the imperial household, who constituted a large part of Paul's Roman audience.[63] Finally, John Byron has sought to establish the Jewish background for slave metaphors in Pauline Christianity, arguing that Exodus was the source of the tradition of (Jewish) slavery to God and that Paul adopted and adapted this tradition to suit his Greco-Roman context.[64]

Plato's use of slavery as a metaphor was pointed out many years ago by Glenn Morrow, followed shortly thereafter by Gregory Vlastos' important article on the topic.[65] Much more recently, A.A. Long has written on slavery as a philosophical metaphor in Plato (and Xenophon), and I have studied metaphors in the *Phaedo* in light of a conception of manumission as social rebirth or healing.[66] In this dialogue, Plato uses metaphorical slavery in two main ways: like real slavery, it could be good, both for the "slave" and for the community as a whole, if it reflected a natural hierarchy, or bad if it entailed an inversion thereof.[67] For Plato, good "slavery" generally involves the subjection of individuals or

---

62 Martin 1990; cf. Byron 2003, 7–12.
63 Brown 2001; cf. Byron 2003, 14–15.
64 Byron 2003. See also Hezser 2005, ch. 15 on the use of slave metaphors in the Hebrew Bible and Jewish writings of the Hellenistic and Roman periods.
65 Morrow 1939, 186–187; Vlastos 1981 [1941]. In a later postscript (1959), Vlastos retracted a bit, saying that slavery is only one of many keys to Plato's philosophy, rather than *the* key; for criticism of Vlastos's retraction, see duBois 2003, 166.
66 See Long 2012, who argues that Socrates pioneered the slave metaphor in philosophy, and Kamen 2013b, in which I argue that Socrates, on the eve of his death, offers a cock to the healing god Asclepius because his soul is about to be freed from "slavery" to his body. For the conception of manumission as healing/rebirth, see Kamen 2012. On the concept of freedom in Plato, Patterson 1991, 156–161, 173–180.
67 On good and bad metaphorical slavery in Plato, see Kamen 2013, 85–90. The double use of the slave metaphor is something that has also been observed in New Testament studies: as Combes 1998 has demonstrated, the early Christians employed slave metaphors to refer not only to "divine slavery," i.e., slavery to God, but also to "human slavery," i.e., slavery to desires and externals. Paul, in fact, uses the metaphor in both of these ways, saying that Chris-

communities to external forces like (good) laws, rulers, and gods (i.e., natural "masters").⁶⁸ Bad "slavery," by contrast, involves either internal subjection (of the soul to the body, or one part of the soul to another part) or external subjection (to a bad ruler or enemy state) or some combination of the two.

Xenophon, too, uses slave metaphors in his philosophical writings. Like Plato, he does not articulate a formal theory of slavery, but we see from some of his works, primarily the *Oikonomikos*, that he gave a lot of thought to the ideal enslaver-enslaved relationship (see ch. 4.1). He also devotes much attention, especially in the *Memorabilia*, to *enkrateia*, that is, self-rule or self-control.⁶⁹ As Tamiolaki demonstrates, these two interests — the master-slave relationship and the virtue of *enkrateia* — dovetail in Xenophon's use of slave metaphors to talk about both "enslavement" to and "mastery" over pleasures and desires.⁷⁰ Indeed, one of the philosophical arguments of the *Oikonomikos* is that one should be "master" over one's pleasures as if they were one's (literal) slaves. Otherwise, one can become a "slave" oneself — and this condition, unlike that of one's own household slaves, represents "bad" slavery.

8.4 Legacies of Greek slavery

A final area of interest in recent years has been the lasting legacy of ancient slavery, both Greek and Roman. Much of this work has focused on the use of ancient slavery in arguments for and against slavery in the modern era, as exemplified by Edith Hall, Richard Alston, and Justine McConnell's edited volume *Ancient Slavery and Abolition: From Hobbes to Hollywood* (2012), the contributors to which explore discussions of slavery and abolition from the late seventeenth century onwards.⁷¹ For example, Margaret Malamud, both in this volume and elsewhere, demonstrates that nineteenth-century abolitionists and Black intellectuals argued that slaves in antiquity, as compared to their counterparts

---

tians escape (bad) human slavery to sin and enter (good) divine slavery to God or Christ. See also Long 2012, who categorizes metaphorical slavery in Plato into three types: culpable slavery to irrational impulses, involuntary slavery to reason, and voluntary slavery to rationality, divinity, and the rule of law.
68 Aristotle likewise argues that most people benefit from (good) "slavery" to rulers, laws, parents, etc., just as natural slaves benefit from their enslavement; see further Patterson 1991, 161–164.
69 See Tamiolaki 2010, ch. 8; Long 2012, 355–357.
70 Tamiolaki 2010, Part III.
71 Hall, Alston, McConnell 2012.

under American slavery, were treated relatively leniently (e.g. enslaved people in antiquity could be manumitted, and when they were, a lack of racial prejudice meant they were able to assimilate into society) and that slavery was bad not only for enslaved people but also for enslavers, making the latter more callous and creating a culture of decadence and decline (here the abolitionists were thinking in particular of Rome). Advocates for slavery, on the other hand, claimed that slavery in America was *milder* than in antiquity; that it benefited both the enslaved and the enslaver; and that it provided the leisure required to produce the glorious civilizations of Greece (especially classical Athens) and Rome.[72]

Perhaps unsurprisingly, Aristotle (see ch. 8.1) played a prominent role in these pro-slavery arguments, and his ideas lingered even after the abolition of slavery into the Jim Crow era.[73] Sara Monoson has examined the use of Aristotle by Confederate academics, politicians, and polemicists in the 1830s–1850s in response to the growing abolitionist movement.[74] Actively engaging with and embracing Aristotle's *Politics* Book 1, they were able to formulate their idea of slavery as a "positive good."[75] Monoson argues further that these writers used Aristotle to shield themselves from accusations of racism under cover of high-minded philosophy; to argue that Northern "wage slavery" was worse and more damaging to its workers than the southern institution; and to support their claim that Africans are naturally suited to be slaves (in fact, some even claimed that they were improving on Aristotle by pinpointing race as the basis for natural slavery). Finally, she notes that these southern writers ignored the fact that Aristotle's defense of slavery was issued in response to contemporary critics of slavery and therefore (deliberately or otherwise) missed the fact that the justice of slavery was not uncontroversial even in Aristotle's time.

Other work in this area has been done specifically on *women* arguing for and against slavery by invoking the Greek and Roman past. Caroline Winterer, for instance, has demonstrated that female advocates on both sides used antiq-

---

[72] Malamud 2012 and 2016, ch. 3. For pro-slavery arguments in America using ancient slavery, see also duBois 2003, 18–21 and 2009, 69–74.
[73] See Greenwood 2022, 348–353, on the afterlife of Aristotle's idea of the slave as property, including the statement of Martin Luther King, Jr., that man is not an "animated tool."
[74] Monoson 2012.
[75] On the shift from presenting slavery as a positive good as opposed to a necessity evil, see Vanderford 2009. He argues that this move, pioneered by professors at the University of Virginia in the 1850s, was part of a shift from thinking in terms of modern natural rights toward the ancient idea of "classic natural right" (a term coined by Leo Strauss to refer to the concept that some men are superior and thus have a right to rule others).

uity differently than their male contemporaries did, primarily in that they focused on women (both free and enslaved) in the ancient world.[76] Of particular interest recently has been the writings of Lydia Maria Child, a nineteenth-century abolitionist who, through various genres (pamphlets, histories, a novel), connected modern slavery to the oppression of women in both antiquity and modernity. Moreover, as Winterer shows, Child equated Athens (where she felt that slaves were treated well) with the free North, full of hardworking industrialists, and Sparta with the South, with enslavers who hate manual labor, love freedom, and abuse their slaves.[77]

Yet other scholarship has explored the nineteenth/early-twentieth-century American classicist Basil Lannau Gildersleeve's defense of Southern slavery.[78] Notably, while the ancient world obviously informs Gildersleeve's thought (e.g. he, like Child and others, compares Athens to the North, Sparta to the South), he does not generally draw on ancient slavery *explicitly* in his discussions of modern slavery. Finally, Hodkinson and Hall have looked at the use of Spartan helotage in late-eighteenth-century British thought, finding that the use of Helots as a point of comparsion was especially prominent during the period of the British parliamentary debates of 1791–1796 about abolishing the slave trade.[79] As they show, helotage is cited by both sides of the debate, with advocates for slavery arguing that their own practices were more lenient than those of the Spartans, and abolitionists arguing that the conditions of Helots, while brutal, were actually superior to those under modern slavery.

Other scholarship on the legacy of ancient slavery has examined its depiction in popular media, including Hollywood films and comic books.[80] Most films featuring ancient slavery, however, are set in Rome (or in the case of *The Ten Commandments*, ancient Egypt), not in Greece. Greek slavery may not be entirely absent from the cinema, however: McConnell has argued that the movie *Sommersby*, which is set in the American South just after slavery has been abolished, uses the *Odyssey*'s Eumaeus and Eurycleia as (implicit) models for two of

---

76 Winterer 2007, ch. 6 (anti-slavery: pp. 169–177; pro-slavery: pp. 177–180).
77 Winterer 2007, 169–175. On Child's use of antiquity, see also Malamud 2016, 112–114, 138–140; Connors n.d., who explores Child's use of Athenian slavery in the novel *Philothea*, arguing that she draws on Plutarch, Euripides, and Plato to persuade her readers of the need for abolition.
78 On Gildersleeve's defense of Southern slavery, see duBois 2003, 13–18; Lupher and Vandiver 2012; Malamud 2016, 137–138, 140–142.
79 Hodkinson and Hall 2012.
80 On the Hollywood reception of ancient slavery, see duBois 2009, ch. 5 and duBois 2014.

its enslaved characters.[81] Helots, in turn, are the focus of Kieron Gillen's five-issue comic series *Three*, which tells the story of three fictional Helots who rebel against the Spartans. This comic is historically well informed (it was written in consultation with Hodkinson) and is framed as a response to the depiction of Sparta in Frank Miller's comic *The 300* (1998) and its subsequent film adaptation (2007).[82]

A final approach to the legacy of ancient slavery is pedagogical: namely, how (and how not) to teach this topic. Dani Bostick has written about the mock slave auctions held at Junior Classical League (JCL) conventions, which she cites as just one example of a pervasive problem in secondary school Classics (another is the treatment of slaves and slavery on the US National Latin Exam).[83] duBois, in turn, has written on teaching ancient slavery at the university level, where she finds it effective to have her students read texts about Greek and Roman slavery alongside slave narratives (especially first-person accounts) from the modern and contemporary worlds, since this shakes up the students' comfort with or easy identification with the ancient material.[84] Finally, Classics PhD student Javal Coleman has pointed out that for some students, like himself, an interest in ancient slavery may be rooted in their own experience as a descendant of enslaved people. Teachers at all levels should not overlook or underestimate this perspective, which in Coleman's case led to a desire to explore the lives and feelings of enslaved individuals in antiquity.[85]

---

81 McConnell 2012.
82 Gillen 2014. There has been surprisingly little scholarship on *Three*, but see Gervais 2014, who reads both versions of *The 300* as well as *Three* as different ways of shaping the meaning of Sparta for modern audiences. See also the "conversation" between Gillen and Hodkinson in Gillen 2014.
83 Bostick 2019. In this piece, she suggests ways for the American Classical League (which sponsors the JCL) to change the culture in secondary school Classics, as well as for teachers in post-secondary education to help out.
84 duBois 2014. She also notes that in her experience, Classics majors are not made especially uncomfortable by references to enslaved people, slavery, and slave torture in the ancient texts they read; general education students, by contrast, tend to identify with ancient slaves, seeing them as underdogs or as heroes that they can sympathize with (an effect, duBois says, that Hollywood movies featuring ancient slavery also aim for).
85 Coleman 2021.

8.5 Conclusion

In studying Greek slavery, as with any area of antiquity, it is important to keep in mind that all of our evidence is a representation and is motivated by ideological, literary, artistic, or other considerations. In this light, scholars have explored the ways that Greek poets, historians, philosophers, and visual artists depicted enslaved people and their condition, representations that in turn reflected and bolstered societal ideas about slavery. Similarly, work has been done on the Greeks' evocative use of slavery as a metaphor to describe various forms of non-servile subjection, particularly in political and philosophical contexts. Finally, scholars have in recent years investigated how later generations have used Greek slavery (including representations and metaphors thereof) in the service of defending and condemning modern slavery, of providing a source of popular entertainment, or of educating students about the harsh realities of the ancient world.

9 Epilogue

In this book, I have sketched out some of the main areas of recent research on Greek slavery. While some topics of study have not changed radically since the time of Finley (e.g. the economics of slavery), many of the questions *within* these topics have, and areas have recently received attention that were nearly or completely ignored in the past (e.g. sex and gender). By tracking the questions that scholars have investigated the past twenty to twenty-five years, I hope also to have provided a roadmap that can serve as a starting point for future research in this area. Indeed, since this book has, by its nature, been more retrospective than prospective, I would like to conclude by briefly mentioning two key areas I see this field progressing in the future.

One is the continued study of Greek slavery vis-à-vis global or comparative slavery. We have already seen some of the tremendous payoffs of looking at Greek slavery (or slaveries) alongside slave systems of contemporaneous Mediterranean and Near Eastern societies, as well as slave societies of the modern and even contemporary world. Not only will further work continue to illuminate areas of Greek slavery we have historically not fully understood, it will also illustrate the ways in which Greek slavery is not so unique in world history (which in turn has important ramifications for overturning long-entrenched ideas about Greek exceptionalism more broadly). A second area likely to develop further in the future is work attempting to access the lived experiences of enslaved and formerly enslaved people in the Greek world. Good scholarship has already begun in this vein, but it is still a relatively new area of research, and much remains to be done. This kind of approach, while inevitably requiring a degree of speculation, is invaluable in providing a vivid sense of what the condition of enslavement might have actually *felt* like. We cannot bring back to life those who were enslaved, but we can redeem some vestige of their humanity by trying to tell their stories.

Works Cited

Acton, P. (2014). *Poiesis: Manufacturing in Classical Athens*. Oxford.
Akrigg, B. (2013). 'Aristophanes, Slaves and History', in: B. Akrigg and R. Tordoff (eds.), *Slaves and Slavery in Ancient Greek Comic Drama*. Cambridge and New York, 111–123.
Akrigg, B. (2019). *Population and Economy in Classical Athens*. Cambridge.
Akrigg, B. and R. Tordoff (eds.) (2013). *Slaves and Slavery in Ancient Greek Comic Drama*. Cambridge and New York.
Alston, R., E. Hall, L. Proffitt (eds.) (2011). *Reading Ancient Slavery*. London.
Alvar Nuño, A. (ed.) (2019). *Historiografía de la esclavitud*. Madrid.
Alvar, J. and L. Hernández Guerra (eds.) (2002). *Jerarquías religiosas y control social en el mundo antiguo*. Valladolid.
Anastasiadis, B.I. and P.N. Doukellis (eds.) (2005). *Esclavage antique et discriminations socio-culturelles*. Bern.
Andreau, J. and R. Descat (2011 [2006]). *The Slave in Greece and Rome*, translated by M. Leopold. Madison.
Arcuri, R., E. Caliri, and A. Pinzone (2012). *Forme di dipendenza nelle società di transizione*. Messina.
Barthe-Deloizy, F. and M.-C. Charpentier (2015). 'Le corps de l'esclave en Grèce ancienne: espace de la représentation ou représentation d'un espace?', in: A. Beltrán, I. Sastra Prats, M. Valdés Guía (eds.), *Los espacios de la esclavitud y la dependencia desde la Antigüedad: homenaje a Domingo Plácido*. Bescançon, 79–95.
Bathrellou E. and K. Vlassopoulos (2022). *Greek and Roman Slaveries*. Hoboken, NJ.
Beltrán, A., I. Sastra Prats, M. Valdés Guía (eds.) (2015). *Los espacios de la esclavitud y la dependencia desde la Antigüedad*. Bescançon.
Bile, M. (2019). '*Woikeus* et *dōlos* à Gortyne au Ve siècle', in: L. Gagliardi and L. Pepe (eds.), *Dike: Essays on Greek Law in Honor of Alberto Maffi*. Milan, 29–47.
Blok, J. and A.P.M.H. Lardinois (eds.) (2006). *Solon of Athens: New Historical and Philological Approaches*. Leiden.
Bodel, J. and W. Scheidel (2017). *On Human Bondage: After Slavery and Social Death*. Malden, MA.
Bömer, F. (1958–63). *Untersuchungen über die Religion der Sklaven in Griechenland und Rom*. 4 vols. Wiesbaden.
Bosher, K. (2013). '"Phlyax" Slaves: From Vase to Stage?', in: B. Akrigg and R. Tordoff (eds.), *Slaves and Slavery in Ancient Greek Comic Drama*. Cambridge and New York, 197–208.
Bostick, D. (2019). 'The Shame of Mock Slave Auctions in Secondary Classics', in: *Sententiae Antiquae*, https://sententiaeantiquae.com/2019/10/29/the-shame-of-mock-slave-auctions-in-secondary-classics/, Accessed December 21, 2022.
Boswell, J. (1990). *The Kindness of Strangers: The Abandonment of Children in Western Europe from Late Antiquity to the Renaissance*. New York.
Bouvier, D. (2008). 'Formes de "retours à la liberté" et statut de l'"affranchissement" dans la poésie homérique', in: A. Gonzales (ed.), *La fin du statut servile? (affranchissement, libération, abolition)*. Vol. 1. Besançon, 9–16.
Bradley, K.R. (1989). *Slavery and Rebellion in the Roman World, 140 B.C.–70 B.C.* Bloomington.
Bradley, K.R. and P. Cartledge (eds.) (2011). *The Cambridge World History of Slavery*. Vol. 1: *The Ancient Mediterranean World*. Cambridge.

Braund, D. (2011). 'The Slave Supply in Classical Greece', in: K. Bradley and P. Cartledge (eds.), *The Cambridge World History of Slavery*. Vol. 1: *The Ancient Mediterranean World*. Cambridge, 112–133.

Breitenfeld, S.B. (2022). *'Someone Get a Whip!' Enslaved Women and Violence in Athenian Oratory, Comedy, and Curses*. Diss. Washington.

Brock, R. (2007). 'Figurative Slavery in Greek Thought', in: A. Serghidou (ed.), *Fear of Slaves—Fear of Enslavement in the Ancient Mediterranean. Peur de l'esclave—Peur de l'esclavage en Méditerranée ancienne (Discours, représentations, pratiques)*. Besançon, 209–215.

Buis, E.J. (2008). 'Les (en)jeux d'un "affranchissement" dramatique: la subjectivité légale de Xanthias dans les *Grenouilles* d'Aristophane', in: A. Gonzales (ed.), *La fin du statut servile? (affranchissement, libération, abolition)*. Vol. 2. Besançon, 419–435.

Byron, J. (2003). *Slavery Metaphors in Early Judaism and Pauline Christianity*. Tübingen.

Cairns, D.L. (1993). *Aidōs: The Psychology and Ethics of Honour and Shame in Ancient Greek Literature*. Oxford.

Cairns, D.L. (1996). '*Hybris*, Dishonour and Thinking Big', in: *Journal of Hellenic Studies* 116, 1–32.

Calderini, A. (1908). *La manomissione e la condizione dei liberti in Grecia*. Milan.

Calvert, B. (1987). 'Slavery in Plato's *Republic*', in: *Classical Quarterly* 37, 367–372.

Cambiano, G. (1987). 'Aristotle and the Anonymous Opponents of Slavery', translated by M. di Gregorio, in: M.I. Finley (ed.), *Classical Slavery*. London, 28–41.

Campa, N.T. (2018). 'Positive Freedom and the Citizen in Athens', in: *Polis* 35, 1–2.

Caneva, S. and A. Delli Pizzi (2015). 'Given to a Deity?: Religious and Social Reappraisal of Human Consecrations in the Hellenistic and Roman East', in: *Classical Quarterly* 65, 167–191.

Canevaro, M. (2018). 'The Public Charge for *Hybris* against Slaves: The Honour of the Victim and the Honour of the *Hybristēs*', in: *Journal of Hellenic Studies* 138, 100–126.

Canevaro, M. (2019). 'L'accusa pubblica di *hybris* contro gli schiavi: L'onore della vittima e l'onore dell'*hybristes*', in: *Rivista di Diritto Ellenico* 9, 43–90.

Canevaro, M. and D.M. Lewis (2014). '*Khoris oikountes* and the Obligations of Freedmen in Late Classical and Early Hellenistic Athens', in: *Incidenza dell'antico* 12, 91–121.

Cartledge, P. (1985). 'Rebels and Sambos in Classical Greece: A Comparative View', in: P. Cartledge and F.D. Harvey (eds.), *Crux: Essays Presented to G. E. M. de Ste. Croix on his 75th Birthday*. London, 16–46.

Cartledge, P. (2002a). 'Greek Civilisation and Slavery', in: T.P. Wiseman (ed.), *Classics in Progress: Essays on Ancient Greece and Rome*. Oxford, 247–262.

Cartledge, P. (2002b). 'The Political Economy of Greek Slavery', in: P. Cartledge (ed.), *Money, Labour and Land: Approaches to the Economies of Ancient Greece*. London, 156–166.

Cartledge, P. (2002c [1973]). *Sparta and Lakonia: A Regional History 1300–362 BC*. London.

Cartledge, P. (2003). 'Raising Hell? The Helot Mirage—A Personal Review', in: N. Luraghi and S.E. Alcock (eds.), *Helots and Their Masters in Laconia and Messenia: Histories, Ideologies, Structures*. Washington, D.C., 12–30.

Cartledge, P. (2011). 'The Helots: A Contemporary Review', in: K. Bradley and P. Cartledge (eds.), *The Cambridge World History of Slavery*. Vol. 1: *The Ancient Mediterranean World*. Cambridge, 74–90.

Christensen, K.A. (1984). 'The Theseion: A Slave Refuge at Athens', in: *American Journal of Ancient History* 9, 23–32.

Cohen, B. (ed.) (2000). *Not the Classical Ideal: Athens and the Construction of the Other in Greek Art*. Leiden.

Cohen, E.E. (1992). *Athenian Economy & Society: A Banking Perspective*. Princeton.
Cohen, E.E. (2000). *The Athenian Nation*. Princeton.
Cohen, E.E. (2003). 'Athenian Prostitution as a Liberal Profession', in: G. Bakewell and J. Sickinger (eds.), *Gestures: Essays in Ancient History, Literature, and Philosophy Presented to Alan L. Boegehold*. Oxford, 214–226.
Cohen, E.E. (2006). 'Free and Unfree Sexual Work: An Economic Analysis of Athenian Prostitution', in: C. Faraone and L. McClure (eds.), *Prostitutes and Courtesans in the Ancient World*. Madison, 95–124.
Cohen, E.E. (2012). 'Juridical Implications of Athenian Slaves' Commercial Activity', in: G. Thür (ed.), *Symposion 2011. Vorträge zur griechischen und hellenistischen Rechtsgeschichte*. Vienna, 213–223.
Cohen, E.E. (2014). 'Sexual Abuse and Sexual Rights: Slaves' Erotic Experience at Athens and Rome', in: T.K. Hubbard (ed.), *A Companion to Greek and Roman Sexualities*. Malden, MA, 184–198.
Cohen, E.E. (2015). *Athenian Prostitution: The Business of Sex*. Oxford.
Cohen, E.E. (2018). 'Slaves Operating Businesses: Legal Ramifications for Ancient Athens—and for Modern Scholarship', in: P. Perlman (ed.), *Ancient Greek Law in the 21st Century*. Austin, 54–69.
Coleman, J. (2021). 'A Black Odyssey: Coming from Slaves and Studying Slavery', in: *Society for Classical Studies Blog*. https://classicalstudies.org/scs-blog/javal-coleman/blog-black-odyssey-coming-slaves-and-studying-slavery, Accessed December 21, 2022.
Combes, I.A.H. (1998). *The Metaphor of Slavery in the Writings of the Early Church: From the New Testament to the Beginning of the Fifth Century*. Sheffield.
Compagno, M., J. Gállego, C. García Mac Gaw (eds.) (2013). *Rapports de subordination personnelle et pouvoir politique dans la Méditerranée antique et au-delà*. Besançon.
Connor, W.R. (1988). '"Sacred" and "Secular": Ἱερὰ καὶ ὅσια and the Classical Athenian Concept of the State', in: *Ancient Society* 19, 161–188.
Cortadella Morral, J., O. Olesti Vila, C. Sierra Martín (eds.) (2018). *Lo viejo y lo nuevo en las sociedades antiguas*. Besançon.
Couvenhes, J.-C. (2014). 'Les kryptoi spartiates', in: *Dialogues d'histoire ancienne*, Supplement 11, 45–76.
Cox, C. (2013). 'Coping with Punishment: The Social Networking of Slaves in Menander', in: B. Akrigg and R. Tordoff (eds.), *Slaves and Slavery in Ancient Greek Comic Drama*. Cambridge and New York, 159–172.
Crone, P. (1987). *Roman, Provincial and Islamic Law: The Origins of the Islamic Patronate*. Cambridge.
Dal Lago, E. and C. Katsari (eds.) (2008). *Slave Systems: Ancient and Modern*. Cambridge.
Darmezin, L. (1999). *Les affranchissements par consécration en Béotie et dans le monde grec hellénistique*. Nancy.
Darwall, S. (1977). 'Two Kinds of Respect', in: *Ethics* 88, 36–49.
Darwall, S. (2013). *Honor, History, and Relationship: Essays in Second-Person Ethics*. Oxford.
Davidson, J.N. (1997). *Courtesans and Fishcakes: The Consuming Passions of Classical Athens*. London.
Davies, P.A. (2017). 'Articulating Status in Ancient Greece: Status (In)consistency as a New Approach', in: *Cambridge Classical Journal* 63, 29–52.
Davis, D.B. (1966). *The Problem of Slavery in Western Culture*. Ithaca.

Deene, M. (2011). 'Naturalized Citizens and Social Mobility in Classical Athens: The Case of Apollodorus', in: *Greece & Rome* 58, 159–175.
Demand, N. (1998). 'Women and Slaves as Hippocratic Patients', in: S.R. Joshel and S. Murnaghan (eds.), *Women and Slaves in Greco-Roman Culture: Differential Equations*. London, 69–84.
Derbew, S. (2018). 'An Investigation of Black Figures in Classical Greek Art', in: *The Iris (Behind the Scenes at the Getty)*. http://blogs.getty.edu/iris/an-investigation-of-black-figures-in-classical-greek-art/, Accessed October 24, 2022.
Derbew, S. (2022). *Untangling Blackness in Greek Antiquity*. Cambridge.
Descat, R. (2011). 'Labour in the Hellenistic Economy: Slavery as a Test Case', in: Z.H. Archibald, J.K. Davies, V. Gabrielsen (eds.), *The Economies of Hellenistic Societies, Third to the First Centuries CE*. Oxford, 207–215.
de Souza, P. (1999). *Piracy in the Graeco-Roman World*. Cambridge.
de Ste. Croix, G.E.M. (1957). 'Slavery [Review of W.L. Westermann's *The Slave Systems of Greek and Roman Antiquity*]', in: *Classical Review* n.s. 7, 54–59.
de Ste. Croix, G.E.M. (1981). *The Class Struggle in the Ancient Greek World from the Archaic Age to the Arab Conquests*. Ithaca.
Dickie, M.W. (2000). 'Who Practiced Love-Magic in Classical Antiquity and in the Late Roman World?', in: *Classical Quarterly* 50, 563–583.
Dimopoulou-Piliouni, A. (2008). '*Apeleutheroi*: Metics or Foreigners?', in: *Dike* 11, 27–50.
Dimopoulou-Piliouni, A. (2012). 'Le rôle des esclaves dans l'économie Athénienne: réponse à Edward Cohen', in: G. Thür (ed.), *Symposion 2011: Vorträge zur griechischen und hellenistischen Rechtsgeschichte*. Vienna, 225–236.
Dmitriev, S. (2016). 'The Protection of Slaves in the Athenian Law against *Hubris*', in: *Phoenix* 70, 64–76.
Doddington, D.S. and E. dal Lago (eds.) (2022). *Writing the History of Slavery*. London.
duBois, P. (1991). *Torture and Truth*. New York and London.
duBois, P. (2003). *Slaves and Other Objects*. Chicago.
duBois, P. (2009). *Slavery: Antiquity and its Legacy*. Oxford.
duBois, P. (2012 [2009]). 'Slavery', in: B. Graziosi, P. Vasunia, G. Boys-Stones (eds.), *The Oxford Handbook of Hellenic Studies*. Oxford. https://doi.org/10.1093/oxfordhb/9780199286140.013.0028
duBois, P. (2014). 'Teaching the Uncomfortable Subject of Slavery', in: N.S. Rabinowitz and F. McHardy (eds.), *From Abortion to Pederasty: Addressing Difficult Topics in the Classics Classroom*. Columbus, 187–198.
duBois, P. (2021). 'How to Tell a Slave', in: S. Hodkinson, M. Kleijwegt, K. Vlassopoulos (eds.), *The Oxford Handbook of Greek and Roman Slaveries*. Oxford. https://doi.org/10.1093/oxfordhb/9780199575251.013.6
Ducat, J. (1990). *Les Hilotes. Bulletin de correspondance hellénique* Supplément 20. Paris.
Ducat, J. (2006). *Spartan Education: Youth and Society in the Classical Period*. Swansea.
Ducat, J. (2015). 'Les hilotes à l'époque archaïque', in: J. Zurbach (ed.), *La main-d'œuvre agricole en Méditerranée archaïque: statuts et dynamiques économiques*. Paris, 165–195.
Ducrey, P. (2022). 'Slaves and War', in: S. Hodkinson, M. Kleijwegt, K. Vlassopoulos (eds.), *The Oxford Handbook of Greek and Roman Slaveries*. Oxford. https://doi.org/10.1093/oxfordhb/9780199575251.013.7
Eidinow, E. (2007). *Oracles, Curses, and Risks among the Ancient Greeks*. Oxford.

Eidinow, E. (2012). '"What Will Happen to Me if I Leave?" Ancient Greek Oracles, Slaves and Slave Owners', in: S. Hodkinson and D. Geary (eds.), *Slaves and Religions in Graeco-Roman Antiquity and Modern Brazil*. Newcastle upon Tyne, 244–278.
Faraone, C. and L. McClure (eds.) (2006). *Prostitutes and Courtesans in the Ancient World*. Madison.
Fenolatea, S. (1984). 'Slavery and Supervision in Comparative Perspective: A Model', in: *Journal of Economic History* 44, 635–668.
Figueira, T.J. (2003). 'The Demography of the Spartan Helots', in: N. Luraghi and S.E. Alcock, (eds.), *Helots and Their Masters in Laconia and Messenia: Histories, Ideologies, Structures*. Washington, D.C., 193–239.
Finley, M.I. (1968). 'Slavery', in: D.L. Sills (ed.), *International Encyclopedia of the Social Sciences*. New York, 307–313.
Finley, M.I. (1973). *The Ancient Economy*. Berkeley.
Finley, M.I. (1981). *Economy and Society in Ancient Greece*, edited by B.D. Shaw and R.P. Saller. New York.
Finley, M.I. (1998 [1980]). *Ancient Slavery and Modern Ideology*, edited by B.D. Shaw. Princeton, NJ.
Fischer, J. (2008). 'Sklaverei und Menschenhandel im mykenischen Griechenland', in: H. Heinen (ed.), *Menschenraub, Menschenhandel und Sklaverei in antiker und moderner Perspektive*. Stuttgart, 45–97.
Fischer, J. (2010a). Review of *Sklaverei und Freilassung in der griechisch-römischen Welt*, by Elisabeth Hermann-Otto. *Gymasium* 117, 616–617.
Fischer, J. (2010b). 'Unfreiheit und Sexualität im klassischen Athen', in: J. Fischer and M. Ulz (eds.), *Unfreiheit und Sexualität von der Antike bis zur Gegenwart*. Hildesheim, 58–82.
Fischer, J. (2014). 'Der Schwarzmeerraum und der antike Sklavenhandel: Bemerkungen zu einigen ausgewählten Quellen', in: M. Frass, H. Graßl, G. Nightingale (eds.), *Akten des 15. Österreichischen Althistorikertages*. Salzburg, 53–71.
Fisher, N.R.E. (1992). *Hybris: A Study in the Values of Honour and Shame in Ancient Greece*. Warminster.
Fisher, N.R.E. (1995). '*Hybris*, Status and Slavery', in: A. Powell (ed.), *The Greek World*. London, 44–84.
Fisher, N.R.E. (2001 [1993]). *Slavery in Classical Greece*. London.
Fisher, N.R.E. (2006). 'Citizens, Foreigners and Slaves in Greek Society', in: K.H. Kinzl (ed.), *A Companion to the Classical Greek World*. Malden, MA, 327–349.
Fisher, N.R.E. (2008). '"Independent" Slaves in Classical Athens and the Ideology of Slavery', in: C. Katsari and E. Dal Lago (eds.), *From Captivity to Freedom: Themes in Ancient and Modern Slavery*. Leicester, 123–146.
Foreman, P.G., *et al*. (n.d.). 'Writing about Slavery/Teaching About Slavery: This Might Help', Community-sourced document, https://docs.google.com/document/d/1A4TEdDgYslX-hlKezLodMIM71My3KTN0zxRv0IQTOQs/, Accessed May 18, 2022.
Forsdyke, S. (2012). *Slaves Tell Tales: And Other Episodes in the Politics of Popular Culture in Ancient Greece*. Princeton.
Forsdyke, S. (2018). 'Slave Agency and Citizenship in Classical Athens', in: G. Thür, U. Yiftach, R. Zelnick-Abramovitz (eds.), *Symposion 2017: Vorträge zur griechischen und hellenistischen Rechtsgeschichte*. Vienna, 345–366.
Forsdyke, S. (2021). *Slaves and Slavery in Ancient Greece*. Cambridge.

Forsdyke, S. (forthcoming). 'How to Find a New Master: Slave Agency in Ancient Greece', in: S.D. Gartland and D. Tandy (eds.), *Voiceless, Invisible, and Countless: The Experience of Subordinates in Greece, 800–300 BC*. Oxford.

Fountoulakis, A. (2004). 'Punishing the Lecherous Slave: Desire and Power in Herondas 5', in: A. Serghidou (ed.), *Fear of Slaves—Fear of Enslavement in the Ancient Mediterranean. Peur de l'esclave—Peur de l'esclavage en Méditerranée ancienne (Discours, représentations, pratiques)*. Besançon, 251–264.

Fynn-Paul, J. (2009). 'Empire, Monotheism and Slavery in the Greater Mediterranean Region from Antiquity to the Early Modern Era', in: *Past & Present* 205, 2–40.

Gagarin, M. and P. Perlman (2016). *The Laws of Ancient Crete c. 650–400 BCE*. Oxford.

Gabrielsen, V. (2003). 'Piracy and the Slave Trade', in: A. Erskine (ed.), *A Companion to the Hellenistic World*. Oxford, 389–404.

Gaca, K.L. (2010). 'The Andrapodizing of War Captives in Greek Historical Memory', in: *TAPA* 140, 117–161.

Gaca, K.L. (2011). 'Girls, Women, and the Significance of Sexual Violence in Ancient Warfare', in: E. Heineman (ed.), *Sexual Violence in Conflict Zones from the Ancient World to the Era of Human Rights*. Philadelphia, 73–88.

Gaca, K.L. (2015). 'Ancient Warfare and the Ravaging Martial Rape of Girls and Women: Evidence from Homeric Epic and Greek Drama', in: M. Masterson, N.S. Rabinowitz, J. Robson (eds.), *Sex in Antiquity*. New York, 278–297.

Gaca, K.L. (2021). 'Controlling Female Slave Sexuality and Men's War-Driven Sexual Desires', in: D. Kamen and C.W. Marshall (eds.), *Slavery and Sexuality in Classical Antiquity*. Madison, 40–65.

Gagarin, M. (1996). 'The Torture of Slaves in Athenian Law', in: *Classical Philology* 91, 1–18.

Gagarin, M. (2010). 'Serfs and Slaves at Gortyn', in: *Zeitschrift der Savigny-Stiftung für Rechtsgeschichte* 127, 14–31.

Garlan, Y. (1988 [1982]). *Slavery in Ancient Greece*, translated by J. Lloyd. Ithaca.

Garlan, Y. (1987). 'War, Piracy and Slavery in the Greek World', translated by M.-J. Roy, in: M.I. Finley (ed.), *Classical Slavery*. London, 9–27.

Garnsey, P. (1996). *Ideas of Slavery from Aristotle to Augustine*. Cambridge.

Garrido-Hory, M. (ed.) (2002). *Routes et marchés d'esclaves*. Besançon.

Genovese, E. (1979). *From Rebellion to Revolution: Afro-American Slave Revolts in the Making of the Modern World*. Baton Rouge.

Gervais, K. (2014). 'This is *my* Sparta! *300* (1998), *300* (2007), and *Three* (2013–14)', in: *The Amphora Issue, Melbourne Historical Journal* 42, 3–19.

Gibbs, L. (trans.) (2002). *Aesop's Fables*. Oxford.

Gillen, K. (2014). *Three*, illustrated by R. Kelly and J. Bellaire. Berkeley.

Glazebrook, A. (2006). 'The Bad Girls of Athens: The Image and Function of *Hetairai* in Judicial Oratory', in: C.A. Faraone and L.K. McClure (eds.), *Prostitutes and Courtesans in the Ancient World*. Madison, 125–138.

Glazebrook, A. (2011). '*Porneion*: Prostitution in Athenian Civic Space', in: A. Glazebrook and M.M. Henry (eds.), *Greek Prostitutes in the Ancient Mediterranean, 800 BCE–200 CE*. Madison, 34–59.

Glazebrook, A. (2014). 'The Erotics of Manumission: Prostitutes and the πρᾶσις ἐπ' ἐλευθερίᾳ', in: *EuGeStA* 4, 53–80.

Glazebrook, A. (ed.) (2015a). *Beyond Courtesans and Whores: Sex and Labor in the Graeco-Roman World*. A Special Issue of *Helios* 42.

Glazebrook, A. (2015b). 'A Hierarchy of Violence?: Sex Slaves, *Parthenoi*, and Rape in Menander's *Epitrepontes*', in: *Helios* 42, 81–101.
Glazebrook, A. (2017). 'Gender and Slavery', in: S. Hodkinson, M. Kleijwegt, K. Vlassopoulos (eds.), *The Oxford Handbook of Greek and Roman Slaveries*. Oxford. https://doi.org/10.1093/oxfordhb/9780199575251.013.13.
Glazebrook, A. (2021a). 'Female Sexual Agency and an Enslaved "Olynthian": Demosthenes 19.196–98', in: D. Kamen and C.W. Marshall (eds.), *Slavery and Sexuality in Classical Antiquity*. Madison, 141–158.
Glazebrook, A. (2021b). *Sexual Labor in the Athenian Courts*. Austin.
Glazebrook, A. and M.M. Henry (eds.) (2011a). *Greek Prostitutes in the Ancient Mediterranean, 800 BCE–200 CE*. Madison.
Glazebrook, A. and M.M. Henry (2011b). 'Introduction: Why Prostitutes? Why Greek? Why Now?', in: A. Glazebrook and M.M. Henry (eds.), *Greek Prostitutes in the Ancient Mediterranean, 800 BCE–200 CE*. Madison, 3–13.
Glazebrook, A. and B. Tsakirgis (eds.) (2016). *Houses of Ill Repute: The Archaeology of Brothels, Houses, and Taverns in the Greek World*. Philadelphia.
Golden, M. (2011). 'Slavery and the Greek Family', in: K. Bradley and P. Cartledge (eds.), *The Cambridge World History of Slavery*. Vol. 1: *The Ancient Mediterranean World*. Cambridge, 134–152.
Gonda, J. (2016). 'An Argument Against Slavery in the *Republic*', in: *Dialogue* 55, 219–244.
Gonzales, A. (ed.) (2008). *La fin du statut servile? (affranchissement, libération, abolition)*. 2 vols. Besançon.
Gonzales, A. (ed.) (2012). *Penser l'esclavage: Modèles antiques, pratiques modernes, problématiques contemporaines*. Besançon.
Gonzales, A. (ed.) (2019). *"Praxis" e ideologías de la violencia. Para una anatomía de las sociedades patriarcales esclavistas desde la Antigüedad*. Besançon.
Gottesman, A. (2014). *Politics and the Street in Democratic Athens*. Cambridge.
Greenwood, E. (2022). 'Reconstructing Classical Philology: Reading Aristotle *Politics* 1.4 After Toni Morrison', in: *American Journal of Philology* 143, 335–357.
Griffith, M. (2002). 'Slaves of Dionysos: Satyrs, Audience, and the Ends of the *Oresteia*', in: *Classical Antiquity* 21, 195–258.
Gschnitzer, F. (1976). *Studien zur griechischen Terminologie der Sklaverei*. Wiesbaden.
Hall, E., R. Alston, J. McConnell (eds.) (2012). *Ancient Slavery and Abolition: From Hobbes to Hollywood*. Oxford.
Hanes, C. (1996). 'Turnover Cost and the Distribution of Slave Labor in Anglo-America', in: *Journal of Economic History* 56, 307–329.
Hansen, M.H. (2010). 'Democratic Freedom and the Concept of Freedom in Plato and Aristotle', in: *Greek, Roman, and Byzantine Studies* 50, 1–27.
Harper, K. (2011). *Slavery in the Late Roman World, AD 275–425*. Cambridge.
Harper, K. (2017). 'Freedom, Slavery, and Female Sexual Honor in Antiquity', in: J. Bodel and W. Scheidel (eds.), *On Human Bondage: After Slavery and Social Death*. Chichester, 109–121.
Harris, E.M. (2002). 'Did Solon Abolish Debt Bondage?', in: *Classical Quarterly* 52, 415–430.
Harris, E.M. (2004). 'Notes on a Lead Letter from the Athenian Agora', in: *Zeitschrift für Papyrologie und Epigraphik* 102, 157–170.
Harris, E.M. (2012). 'Homer, Hesiod and the "Origins" of Greek Slavery', in: *Revue des études anciennes* 114, 345–366.

Harris, E.M. (2020). 'Slavery in Hesiod and Homer', in: C.O. Pache (ed.), *The Cambridge Guide to Homer*. Cambridge, 387–389.
Harris, E.M. (forthcoming). 'The Dedication of *Phialai* by Metics and Citizens: Or, Applying Ockham's Razor to the Interpretation of Some Attic Inscriptions'.
Harris, W.V. (ed.) (2013). *Moses Finley and Politics*. Leiden.
Harrison, T. (2019). 'Classical Greek Ethnography and the Slave Trade', in: *Classical Antiquity* 38, 36–57.
Hartman, S. (2007). *Lose Your Mother: A Journey along the Atlantic Slave Route*. New York.
Hartman, S. (2008). 'Venus in Two Acts', in: *Small Axe* 26, 1–14.
Harvey, D. (2004). 'The Clandestine Massacre of the Helots (Thucydides 4.80)', in: T.J. Figueira (ed.), *Spartan Society*. Swansea, 199–217.
Harvey, D. (2007). '"Help! I'm Dying Here": A Letter from a Slave', in: *Zeitschrift für Papyrologie und Epigraphik* 163, 49–50.
Heath, M. (2008). 'Aristotle on Natural Slavery', in: *Phronesis* 53, 243–270.
Hermann-Otto, E. (2009). *Sklaverei und Freilassung in der griechisch-römischen Welt*. Hildesheim.
Hezser, C. (2005). *Jewish Slavery in Antiquity*. Oxford.
Hezser, C. (2016). 'Greek and Roman Slaving in Comparative Ancient Perspective: The Level of Integration', in: S. Hodkinson, M. Kleijwegt, K. Vlassopoulos (eds.), *The Oxford Handbook of Greek and Roman Slaveries*. Oxford. https://doi.org/10.1093/oxfordhb/978019957525 1.013.16
Higgins, K.J. (1999). *"Licentious Liberty" in a Brazilian Gold-Mining Region: Slavery, Gender, and Social Control in Eighteenth-Century Sabará, Minas Gerais*. University Park, Penn.
Himmelmann, N. (1971). *Archäologisches zum Problem der griechischen Sklaverei*. Mainz.
Hinsch, M. (2021). *Ökonomik und Hauswirtschaft im klassischen Griechenland*. Stuttgart.
Hodkinson, S. (2003). 'Spartiates, Helots and the Direction of the Agrarian Economy: Towards an Understanding of Helotage in Comparative Perspective', in: N. Luraghi and S.E. Alcock (eds.), *Helots and Their Masters in Laconia and Messenia: Histories, Ideologies, Structures*. Washington, D.C., 248–285.
Hodkinson, S. (2008). 'Spartiates, Helots and the Direction of the Agrarian Economy: Toward an Understanding of Helotage in Comparative Perspective', in: E. Dal Lago and C. Katsari (eds.), *Slave Systems: Ancient and Modern*. Cambridge, 285–320.
Hodkinson, S. and D. Geary (eds.) (2012). *Slaves and Religions in Graeco-Roman Antiquity and Modern Brazil*. Newcastle upon Tyne.
Hodkinson, S. and E. Hall (2012). 'Appropriations of Spartan Helotage in British Anti-Slavery Debate of the 1790s', in: E. Hall, R. Alston, J. McConnell (eds.), *Ancient Slavery and Abolition: From Hobbes to Hollywood*. Oxford, 65–102.
Hodkinson, S., M. Kleijwegt, K. Vlassopoulos (eds.) (2016–). *The Oxford Handbook of Greek and Roman Slaveries*. Oxford. https://doi.org/10.1093/oxfordhb/9780199575251.001. 0001
Hopkins, K. (1978). *Conquerors and Slaves*. Cambridge.
Honoré, A.M. (1961). 'Ownership', in: A.G. Guest (ed.), *Oxford Essays in Jurisprudence*. Oxford, 107–147.
Huemoeller, K. (2018). Review of *Ancient Greek and Roman Slavery*, by Peter Hunt. *Bryn Mawr Classical Review* 2018.09.53.
Hunnings, L. (2011). 'The Paradigms of Execution: Managing Slave Death from Homer to Virginia', in: R. Alston, E. Hall, L. Proffitt (eds.), *Reading Ancient Slavery*. London, 51–71.

Hunt, P. (1998). *Slaves, Warfare and Ideology in the Greek Historians*. Cambridge.
Hunt, P. (2001). 'The Slaves and Generals of Arginusae', in: *American Journal of Philology* 122, 359–380.
Hunt, P. (2006). 'Arming Slaves and Helots in Classical Greece', in: C.L. Brown and P.D. Morgan (eds.), *Arming Slaves: From Classical Times to the Modern Age*. New Haven, 14–39.
Hunt, P. (2011). 'Slaves in Greek Literary Culture', in: K. Bradley and P. Cartledge (eds.), *The Cambridge World History of Slavery*. Vol. 1: *The Ancient Mediterranean World*. Cambridge, 22–47.
Hunt, P. (2012). Review of *The Slave in Greece and Rome*, by Jean Andreau and Raymond Descat. *Bryn Mawr Classical Review* 2012.10.26.
Hunt, P. (2015a). 'Slavery', in: C. Benjamin (ed.), *The Cambridge World History*. Vol. 4: *A World with States, Empires, and Networks, 1200 BCE to 900 CE*. Cambridge, 76–100.
Hunt, P. (2015b). 'Trojan Slaves in Classical Athens: Ethnic Identity among Slaves at Athens', in: C. Taylor and K. Vlassopoulos (eds.), *Communities and Networks in the Ancient Greek World*. Oxford, 128–154.
Hunt, P. (2016). 'Violence against Slaves in Classical Greece', in: W. Riess and G. Fagan (eds.), *The Topography of Violence in the Greco-Roman World*. Ann Arbor, 136–161.
Hunt, P. (2017a). 'Slaves as Active Subjects: Individual Strategies', in: S. Hodkinson, M. Kleijwegt, K. Vlassopoulos (eds.), *The Oxford Handbook of Greek and Roman Slaveries*. Oxford. https://doi.org/10.1093/oxfordhb/9780199575251.013.19
Hunt, P. (2017b). 'Slaves or Serfs?: Patterson on the Thetes and Helots of Ancient Greece', in: W. Scheidel and J. Bodel (eds.), *On Human Bondage: After Slavery and Social Death*. Malden, MA, 55–80.
Hunt, P. (2018a). 'Ancient Greece as a "Slave Society"', in: N. Lenski and C.M. Cameron (eds.), *What is a Slave Society? The Practice of Slavery in Global Perspective*. Cambridge, 61–85.
Hunt, P. (2018b). *Ancient Greek and Roman Slavery*. Hoboken, NJ.
Hunter, V. (1992). 'Constructing the Body of the Citizen: Corporal Punishment in Classical Athens', in: *Echos du monde classique: Classical Views* 36, 271–291.
Hunter, V. (1994). *Policing Athens: Social Control in the Attic Lawsuits*. Princeton.
Iriarte Goñi, A. (2007). *Resistencia, sumisión e interiorización de la dependencia*. Salamanca.
Ismard, P. (2014a). 'Classes, ordres, statuts: la reception française de la sociologie finleyenne et le cas Pierre Vidal-Naquet', in: *Anabases* 19, 39–53.
Ismard, P. (2014b). 'The Single Body of the City: Public Slaves and the Question of the Greek State', translated by J. Stephens, in: *Annales HSS* 69, 505–532.
Ismard, P. (2017a [2015]). *Democracy's Slaves: A Political History of Ancient Greece*, translated by J.M. Todd. Cambridge, MA.
Ismard, P. (2017b). 'Écrire l'histoire de l'esclavage. Entre approche globale et perspective comparatiste', in: *Annales HSS* 72, 9–43.
Ismard, P. (2019). *La cité et ses esclaves*. Paris.
Jameson, M.H. (1977–78). 'Agriculture and Slavery in Classical Athens', in: *Classical Journal* 73, 122–145.
Jameson, M.H. (2002). 'On Paul Cartledge, "The Political Economy of Greek Slavery"', in: P. Cartledge (ed.), *Money, Labour and Land: Approaches to the Economies of Ancient Greece*. London, 167–174.
Jew, D., R. Osborne, and M. Scott (eds.) (2016). *M. I. Finley: An Ancient Historian and his Impact*. Cambridge.
Johnson, W. (2003). 'On Agency', in: *Journal of Social History* 37, 113–124.

Johnstone, S. (1998). 'Cracking the Code of Silence: Athenian Legal Oratory and the Histories of Slaves and Women', in: S.R. Joshel and S. Murnaghan (eds.), *Women and Slaves in Greco-Roman Culture: Differential Equations*. London, 221–236.
Jones, A.H.M. (1952). 'The Economic Basis of the Athenian Democracy', in: *Past & Present* 1, 13–31.
Jones, C. (2008). 'Hyperides and the Sale of Slave Families', in: *Zeitschrift für Papyrologie und Epigraphik* 164, 19–20.
Jordan, D.R. (2000). 'A Personal Letter Found in the Athenian Agora', in: *Hesperia* 69, 91–103.
Joshel, S.R. and S. Murnaghan (eds.) (1998a). *Women and Slaves in Greco-Roman Culture: Differential Equations*. London.
Joshel, S.R. and S. Murnaghan (1998b). 'Introduction: Differential Equations', in: S.R. Joshel and S. Murnaghan (eds.), *Women and Slaves in Greco-Roman Culture: Differential Equations*. London, 1–21.
Joshel, S.R. (2013). 'Geographies of Slave Containment and Movement', in: M. George (ed.), *Roman Slavery and Roman Material Culture*. Toronto, 99–128.
Joshel, S.R. and L.H. Petersen (2014). *The Material Life of Roman Slaves*. Cambridge.
Kamen, D. (2005). Review of *Not Wholly Free: The Concept of Manumission and the Status of Manumitted Slaves in the Ancient Greek World*, by Rachel Zelnick-Abramovitz. *Bryn Mawr Classical Review* 2005.11.21.
Kamen, D. (2009). 'Servile Invective in Classical Athens', in: *Scripta Classica Israelica* 28, 43–56.
Kamen, D. (2010). 'A Corpus of Inscriptions: Representing Slave Marks in Antiquity', in: *Memoirs of the American Academy in Rome* 60, 95–110.
Kamen, D. (2011). 'Reconsidering the Status of *Khōris Oikountes*', in: *Dike* 14, 43–53.
Kamen, D. (2012). 'Manumission, Social Rebirth, and Healing Gods in Ancient Greece', in: S. Hodkinson and D. Geary (eds.), *Slaves and Religions in Graeco-Roman Antiquity and Modern Brazil*. Newcastle upon Tyne, 174–194.
Kamen, D. (2013a). *Status in Classical Athens*. Princeton.
Kamen, D. (2013b). 'The Manumission of Socrates: A Rereading of Plato's *Phaedo*', in: *Classical Antiquity* 32, 78–100.
Kamen, D. (2014a). 'Sale for the Purpose of Freedom: Slave-Prostitutes and Manumission in Ancient Greece', in: *Classical Journal* 109, 281–307.
Kamen, D. (2014b). 'Slave-Prostitutes and ἐργασία in the Delphic Manumission Inscriptions', in: *Zeitschrift für Papyrologie und Epigraphik* 188, 149–153.
Kamen, D. (2016). 'Manumission and Slave-Allowances in Classical Athens', in: *Historia* 65, 413–426.
Kamen, D. (2020 [2013]). 'Slavery, Greece', in: R. Bagnall et al. (eds.), *Encyclopedia of Ancient History*. Malden, MA, 6280–6282.
Kamen, D. (2020). *Insults in Classical Athens*. Madison.
Kamen, D. (2021). Review of *Greek Slave Systems in their Eastern Mediterranean Context*, by David M. Lewis. *Ancient West & East* 20, 402–404.
Kamen, D. and S. Levin-Richardson (2022a). 'Epigraphy and Critical Fabulation: Imagining Narratives of Greco-Roman Sexual Slavery', in: E.H. Cousins (ed.), *Dynamic Epigraphy: New Approaches to Inscriptions*. Barnsley, 201–221.
Kamen, D. and S. Levin-Richardson (2022b). 'Approaching Emotions and Agency in Greek and Roman Slavery', in: A. Pałuchowski (ed.), *Les lectures contemporaines de l'esclavage: problématiques, méthodologies et analyses depuis les années 1990*. Besançon, 25–45.

Kamen, D. (forthcoming). 'Varying Statuses, Varying Rights: A Case Study of the *graphē hubreōs*', in: S.D. Gartland and D. Tandy (eds.), *Voiceless, Invisible, and Countless: The Experience of Subordinates in Greece, 800–300 BC*. Oxford.

Kamen, D. and C.W. Marshall (eds.) (2021). *Slavery and Sexuality in Classical Antiquity*. Madison.

Kamtekar, R. (2016). 'Studying Ancient Political Thought through Ancient Philosophers: The Case of Aristotle and Natural Slavery', in: *Polis* 33, 150–171.

Kapparis, K. (2018). *Prostitution in the Ancient Greek World*. Berlin.

Katsari, C., E. Dal Lago (eds.) (2008). *From Captivity to Freedom: Themes in Ancient and Modern Slavery*. Leicester.

Kazakévich, E.G. (2008). 'Were the *Khōris Oikountes* Slaves?', edited by D. Kamen, in: *Greek, Roman, and Byzantine Studies* 48, 343–380.

Kennedy, R.F. (2015). 'Elite Citizen Women and the Origins of the *Hetaira* in Classical Athens', in: *Helios* 42, 61–79.

Klees, H. (1998). *Sklavenleben im Klassischen Griechenland*. Stuttgart.

Klees, H. (2000). 'Die rechtliche und gesellschaftliche Stellung der Freigelassenen im klassischen Griechenland', in: *Laverna* 11, 1–43.

Konstan, D. (2013). 'Menander's Slaves: The Banality of Violence', in: B. Akrigg and R. Tordoff (eds.), *Slaves and Slavery in Ancient Greek Comic Drama*. Cambridge and New York, 144–158.

Kurke, L. (1997). 'Inventing the *Hetaira*: Sex, Politics, and Discursive Conflict in Archaic Greece', *Classical Antiquity* 16, 106–150.

Kurke, L. (1999). *Coins, Bodies, Games, and Gold: The Politics of Meaning in Archaic Greece*. Princeton.

Kurke, L. (2010). *Aesopic Conversations: Popular Tradition, Cultural Dialogue, and the Invention of Greek Prose*. Princeton.

Kyrtatas, D. J. (2011). 'Slavery and Economy in the Greek World', in: K. Bradley and P. Cartledge (eds.), *The Cambridge World History of Slavery*. Vol. 1: *The Ancient Mediterranean World*. Cambridge, 91–111.

Labarre, G. (1998). 'Les métiers du textile en Grèce ancienne', in: *Topoi* 8, 791–814.

Lakoff, G. and M. Johnson (1980). *Metaphors We Live By*. Chicago.

Langerwerf, L. (2012). 'Universal Slave Revolts: C.L.R. James's Use of Classical Literature in *The Black Jacobins*', in: E. Hall, R. Alston, J. McConnell (eds.), *Ancient Slavery and Abolition: From Hobbes to Hollywood*. Oxford, 353–384.

Lanni, A. (2006). *Law and Justice in the Courts of Classical Athens*. Cambridge.

Lape, S. (2010). *Race and Citizen Identity in the Classical Athenian Democracy*. Cambridge.

Lape, S. (2013). 'Slavery, Drama and the Alchemy of Identity in Aristophanes', in: B. Akrigg and R. Tordoff (eds.), *Slaves and Slavery in Ancient Greek Comic Drama*. Cambridge and New York, 76–90.

Lauffer, S. (1979 [1956]). *Die Bergwerkssklaven von Laureion*. Weisbaden.

Lee, M. (2015). 'Other "Ways of Seeing": Female Viewers of the Knidian Aphrodite', in: *Helios* 42, 103–122.

Lenski, N. (2018a). 'Ancient Slaveries and Modern Ideology', in: N. Lenski and C.M. Cameron (eds.), *What is a Slave Society? The Practice of Slavery in Global Perspective*. Cambridge, 106–147.

Lenski, N. (2018b). 'Framing the Question: What is a Slave Society?', in: N. Lenski and C.M. Cameron (eds.), *What is a Slave Society? The Practice of Slavery in Global Perspective*. Cambridge, 15–57.

Lenski, N. and C.M. Cameron (2018a). *What is a Slave Society? The Practice of Slavery in Global Perspective*. Cambridge.

Lenski, N. and C.M. Cameron (2018b). 'Introduction: Slavery and Society in Global Perspective', in: N. Lenski and C.M. Cameron (eds.), *What is a Slave Society? The Practice of Slavery in Global Perspective*. Cambridge, 1–14.

Levin-Richardson, S. (forthcoming). 'Emotional Labor in Antiquity: The Case of Greco-Roman Prostitution', in: K. Bowes and M. Flohr (eds.), *Penn-Leiden XI: Valuing Labor in Antiquity*. Leiden.

Lewis, D.M. (2011). 'Near Eastern Slaves in Classical Attica and the Slave Trade with Persian Territories', in: *Classical Quarterly* 61, 91–113.

Lewis, D.M. (2013). 'Slave Marriages in the Laws of Gortyn: A Matter of Rights?', in: *Historia* 62, 390–416.

Lewis, D.M. (2015). 'Slavery and Manumission', in: E.M. Harris and M. Canevaro (eds.), *The Oxford Handbook of Ancient Greek Law*. Oxford. https://doi.org/10.1093/oxfordhb/9780199599257.013.21

Lewis, D.M. (2016). 'The Market for Slaves in the Fifth and Fourth Century Aegean: Achaemenid Anatolia as a Case Study', in: E.M. Harris, D.M. Lewis, M. Woolmer (eds.), *The Ancient Greek Economy: Markets, Households and City-States*. New York, 316–336.

Lewis, D.M. (2017). 'Orlando Patterson, Property, and Ancient Slavery: The Definitional Problem Revisited', in: W. Scheidel and J. Bodel (eds.), *On Human Bondage: After Slavery and Social Death*. Malden, MA, 31–54.

Lewis, D.M. (2018a). *Greek Slave Systems in their Eastern Mediterranean Context, c. 800–146 BC*. Oxford.

Lewis, D.M. (2018b). 'Notes on Slave Names, Ethnicity, and Identity in Classical and Hellenistic Greece', in: *Studia Źródłoznawcze. U Schyłku Starożytności* 16, 169–199.

Lewis, D.M. (2018c). 'Classical and Near Eastern Slavery in the First Millennium BCE', in: S. Hodkinson, M. Kleijwegt, K. Vlassopoulos (eds.), *The Oxford Handbook of Greek and Roman Slaveries*. Oxford. https://doi.org/10.1093/oxfordhb/9780199575251.013.42

Lewis, D.M. (2019). 'Piracy and Slave Trading in Action in Classical and Hellenistic Greece', in: *Mare Nostrum* 10, 79–108.

Lewis, D.M. (2020). 'Legal Knowledge in Gortyn: Debt Bondage and the Liability of Slaves in Gortynian Law', in: C. Ando and W.P. Sullivan (eds.), *The Discovery of the Fact*. Ann Arbor, 72–90.

Lewis, D.M. (2021). 'Helots', in: *Oxford Classical Dictionary*. Oxford. https://doi.org/10.1093/acrefore/9780199381135.013.3000

Lewis, D.M. (2022a). 'A Cargo of Slaves? Demosthenes 34.10', in: *The Mariner's Mirror* 108, 135–148.

Lewis, D.M. (2022b). 'Global Slavery for Greek Historians: Prospects and Pitfalls', in: A. Pałuchowski (ed.), *Les lectures contemporaines de l'esclavage: problématiques, méthodologies et analyses depuis les années 1990*. Besançon, 47–62.

Lewis, D.M. (2022c). 'The Homeric Roots of Helotage', in: J.C. Bernhardt and M. Canevaro (eds.), *From Homer to Solon: Continuity and Change in Archaic Greece*. Leiden, 64–92.

Lewis, D.M. (2022d). 'Defining Slavery in Global Perspective', in: D.S. Doddington and E. dal Lago (eds.), *Writing the History of Slavery*. London, 19–39.

Lewis, D.M. (forthcoming). 'Did Serfdom Exist in Classical and Hellenistic Crete?', in: P. Scheibelreiter (ed.), *Symposion 2022: Akten der Gesellschaft für griechische und Hellenistische Rechtsgeschichte*. Vienna.
Lewis, D.M., P. Morton, T. Parkin (2022). '(Re)producing Slaves: Demand, Supply, and Demography', in: S. Hodkinson, M. Kleijwegt, K. Vlassopoulos (eds.), *The Oxford Handbook of Greek and Roman Slaveries*. Oxford. https://doi.org/10.1093/oxfordhb/9780199575251.013.29
Lewis, D.M. and S. Zanovello (2017). 'Freedmen/Freedwomen, Greek', in: *Oxford Classical Dictionary*. https://doi.org/10.1093/acrefore/9780199381135.013.8019
Lewis, J. (2004). 'Slavery and Lawlessness in Solonian Athens', in: *Dike* 7, 19–40.
Lewis, S. (1998/9). 'Slaves as Viewers and Users of Athenian Pottery', in: *Hephaistos* 16/17, 71–89.
Liddel, P. (2007). *Civic Obligation and Individual Liberty in Ancient Athens*. Oxford.
Link, S. (1994). *Das griechische Kreta: Untersuchungen zu seiner staatlichen und gesellschaftlichen Entwicklung vom 6. bis zum 4. Jahrhundert v. Chr*. Stuttgart.
Link, S. (2001). '"Dolos" und "Woikeus" im Recht von Gortyn', in: *Dike* 4, 87–112.
Link, S. (2006). 'Zur Entstehungsgeschichte der spartanischen Krypteia', in: *Klio* 88, 34–43.
Lissarague, F. (2000). 'Aesop, Between Man and Beast: Ancient Portraits and Illustrations', in: B. Cohen (ed.), *Not the Classical Ideal: Athens and the Construction of the Other in Greek Art*. Leiden, 132–149.
Long, A.A. (2012). 'Slavery as Philosophical Metaphor in Plato and Xenophon', in: R. Patterson et al. (eds.), *Presocratics and Plato*. Las Vegas, 351–366.
Lupher, D. and E. Vandiver (2012). 'Yankee She-Men and Octoroon Electra: Basil Lanneau Gildersleeve on Slavery, Race, and Abolition', in: E. Hall, R. Alston, J. McConnell (eds.), *Ancient Slavery and Abolition: From Hobbes to Hollywood*. Oxford, 319–351.
Luraghi, N. (2002). 'Helotic Slavery Reconsidered', in: A. Powell and S. Hodkinson (eds.), *Sparta: Beyond the Mirage*. Swansea, 227–248.
Luraghi, N. (2003). 'The Imaginary Conquest of the Helots,' in: N. Luraghi and S.E. Alcock (eds.), *Helots and Their Masters in Laconia and Messenia: Histories, Ideologies, Structures*. Washington, D.C., 109–141.
Luraghi, N. (2009). 'The Helots: Comparative Approaches, Ancient and Modern', in: S. Hodkinson (ed.), *Sparta: Comparative Approaches*. Swansea, 261–304.
Luraghi, N. (2022). Review of *Historicising Ancient Slavery*, by Kostas Vlassopoulos. *Bryn Mawr Classical Review* 2022.10.04.
Luraghi, N. and S.E. Alcock (eds.) (2003). *Helots and their Masters in Laconia and Messenia: Histories, Ideologies, Structures*. Washington, D.C.
MacDowell, D. (ed. and trans.) (1990). *Demosthenes against Meidias*. Oxford.
Mactoux, M.-M. (2008). 'Regards sur la proclamation de l'affranchissement au théâtre à Athènes,' in: A. Gonzales (ed.), *La fin du statut servile? (Affranchissement, libération, abolition)*. Vol. 2. Besançon, 437–451.
Maffi, A. (2008). 'Economia e diritto nell'Atene del IV secolo', in: E.M. Harris and G. Thür (eds.), *Symposion 2007: Vorträge zur Griechischen und Hellenistischen Rechtsgeschichte*, Vienna, 203–222.
Maffi, A. (2014). 'Identificare gli schiavi nei documenti greci', in: M. DePauw and S. Coussement (eds.), *Identifiers and Identification Methods in the Ancient World*. Leuven, 197–206.

Malamud, M. (2012). 'The *Auctoritas* of Antiquity: Debating Slavery through Classical Exempla in the Antebellum USA', in: E. Hall, R. Alston, J. McConnell (eds.), *Ancient Slavery and Abolition: From Hobbes to Hollywood*. Oxford, 279–317.

Malamud, M. (2016). *African Americans and the Classics: Antiquity, Abolition and Activism*. London.

Marincola, J. (2007). 'The Persian Wars in Fourth-Century Oratory and Historiography', in: E. Bridges, E. Hall, P.J. Rhodes (eds.), *Cultural Responses to the Persian Wars: Antiquity to the Third Millennium*. Oxford, 105–126.

Marshall, C.W. (2013). 'Sex Slaves in New Comedy', in: B. Akrigg and R. Tordoff (eds.), *Slaves and Slavery in Ancient Greek Comic Drama*. Cambridge and New York, 173–196.

Marshall, C.W. (2017). 'Breastfeeding in Greek Literature and Thought', in: *Illinois Classical Studies* 42, 185–201.

Marshall, C.W. (2021). 'Love-Sick in a Different Way: Sex and Desire in Lysias 4', in: D. Kamen and C.W. Marshall (eds.), *Slavery and Sexuality in Classical Antiquity*. Madison, 124–140.

Martin, D.B. (1990). *Slavery as Salvation: The Metaphor of Slavery in Pauline Christianity*. New Haven.

Martin, R.P. (2006). 'Solon in No Man's Land', in: J. Blok and A.P.M.H. Lardinois (eds.), *Solon of Athens: New Historical and Philological Approaches*. Leiden, 157–172.

Martínez Lacy, R. (ed.) (2018). *Hermenéutica de la esclavitud*. Besançon.

Matuszewski, R. (2021). 'Same-Sex Relations between Free and Slave in Democratic Athens', in: D. Kamen and C.W. Marshall (eds.), *Slavery and Sexuality in Classical Antiquity*. Madison, 104–123.

McArthur, M. (2019). 'Kittos and the *Phialai Exeleutherikai*', *Annual of the British School at Athens* 114, 263–291.

McCarthy, K. (2000). *Slaves, Masters, and the Art of Authority in Plautine Comedy*. Princeton.

McClure, L. (2003). *Courtesans at Table: Gender and Greek Literary Culture in Athenaeus*. New York.

McConnell, J. (2012). 'Eumaeus and Eurycleia in the Deep South: Odyssean Slavery in *Sommersby*', in: E. Hall, R. Alston, J. McConnell (eds.), *Ancient Slavery and Abolition: From Hobbes to Hollywood*. Oxford, 385–407.

McCoskey, D. (1998). '"I, Whom She Detested So Bitterly": Slavery and the Violent Division of Women in Aeschylus' *Oresteia*', in: S.R. Joshel and S. Murnaghan (eds.), *Women and Slaves in Greco-Roman Culture: Differential Equations*. London, 35–55.

McKeown, N. (2002). 'Seeing Things: Examining the Body of the Slave in Greek Medicine', in: T. Wiedemann and J. Gardner (eds.), *Representing the Body of the Slave*. London, 29–40.

McKeown, N. (2007). *The Invention of Ancient Slavery?* London.

McKeown, N. (2011). 'Resistance Among Chattel Slaves in the Classical Greek World', in: K. Bradley and P. Cartledge (eds.), *The Cambridge World History of Slavery*. Vol. 1: *The Ancient Mediterranean World*. Cambridge, 153–175.

McKeown, N. (2019). 'Slaves as Active Subjects: Collective Strategies', in: S. Hodkinson, M. Kleijwegt, K. Vlassopoulos (eds.), *The Oxford Handbook of Greek and Roman Slaveries*. Oxford. https://doi.org/10.1093/oxfordhb/9780199575251.013.25

Meyer, E.A. (2002). Review of *Inscriptions du sanctuaire de la Mère des Dieux autochtone de Leukopétra (Macédoine)*, edited by P.M. Petsas et al., in: *American Journal of Philology* 123, 136–140.

Meyer, E.A. (2010). *Metics and the Athenian* Phialai-*Inscriptions: A Study in Athenian Epigraphy and Law*. Stuttgart.

Miller, J.C. (2008). 'Slaving as Historical Process: Examples from the Ancient Mediterranean and the Modern Atlantic', in: E. Dal Lago and C. Katsari (eds.), *Slave Systems: Ancient and Modern*. Cambridge, 70–102.

Millett, P. (2007). 'Aristotle and Slavery in Athens', in: *Greece & Rome* 54, 178–209.

Miner, J. (2003). 'Courtesan, Concubine, Whore: Apollodorus' Deliberate Use of Terms for Prostitutes', in: *American Journal of Philology* 124, 19–37.

Mirhady, D. (1996). 'Torture and Rhetoric in Athens', in: *Journal of Hellenic Studies* 116, 119–131.

Monoson, S.S. (2011). 'Navigating Race, Class, Polis and Empire: The Place of Empirical Analysis in Aristotle's Account of Natural Slavery', in: R. Alston, E. Hall, L. Proffitt (eds.), *Reading Ancient Slavery*. London, 133–151.

Monoson, S.S. (2012). 'Recollecting Aristotle: Pro-Slavery Thought in Antebellum America and the Argument of *Politics* Book 1', in: E. Hall, R. Alston, J. McConnell (eds.), *Ancient Slavery and Abolition: From Hobbes to Hollywood*. Oxford, 247–277.

Morris, I. (1986). 'The Use and Abuse of Homer', in: *Classical Antiquity* 5, 81–138.

Morris, I. (2011). 'Archaeology and Greek Slavery', in: K. Bradley and P. Cartledge (eds.), *The Cambridge World History of Slavery*. Vol. 1: *The Ancient Mediterranean World*. Cambridge, 176–193.

Morris, S.P. (2018). 'Material Evidence: Looking for Slaves? The Archaeological Record: Greece', in: S. Hodkinson, M. Kleijwegt, K. Vlassopoulos (eds.), *The Oxford Handbook of Greek and Roman Slaveries*. Oxford. https://doi.org/10.1093/oxfordhb/9780199575251.013.8

Morris, S.P. and J. Papadopoulos. (2005). 'Greek Towers and Slaves: An Archaeology of Exploitation', in: *American Journal of Archaeology* 109, 155–225.

Morrow, G.R. (1939). 'Plato and Greek Slavery', in: *Mind* n.s. 48, 186–201.

Mulliez, D. (2016). 'La loi, la norme et l'usage dans les relations entre maîtres et esclaves à travers la documentation delphique (200 av. J.-C.–100 ap. J.-C.)', in: M. Dondin-Payre and N. Tran (eds.), *Esclaves et maîtres dans le monde romain. Expressions épigraphiques de leurs relations*. Rome. https://books.openedition.org/efr/3192, Accessed October 24, 2022.

Mulliez, D. (2019). *Corpus des inscriptions de Delphes V: Les actes d'affranchissement*. Vol. 1: *Prêtrises I à IX* (Nos. 1–722). Athens.

Mulliez, D. (2021a). 'Esclaves et affranchis à Delphes: une main-d'œuvre indifférenciée, mais indispensable', in: S. Maillot and J. Zurbach (eds.), *Statuts personnels et main-d'œuvre en Méditerranée hellénistique*. Clermont-Ferrand, 141–164.

Mulliez, D. (2021b). 'Le recours à l'arbitrage privé dans les actes d'affranchissement delphiques', in: K. Kalogeropoulos, D. Vassilikou, M. Tiverios (eds.), *Sidelights on Greek Antiquity: Archaeological and Epigraphical Essays in Honour of Vasileios Petrakos*. Berlin, 117–136.

Mulliez, D. (forthcoming a). 'Familles d'esclaves dans la documentation delphique', in: R. Bouchon, L. Lamoine, S. Maillot (eds.), *Familles d'esclaves, esclaves dans la famille, dans le monde grec et romain (IVᵉ s. a.C.–IIᵉ s. p.C.)*. Clermont-Ferrand.

Mulliez, D. (forthcoming b). *Corpus des inscriptions de Delphes V: Les actes d'affranchissement*. Vol. 2 : *Prêtrises X à XXXV* (Nos. 723–1341). Athens.

Nafissi, M. (2015). '*Krypteiai* spartane', in: A. Beltran, I. Sastre, M. Valdé (eds.), *Los espacios de la esclavitud y la dependencia desde la antigüedad*. Besançon, 201–229.

Nakassis, D. (2013). *Individuals and Society in Mycenaean Pylos*. Leiden.

N'Doye, M. (2008). 'L'affranchissement dans les poèmes homériques: de la parenté illusoire à l'adoption', in: A. Gonzales (ed.), *La fin du statut servile? (affranchissement, libération, abolition)*. Vol. 1. Besançon, 17–27.

Nikolsky, B. (2011). 'Slavery and Freedom in Euripides' *Cyclops*', in: R. Alston, E. Hall, L. Proffitt (eds.), *Reading Ancient Slavery*. London, 121–132.

North, J.A. (2020). 'Slaves and Religion', in: S. Hodkinson, M. Kleijwegt, K. Vlassopoulos (eds.), *The Oxford Handbook of Greek and Roman Slaveries*. Oxford. https://doi.org/10.1093/oxfordhb/9780199575251.013.26

Oakley, J. (2000). 'Some "Other" Members of the Athenian Household: Maids and their Mistresses in Fifth-Century Athenian Art', in: B. Cohen (ed.), *Not the Classical Ideal: Athens and the Construction of the Other in Greek Art*. Leiden, 227–247.

Olivier, J.P. (1987). 'Des extraits de contrats de vente d'esclaves dans les tablettes de Knossos', in: *Minos* 20–22, 479–498.

Olson, S.D. (2013). 'Slaves and Politics in Early Aristophanic Comedy', in: B. Akrigg and R. Tordoff (eds.), *Slaves and Slavery in Ancient Greek Comic Drama*. Cambridge and New York, 63–75.

Ormand, K. (2018 [2008]). *Controlling Desires: Sexuality in Ancient Greece and Rome*. Austin.

Osborne, R. (1995). 'The Economics and Politics of Slavery at Athens', in: A. Powell (ed.), *The Greek World*. London, 27–43.

Osborne, R. (2000). 'Religion, Imperial Politics, and the Offering of Freedom to Slaves', in: V. Hunter and J. Edmondson (eds.), *Law and Social Status in Classical Athens*. Oxford, 75–92.

Osborne, R. (2017). 'Visual Evidence—of What?', in: S. Hodkinson, M. Kleijwegt, K. Vlassopoulos (eds.), *The Oxford Handbook of Greek and Roman Slaveries*. Oxford. https://doi.org/10.1093/oxfordhb/9780199575251.013.27.

Owens, E.A. (2017). 'Promises: Sexual Labor in the Space Between Slavery and Freedom', in: *Louisiana History* 58, 179–216.

Paiaro, D. and M.J. Requena (2015). '"Muchas veces pegarías a un ateniense creyendo que era un esclavo"… (Ps.-X., 1, 10): Espacios democráticos y relaciones de dependencia en la Atenas Clásica', in: A. Beltrán, I. Sastra Prats, M. Valdés Guía (eds.), *Los espacios de la esclavitud y la dependencia desde la Antigüedad: homenaje a Domingo Plácido*. Besçancon, 153–170.

Pałuchowski, A. (2017). 'La condition servile en Crète aux époques classique et hellénistique à la lumière de l'apparente absence de châtiments corporels à l'égard des individus de statut non-libre', in: *Klio* 99, 51–88.

Pałuchowski, A. (2018). 'L'évolution contextualisée du modèle de l'esclavage crétois de l'époque archaïque à l'époque hellénistique', in: *Proceedings of the 12th International Congress of Cretan Studies*. Heraklion, 1–16. https://12iccs.proceedings.gr/en/proceedings/category/38/32/362, Accessed October 24, 2022.

Pałuchowski, A. (ed.) (2022). *Les lectures contemporaines de l'esclavage: problématiques, méthodologies et analyses depuis les années 1990*. Besançon.

Paradiso, A. (1999). 'Schiavitù femminile e violenza varnale: *Strupro* e coscienza dello *stupro* sullle schiave in Grecia', in: F. Merola and A. Storchi-Marino (eds.), *Femme-esclaves: Modèles d'interprétation anthropologique, économique, juridique*. Naples, 145–162.

Paradiso, A. (2004). 'The Logic of Terror: Thucydides, Spartan Duplicity and an Improbable Massacre', in: T.J. Figueira (ed.), *Spartan Society*. Swansea, 179–198.

Paradiso, A. (2008). 'Politiques de l'affranchissement chez Thucydide', in: A. Gonzales (ed.), *La fin du statut servile? (affranchissement, libération, abolition)*. Vol. 1. Besançon, 65–76.
Parmenter, C.S. (2020). 'Journeys into Slavery along the Black Sea Coast, c. 550–450 BCE', in: *Classical Antiquity* 39, 57–94.
Patterson, C. (1985). '"Not Worth the Rearing": The Causes of Infant Exposure in Ancient Greece', in: *TAPA* 115, 103–123.
Patterson, O. (1982). *Slavery and Social Death: A Comparative Study*. Cambridge, MA.
Patterson, O. (1991). *Freedom*. Vol. 1: *Freedom in the Making of Western Culture*. New York.
Patterson, O. (2003). 'Helots and The Masters in Laconia and Messenia: Histories, Ideologies, Structures', in: N. Luraghi and S.E. Alcock (eds.), *Helots and Their Masters in Laconia and Messenia: Histories, Ideologies, Structures*. Washington, D.C., 289–307.
Patterson, O. (2012). 'Trafficking, Gender and Slavery: Past and Present', in: J. Allain (ed.), *The Legal Understanding of Slavery: From the Historical to the Contemporary*. Oxford, 322–359.
Petsas, P.M. et al. (eds.) (2000). *Inscriptions du sanctuaire de la Mère des Dieux autochtone de Leukopétra (Macédoine)*. Athens.
Porter, J.D. (2019). 'Slavery and Athens' Economic Efflorescence: Mill Slavery as a Case Study', in: *Mare Nostrum* 10, 25–50.
Porter, J.D. (2021a). 'The Archaic Roots of Paternalism: Continuity in Attitudes towards Slaves and Slavery in the *Odyssey*, Xenophon's *Oeconomicus*, and Beyond', *Greece & Rome* 68, 255–277.
Porter, J.D. (2021b). 'The Sexual Agency of Slaves in Classical Athens', in: D. Kamen and C.W. Marshall (eds.), *Slavery and Sexuality in Classical Antiquity*. Madison, 104–123.
Porter, J.D. (2021/22). 'The *Apophora* and the 'Leasing' of Property to Slaves and Manumitted Slaves in Classical Athens', in: *Historia* 70, 185–205.
Porter, J.D. (forthcoming a). *Slaving Strategies in Classical Athens*. Edinburgh.
Porter, J.D. (forthcoming b). 'Slave Hierarchies and Honour as a Privilege in Classical Athens and Comparative History', in: D. Cairns, M. Canavero, D.M. Lewis (eds.), *Slavery and Honour in the Ancient Greek World*. Edinburgh.
Pritchard, D.M. (2020). 'The Social Structure of Democratic Athens', in: C.D. de Souza and M.A. de Oliveira Silva (eds.), *Morte e vida na Grécia Antiga: olhares interdisciplinares*. Teresina, 102–132.
Pritchett, W.K. (1953). 'The Attic Stelai, Part I', in: *Hesperia* 22, 225–299.
Pritchett, W.K. (1956). 'The Attic Stelai: Part II', in: *Hesperia* 25, 178–328.
Pritchett, W.K. (1961). 'Five New Fragments of the Attic Stelai', in: *Hesperia* 30, 23–29.
Proffitt, L. (2011). 'Family, Slavery and Subversion in Menander's *Epitrepontes*', in: R. Alston, E. Hall, L. Proffitt (eds.), *Reading Ancient Slavery*. London, 152–174.
Rabbås, Ø. (2015). 'Virtue, respect, and morality in Aristotle', in: *The Journal of Value Inquiry* 49, 619–643.
Rädle, H. (1969). *Untersuchungen zum griechischen Freilassungswesen*. Diss. Munich.
Rabinowitz, N.S. (1998). 'Women and Class in Euripidean Tragedy', in: S.R. Joshel and S. Murnaghan (eds.), *Women and Slaves in Greco-Roman Culture: Differential Equations*. London and New York, 56–68.
Rankine, P. (2011). 'Odysseus as Slave: The Ritual of Domination and Social Death in Homeric Society', in: R. Alston, E. Hall, L. Proffitt (eds.), *Reading Ancient Slavery*. London, 34–50.
Reduzzi Merola, F. (ed.) (2014). *Dipendenza ed emarginazione nel mondo antico e moderno*. Rome.

Reduzzi Merola, F., A. Caravaglios, M. Vittoria Bramante (eds.) (2020). *Le realtà della schiavitù: identità e biografie da Eumeo a Frederick Douglass*. Naples.

Richlin, A. (2017). *Slave Theater in the Roman Republic: Plautus and Popular Comedy*. Cambridge.

Ricl, M. (2001). 'Donations of Slaves and Freeborn Children to Deities in Roman Macedonia and Phrygia: A Reconsideration', in: *Tyche* 16, 127–160.

Rihll, T. (1996). 'The Origin and Establishment of Ancient Greek Slavery', in: M.L. Bush (ed.), *Serfdom and Slavery: Studies in Legal Bondage*. London, 89–111.

Rihll, T. (2011). 'Classical Athens', in: K. Bradley and P. Cartledge (eds.), *The Cambridge World History of Slavery*. Vol. 1: *The Ancient Mediterranean World*. Cambridge, 48–73.

Rihll, T. (2022). 'Slave Labor and Production', in: S. Hodkinson, M. Kleijwegt, K. Vlassopoulos (eds.), *The Oxford Handbook of Greek and Roman Slaveries*. Oxford. https://doi.org/10.1093/oxfordhb/9780199575251.013.32

Robertson, B. (2008). 'The Slave Names of IG I^3 1032 and the Ideology of Slavery at Athens', in: C. Cooper (ed.), *Epigraphy and the Greek Historian*. Toronto, 79–116.

Rosivach, V.J. (1989). '*Talasiourgoi* and *Paidia* in *IG* 2^2 1553–78: A Note on Athenian Social History', in: *Historia* 38, 365–370.

Rosivach, V.J. (1999). 'Enslaving *Barbaroi* and the Athenian Ideology of Slavery', in: *Historia* 48, 129–157.

Sabnis, S. (2021). 'Literary Evidence: Fiction', in: S. Hodkinson, M. Kleijwegt, K. Vlassopoulos (eds.), *The Oxford Handbook of Greek and Roman Slaveries*. Oxford. https://doi.org/10.1093/oxfordhb/9780199575251.013.34

Sallares, R. (1991). *The Ecology of the Ancient Greek World*. London.

Sargent, R. (1924). *The Size of the Slave Population at Athens during the Fifth and Fourth Centuries before Christ*. Urbana.

Scafuro, A. (2016). 'Note to the *Phialai Exeleutherikai*: Response to Velissaroulos-Karakostas', in: D.F. Leão and G. Thür (eds.), *Symposion 2015: Vorträge zur griechischen und hellenistischen Rechtsgeschichte*, Vienna, 75–89.

Scheidel, W. (2003). 'Helot Numbers: A Simplified Model', in: N. Luraghi and S.E. Alcock (eds.), *Helots and their Masters in Laconia and Messenia: Histories, Ideologies, Structures*. Washington, D.C., 240–247.

Scheidel, W. (2005). 'Real Slave Prices and the Relative Cost of Slave Labor in the Greco-Roman World', in: *Ancient Society* 35, 1–17.

Scheidel, W. (2008). 'The Comparative Economics of Slavery in the Greco-Roman World', in: E. Dal Lago and C. Katsari (eds.), *Slave Systems Ancient and Modern*. Cambridge, 105–126.

Schipp, O. (2010). Review of *Sklaverei und Freilassung in der griechisch-römischen Welt*, by Elisabeth Hermann-Otto. *Bryn Mawr Classical Review* 2010.11.06.

Scott, J.C. (1985). *Weapons of the Weak: Everyday Forms of Peasant Resistance*. New Haven.

Scott, J.C. (1990). *Domination and the Arts of Resistance*. New Haven.

Sells, D. (2013). 'Slaves in the Fragments of Old Comedy', in: B. Akrigg and R. Tordoff (eds.), *Slaves and Slavery in Ancient Greek Comic Drama*. Cambridge and New York, 91–110.

Serghidou, A. (2004). 'Herodotus and the Rhetoric of Slavery', in: V. Karageorghis and I. Taifacos (eds.), *The World of Herodotus*. Nicosia, 179–197.

Serghidou, A. (ed.) (2007). *Fear of Slaves—Fear of Enslavement in the Ancient Mediterranean. Peur de l'esclave—Peur de l'esclavage en Méditerranée ancienne (Discours, représentations, pratiques)*. Besançon.

Serghidou, A. (2008). 'Aspects culturels de la liberté personnelle chez Hérodote', in: A. Gonzales (ed.), *La fin du statut servile? (affranchissement, libération, abolition)*. Vol. 1. Besançon, 175–184.
Severy-Hoven, B. (2012). 'Master Narratives and the Wall Painting of the House of the Vettii, Pompeii', in: *Gender & History* 24, 540–580.
Shaw, B.D. (1998). '"A Wolf by the Ears": M.I. Finley's *Ancient Slavery and Modern Ideology* in Historical Context', in: M.I. Finley, *Ancient Slavery and Modern Ideology*, edited by B.D. Shaw. Princeton, 3–74.
Silver, M. (2015). '"Living Apart", *Apeleutheroi* and *Paramone*-Clause. A Response to Canevaro and Lewis', in: *Incidenza dell'Antico* 13, 139–161.
Simpson, P. (2006). 'Aristotle's Defensible Defence of Slavery', in: *Polis* 23, 95–115.
Sosin, J.D. (2015). 'Manumission with *Paramone*: Conditional Freedom?' in: *TAPA* 145, 325–381.
Stewart, R. (2012). *Plautus and Roman Slavery*. Malden, MA.
Synodinou, K. (1997). *On the Concept of Slavery in Eyripides*. Ionnina.
Tamiolaki, M. (2008). 'La libération et la citoyenneté des esclaves aux Arginuses: Platéens ou Athéniens? Un vers controversé d'Aristophane (*Gren.* 694) et l'idéologie de la société athénienne', in: A. Gonzales (ed.), *La fin du statut servile? Affranchissement, libération, abolition*. Vol. 1. Besançon, 53–63.
Tamiolaki, M. (2010). *Liberté et esclavage chez les historiens grecs classiques*. Paris.
Taylor, C. (2015). 'Social Networks and Social Mobility in Fourth-Century Athens', in: C. Taylor and K. Vlassopoulos (eds.), *Communities and Networks in the Ancient Greek World*. Oxford, 35–53.
Thalmann, W.G. (1996). 'Versions of Slavery in the *Captivi* of Plautus', in: *Ramus* 25, 112–145.
Thalmann, W.G. (1998). *The Swineherd and the Bow: Representations of Class in the* Odyssey. Ithaca.
Thalmann, W.G. (2011). 'Some Ancient Greek Images of Slavery', in: R. Alston, E. Hall, L. Proffitt (eds.), *Reading Ancient Slavery*. London, 72–96.
Thompson, F.H. (2003). *The Archaeology of Greek and Roman Slavery*. London.
Todd, S.C. (1995). *The Shape of Athenian Law*. Oxford.
Todd, S.C. (2013). 'Male Slave Sexuality and the Absence of Moral Panic in Classical Athens', *Bulletin of the Institute of Classical Studies* 56, 37–53.
Todd, S.C. (2018). 'Slave Manumission and *Paramonē*—Some Remaining Problems? Response to Rachel Zelnick-Abramovitz', in: G. Thür, U. Yiftach, R. Zelnick-Abramovitz (eds.), *Symposion 2017: Vorträge zur griechischen und hellenistischen Rechtsgeschichte*. Vienna, 403–409.
Tompkins, D. (2013). 'Moses Finkelstein and the American Scene: The Political Formation of Moses Finley, 1932–1955', in: W.V. Harris (ed.), *Moses Finley and Politics*. Leiden, 5–30.
Tompkins, D. (2014). 'La formation de Moses Finley d'après les documents américains, 1932–1955', in: *Anabases* 19, 111–129.
Topper, K. (2012). *The Imagery of the Athenian Symposium*. Cambridge.
Tordoff, R. (2013). 'Introduction: Slaves and Slavery in Ancient Greek Comedy', in: B. Akrigg and R. Tordoff (eds.), *Slaves and Slavery in Ancient Greek Comic Drama*. Cambridge and New York, 1–62.
Tordoff, R. (2017). 'Slaves and Slavery', in: A. Glazebrook and C. Vester (eds.), *Themes in Greek Society and Culture: An Introduction to Ancient Greece*. Oxford, 218–240.
Trevett, J. (2017). 'Status and Class', in: A. Glazebrook and C. Vester (eds.), *Themes in Greek Society and Culture: An Introduction to Ancient Greece*. Oxford, 196–217.

Tsetskhladze, G.R. (2008). 'Pontic Slaves in Athens: Orthodoxy and Reality', in: P. Mauritsch et al. (eds.), *Antike Lebenswelten. Konstanz—Wandel—Wirkungsmacht Festschrift für Ingomar Weiler zum 70. Geburtstag.* Wiesbaden, 309–219.

Tucker, C.W. (1982). 'Women in Manumission Inscriptions at Delphi', in: *TAPA* 112, 225–236.

Urbainczyk, T. (2008). *Slave Revolts in Antiquity.* London.

Urbainczyk, T. (2021). 'Literary Evidence: Non-Fiction', in: S. Hodkinson, M. Kleijwegt, K. Vlassopoulos (eds.), *The Oxford Handbook of Greek and Roman Slaveries.* Oxford. https://doi.org/10.1093/oxfordhb/9780199575251.013.37

Vanderford, C. (2009). 'Proslavery Professors: Classic Natural Right and the Positive Good Argument in Antebellum Virginia', in: *Civil War History* 55, 5–30.

Van Wees, H. (2003). 'Conquerors and Serfs: Wars of Conquest and Forced Labour in Archaic Greece', in: N. Luraghi and S. Alcock (eds.), *Helots and their Masters in Laconia and Messenia: Histories, Ideologies, Structures.* Washington, D.C., 33–80.

Van Wees, H. (2011). 'Demetrius and Draco: Athens' Population and Property Classes in and before 317 BC', in: *Journal of Hellenic Studies* 131, 95–114.

Van Wees, H. (2021). 'Slaving Practices in the Early Greek World', in: S. Hodkinson, M. Kleijwegt, K. Vlassopoulos (eds.), *The Oxford Handbook of Greek and Roman Slaveries.* Oxford. https://doi.org/10.1093/oxfordhb/9780199575251.013.40

Velissaropoulos-Karakostas, J. (2016). 'Note sur les *phialai exeleutherikai*', in: D.F. Leão and G. Thür (eds.), *Symposion 2015: Vorträge zur griechischen und hellenistischen Rechtsgeschichte.* Vienna, 75–89.

Vester, C. (2013). 'Tokens of Identity in Menander's *Epitrepontes*: Slaves, Citizens and In-Betweens', in: B. Akrigg and R. Tordoff (eds.), *Slaves and Slavery in Ancient Greek Comic Drama.* Cambridge and New York, 209–227.

Vlassopoulos, K. (2007). 'Free Spaces: Identity, Experience and Democracy in Classical Athens', in: *Classical Quarterly* 57, 33–52.

Vlassopoulos, K. (2009). 'Slavery, Freedom and Citizenship in Classical Athens: Beyond a Legalistic Approach', in: *European Review of History: Revue européenne d'histoire* 16, 347–363.

Vlassopoulos, K. (2010). 'Athenian Slave Names and Athenian Social History', in: *Zeitschrift für Papyrologie und Epigraphik* 175, 113–144.

Vlassopoulos, K. (2011a). 'Greek Slavery: From Domination to Property and Back Again', in: *Journal of Hellenic Studies* 131, 115–130.

Vlassopoulos, K. (2011b). 'Two Images of Ancient Slavery: The "Living Tool" and the *koinōnia*', in: E. Herrmann-Otto (ed.), *Sklaverei und Zwangsarbeit zwischen Akzeptanz und Widerstand.* Zurich, 467–477.

Vlassopoulos, K. (2011c). Review of *Metics and the Athenian Phialai-Inscriptions: A Study in Athenian Epigraphy and Law*, by Elizabeth Meyer. *Bryn Mawr Classical Review* 2011.02.48.

Vlassopoulos, K. (2015). 'Plotting Strategies, Networks, and Communities in Classical Athens: The Evidence of Slave Names', in: C. Taylor and K. Vlassopoulos (eds.), *Communities and Networks in the Ancient Greek World.* Oxford, 101–127.

Vlassopoulos, K. (2016a). 'Finley's Slavery', in: D. Jew, R. Osborne, and M. Scott (eds.), *M. I. Finley: An Ancient Historian and His Impact.* Cambridge, 76–99.

Vlassopoulos, K. (2016b). 'Does Slavery Have a History? The Consequences of a Global Approach', in: *Journal of Global Slavery* 1, 5–27.

Vlassopoulos, K. (2018). 'Hope and Slavery', in: G. Kazantzidis and D. Spatharas (eds.), *Hope in Ancient Literature, History, and Art: Ancient Emotions I.* Berlin, 235–258.

Vlassopoulos, K. (2019). 'The End of Enslavement, "Greek Style"', in: S. Hodkinson, M. Kleijwegt, K. Vlassopoulos (eds.), *The Oxford Handbook of Greek and Roman Slaveries*. Oxford. https://doi.org/10.1093/oxfordhb/9780199575251.013.39
Vlassopoulos, K. (2021). *Historicising Ancient Slavery*. Edinburgh.
Vlastos, G. (1981 [1941]). 'Slavery in Plato's Thought', in: *Platonic Studies*. Princeton, 147–163.
Vlastos, G. (1981 [1968]). 'Does Slavery Exist in Plato's *Republic*?', in: *Platonic Studies*. Princeton, 140–146.
Vogt, J. (1975 [1965]). *Ancient Slavery and the Ideal of Man*, translated by T. Wiedemann. Cambridge, MA.
Walin, D. (2009). 'An Aristophanic Slave: *Peace* 819–1126', in: *Classical Quarterly* 59, 30–45.
Walin, D. (2012). *Slaves, Sex, and Transgression in Greek Old Comedy*. Diss. Berkeley.
Watson, J. L. (1980). 'Introduction: Slavery as an Institution: Open and Closed Systems', in: J.L. Watson (ed.), *Asian and African Systems of Slavery*. Berkeley, 1–15.
Weiler, I. (2001). 'Eine Sklavin wird frei. Zur Rolle des Geschlechts bei der Freilassung', in: H. Bellen and H. Heiner (eds.), *Fünfzig Jahre Forschungen zur antiken Sklaverei an der Mainzer Akademie, 1950–2000: Miscellanea zum Jubiläum*. Stuttgart, 113–132.
Welwei, K.-W. (2004). 'War die Krypteia ein grausames Terrorinstrument? Zur Entstehung einer Fiction', in: *Laverna* 15, 33–46.
Welwei, K.-W. (2006). 'Überlegungen zur frühen Helotie in Lakonien', in: A. Luther, M. Meier, T. Thommen (eds.), *Das frühe Sparta*. Stuttgart, 29–41.
Wiedemann, T. (1981). *Greek & Roman Slavery*. London.
Wiedemann, T. and J. Gardner (eds.) (2002). *Representing the Body of the Slave*. London.
Willetts, R.F. (1967). *The Law Code of Gortyn*. Berlin.
Wilson, E. (2021). 'Slaves and Sex in the *Odyssey*', in: D. Kamen and C.W. Marshall (eds.), *Slavery and Sexuality in Classical Antiquity*. Madison, 15–39.
Winterer, C. (2007). *The Mirror of Antiquity: American Women and the Classical Tradition, 1750–1900*. Ithaca.
Wood, E.M. (1988). *Peasant-Citizen and Slave: The Foundations of Athenian Democracy*. London.
Wrenhaven, K.L. (2009). 'The Identity of the "Wool-Workers" in the Attic Manumissions', in: *Hesperia* 78, 367–386.
Wrenhaven, K.L. (2011). 'Greek Representations of the Slave Body: A Conflict of Ideas?', in: R. Alston, E. Hall, L. Proffitt (eds.), *Reading Ancient Slavery*. London, 97–120.
Wrenhaven, K.L. (2012). *Reconstructing the Slave: The Image of the Slave in Ancient Greece*. London.
Wrenhaven, K.L. (2013a). 'Barbarians at the Gate: Foreign Slaves in Greek City-States', in: *Electryone* 1, 1–17.
Wrenhaven, K.L. (2013b) 'A Comedy of Errors: The Comic Slave in Greek Art', in: B. Akrigg and R. Tordoff (eds.), *Slaves and Slavery in Ancient Greek Comic Drama*. Cambridge and New York, 124–143.
Wrenhaven, K.L. (2021). 'Slaves and Sex in Classical Greek Art', in: D. Kamen and C.W. Marshall (eds.), *Slavery and Sexuality in Classical Antiquity*. Madison, 66–88.
Zanovello, S. (2017). *From Slave to Free: A Legal Perspective on Greek Manumission*. Diss. Padova/Edinburgh.
Zanovello, S. (2018). 'Some Remarks on Manumission and Consecration in Hellenistic Chaeronea', in: *Journal of Global Slavery* 3, 129–151.

Zanovello, S. (2021). *From Slave to Free: A Legal Perspective on Greek Manumission*. Alessandria.

Zanovello, S. (2022). 'Homer and the Vocabulary of Manumission', in: J.C. Bernhardt and M. Canevaro (eds.), *From Homer to Solon: Continuity and Change in Archaic Greece*. Leiden, 93–114.

Zelnick-Abramovitz, R. (2005). *Not Wholly Free: The Concept of Manumission and the Status of Manumitted Slaves in the Ancient Greek World*. Leiden.

Zelnick-Abramovitz, R. (2013). *Taxing Freedom in Thessalian Manumission Inscriptions*. Leiden.

Zelnick-Abramovitz, R. (2014). 'Greek Slavery', in: C. Clayman (ed.), *Oxford Bibliographies Online: Classics*. Oxford. https://doi.org/10.1093/OBO/9780195389661-0041

Zelnick-Abramovitz, R. (2018). 'The Status of Slaves Manumitted under *Paramonē*: A Reappraisal', in: G. Thür, U. Yiftach, R. Zelnick-Abramovitz (eds.), *Symposion 2017: Vorträge zur griechischen und hellenistischen Rechtsgeschichte*. Vienna, 377–401.

Index Locorum

Aelian
Varia historia
2.7	36

Aeschines
1.17	58, 59 n. 46
1.139	69
2.79	53
3.41–42	84

Aeschylus
Choephoroe
747–764	62–63 n. 9

Agora Inventory
I 1580	85 n. 13
I 3183	85 n. 13
I 4665	85 n. 13
I 4763	85 n. 13
I 5656	85 n. 13
I 5774	85 n. 13
I 7180	52
IL 1702	51

Andocides
1.12–18	85
1.27–28	85

Anecdota Graeca
I 316.11	97 n. 60

Antiphon
5.47	57
5.69	79
6.4	57

Aristophanes
Acharnenses
271–275	67

Equites
24–29	70
1311–1312	57
1384–1386	67 n. 32

Pax
1138–1139	67

Ranae
33	85
190–192	85
542–548	70
616–622	54
693–695	85
694	103 n. 14

Thesmophorizusae
490–492	69

Vespae
435	52
500–502	70
1291–1295	52

Aristotle
Athēnaiōn politeia
6.1	18
12.4	18
57.3	58
58.3	86

Politica
1253b1–1255b40	105
1253b33	9
1254a14–18	9 n. 41
1254d32–34	105
1255a1–2	105
1255a6–7	34
1264a21–22	26
1269a29–1271b19	24 n. 50
1269a36–b5	25
1269b7–12	54 n. 32
1271b20–1272b23	24 n. 50
1272b16–22	25

[Aristotle]
Oikonomika
1344a25–26	49 n. 11
1344a29–31	49
1344a35–b11	50
1344b17–18	70

Athenaeus
6.265bc	20
6.265d–266e	79–80
6.267b	93 n. 41
6.272bd	37
6.272c	36–37
13.604c	67–68

Cicero
Orator
93–94	109

Corpus des inscriptions de Delphes
V 1.388	91

Demosthenes
4.36–37	97
19.196–198	53 n. 28
21.46	58, 58–59 n. 46
22.55	50
23.71	58
27.9	42
29.25–26	83
30.37	53 n. 29
34.10	32 n. 2
36.8	98
46.13	98
47.55	63
47.56	63
47.68–73	58

[Demosthenes]
59	65, 97–98
59.2	98
59.29–31	84
59.31–32	65
59.40	98

Digest
40.7	94
40.7.1.pr.	94
40.7.9.pr.	94

Dio Chrysostomus
15.25	34

Diodorus Siculus
5.38.1	41 n. 49

Diogenes Laertius
3.19–20	111

Ephorus Historicus
BNJ 70 F 117	21 n. 29, 22–23

Euripides
Ion
128–140	102 n. 6

Hellenica Oxyrhynchia
17.4	78

Hellanicus Historicus
BNJ 4 F 188	21 n. 29

Herodotus
2.134	74
2.135	65
4.1–4	69
9.10.1	23
9.28.2	23
9.29.1	23

Herondas
Mime 5   69

Hesiod
Opera et Dies
403–406	17

Homer
Odyssey
1.427–435	47–48 n. 5
17.322–323	17 n. 10
18.320–326	48 n. 6
19.392–393	62
19.471–472	62

Iliad
6.463	17

Hyperides
3	42, 64, 68, 84
3.22	42

fr. 29 Jensen 37
fr. *Against Timandrus* 71

Inscriptiones Creticae
IV 72 24

Inscriptiones Graecae
II² 1469 86
II² 1553–1578 85 n. 13
II² 1554 75 n. 8
II² 1578 86, 87
V 2.429 88 n. 27
VII 1779 88
VII 3321 89

Isaeus
8.12 53 n. 29

Isocrates
4.181 112 n. 59

Lysias
1.12 67
1.18 43
3 68
4 68
13.19 53

Meiggs and Lewis
8 20

Menander
Epitrepontes
267 71
Hērōs
2–3 52

Myron
BNJ 106 F 2 55

Pausanias
1.29.8 80

Philochorus
BNJ 328 F 177 78

Plato
Gorgias
483b 71
Leges
633bc 56
776d 57
777d 48
777e–778a 49
879ab 57
915a 93 n. 41
936ce 57
Respublica
575d 110
577c 110
578e 79

Plutarch
Lycurgus
28.1 55
28.2–3 55
28.3 56
28.4 55, 56
28.5 55
28.6 55
Solon
15.3 18
22.2 54–55

Pollux
3.83 22, 96

Polyaenus Historicus
1.43.1 80 n. 29

Sammlung der griechischen Dialektinschriften
II 1689 91

Solon
fr. 9 West 110
fr. 11 West 110
fr. 36 West 110

Theopompus Historicus
BNJ 115 F13 21 n. 29, 54

Thucydides
1.101–102	80
4.80.2–4	56
5.116.4	111 n. 57
6.27.2	85
7.27.5	37, 78
8.40.2	20, 78

Vita Aesopi Westermanniana
1	78
75	69

Xenophon
Hellenica
1.6.24	85

Hiero
10.4	79

Oikonomikos
3.4	52
7.20	62
7.21–25	62
9.5	70
9.11–13	41
10.12	67
12.3–15.1	41
13.9–12	49
14.9	49

Symposium
4.53–54	67

[Xenophon]
Athēnaiōn politeia
1.10	96, 107

General Index

Aegina 37
Aesop 69, 77–78
agency 6, 7, 8, 42, 73–76, 78, 82, 109
agricultural labor 17–18, 22, 26, 30, 38–40, 46
Akrigg, Ben 8, 102–103
Alston, Richard 8, 113
American slavery 7, 23–24, 35, 76, 81, 82, 95, 113–116
amphipolos 17
andrapodon 17, 37, 50–51, 78
Andreau, Jean 4
apeleutheros 90, 96
Apollo 88, 89, 91
apophora 42
Aristotle 9, 10, 24–25, 26, 38, 49–50, 55–56, 105–106, 114
art, Greek 107–109
Artemidorus 74–74
Attic Stelai 32, 33, 35, 45
banking 38, 42, 84, 98
basanos 29, 51, 53–54
Bathrello, Eftychia 5
beating 52, 53, 54, 55
Bodel, John 8
Bömer, Franz 75
Bradley, Keith 8–9
branding 52–53
Braund, David 33, 36
Brazil 7–8, 12–13, 75, 95
Cameron, Catherine 13
Canevaro, Mirko 58, 59, 93
Cartledge, Paul 1–2, 8–9, 40, 56, 81
chains 51, 52, 53
Child, Lydia Maria 115
Chios 20, 24, 78, 79–80
chōris oikountes 97
Cohen, Edward 28, 53, 59, 68
comedy, Greek 8, 39, 52, 54, 67, 69, 70, 102–104
commerce 20, 38, 42–43
communities, enslaved people's 6, 29, 74, 75, 80, 82

comparative slavery studies 2, 5, 7–8, 13, 15, 24, 29, 36, 52, 72, 118
consecration, manumission through 88–91, 99
Corinth 37
Crete 24–26
Dal Lago, Enrico 7
Davies, Peter 27–28, 29–30
debt bondage 18–19, 20, 24, 26, 36, 110
Deceleia 37, 78
Delphi 35, 65–66, 71, 91–92
democracy 3–4, 19–20, 28, 40, 43, 111
Descat, Raymond 4
dikē apostasiou 85–87
dikē blabēs 58
dikē emmēnos 86–87
dikē phonou 58
dishonor 9, 11–12, 58–59, 61
do-e-ro/do-e-ra 15
Dodona 75
dōlos 25
domestic labor 17, 38, 40–41, 43, 44
domination, slavery as 6, 9–12
doulos 10, 16, 17, 22, 26, 27, 112
Drimacus 79–80
duBois, Page 3, 50, 53, 54, 101, 109
Eidinow, Esther 75
eleutheros/eleutheria 10, 49, 61, 65, 84, 88, 89, 90, 91, 92, 98
Eumaeus 17, 115–116
Eurycleia 17, 47, 62, 115–116
Fenoaltea, Stefano 44
fetters 51, 52, 53
Finley, Moses 1, 2, 6, 9, 12–14, 19–20, 22, 26, 27, 37–38, 118
Fisher, N.R.E. 38, 58
Forsdyke, Sara 5, 11–12, 29, 30, 36, 74, 80
Fynn-Paul, Jeffrey 45
Gaca, Kathy 58–59, 66
Gardner, Jane 7
Garlan, Yvon 34
Geary, Dick 7, 75
gender 9, 41, 61–64, 71–72, 102, 118

Genovese, Eugene 81
Gildersleeve, Basil Lannau 115
Glazebrook, Allison 53, 62, 64, 65
global slavery studies 2, 23, 15, 118
Gonzales, Antonio 7, 8
Gottesman, Alex 78
graphē aprostasiou 87
graphē hubreōs 59
Greenwood, Emily 106
Hall, Edith 8, 113, 115
Hanes, Christopher 44
Harper, Kyle 45, 61
Harpocration 86, 96, 97
Harris, Edward 18, 19, 20, 51
hektēmoros 18
Helots 21–24, 54–57, 73, 80–81, 115–116
Hermann-Otto, Elisabeth 4–5
Hesiod 17–18
hetaira 64–65
Hinsch, Moritz 40
historians, Greek 2–3, 32, 104, 109, 110–111
Hodkinson, Stephen 7–8, 9, 23–24, 75, 116
Homer 17, 18, 20, 22, 34, 47, 48, 62, 101, 115–116
honor 12, 45, 49, 58–59, 61, 80, 97
Honoré, A.M. 11
hubris 48, 49–50, 58–59, 60, 68
Hunt, Peter 2–3, 5, 50, 57, 77, 104
Hunter, Virginia 50
Ismard, Paulin 3–4, 27, 43
Jameson, Michael 39–40
Johnson, Walter 76
Jones, A.H.M. 39
Jones, Christopher 71
Joshel, Sandra 61
Kapparis, Konstantinos 53
Katsari, Constantina 7
Kleijwegt, Marc 9
krypteia 55–56
Laconia 21
Lenski, Noel 11, 13–14
Lesis 51, 57
Lewis, David 5–6, 11, 14, 18, 22, 25, 26, 27, 30, 39, 45, 93
Long, A.A. 112

Luraghi, Nino 7, 21, 24
Maffi, Alberto 42
Malamud, Margaret 113–114
manufacturing 20, 38, 42
manumission 4–5, 7, 35, 61, 63–64, 65–66, 67, 71, 75, 83–100, 101, 102, 103, 112
marriage 25–26, 70, 71, 98
Marshall, C.W. 8, 68, 104
Matuszewski, Rafał 67, 68, 108
McConnell, Justine 113, 115
McKeown, Niall 1–2, 74, 76–77
medical writers 104
Messenia 21, 56–57, 80, 81
metaphors 10, 101, 105, 109–113
metics 27, 28, 29, 30, 36, 37, 51, 58, 96, 97
Meyer, Elizabeth 85, 87
mining 20, 37, 38, 41, 44, 51
Mirhady, David 54
Monoson, Sara 114
Morrow, Glenn 112
Mulliez, Dominique 71
Murnaghan, Sheila 61
Mycenaean period 16
Nakassis, Dimitri 16
Neaira 65, 97–99
New Testament 112
North, John 75–76
numbers, slave 23, 35, 36–37, 40, 81
oikogenēs 34, 35
oiketēs 27, 37, 78
Paiaro, Diego 28–29
paidagōgos 62, 63
Paradiso, Annalisa 56, 57
Parmenter, Christopher 36
Pasion 98
Patterson, Orlando 8, 9–12, 73–75
Peloponnesian War 37, 56, 78, 84, 103, 111
Persian Wars 110–111
phialai exeleutherikai 66, 85–87, 99
philosophers, Greek 9, 10, 24–25, 26, 37, 38, 48, 49–50, 55–56, 57, 58, 79, 104–106, 110, 111–113, 114
Phormion 98
Phrygia 33, 77

Plato 10, 48, 55–56, 57, 79, 104–105, 110, 111, 112–113
popular culture 115–116
pornē 64–65
Porter, Jason 42, 48, 49
prasis ep' eleutheriai 65, 84
Proffitt, Laura 8
property, slave as VII, 6, 9–11, 14, 18, 22, 30, 32, 34, 52, 57, 58, 67, 89–90, 93, 106
prostitution 12, 41, 44, 53, 61, 63, 64–66, 67, 70, 71, 97–99, 104
Pseudo-Aristotle 38, 49–50, 70
public slaves 3–4, 43, 51–52
Raaflaub, Kurt 110
rape 24, 66–68
religion 7–8, 9, 16, 29, 75–76, 87–92, 99, 112
Requena, Mariano 28–29
resistance 3, 7, 76–79, 82, 103, 109
revolt 24–25, 55, 56, 79–81
Rihll, Tracey 20
sale, manumission through 65, 84, 88, 91, 99
Scheidel, Walter 8, 23, 44–45
Scott, James C. 77
Scythia 33, 69–70
seisachtheia 18–19
serfdom 22, 23–24, 25, 26, 30
Serghidou, Anastasia 7
sex 5, 8, 12, 41, 44, 53, 61, 63–71, 76–77, 84, 97–99, 101, 103, 104, 108, 118
shackles 51, 52, 53
slave societies 6, 12–14, 20, 22, 26, 29, 30, 35, 47, 63, 94, 118
slaving strategies 6, 14, 47–50, 51
social death 8, 9–10, 11, 14, 73–74
Solon 18–21, 42–43, 110
Sosin, Joshua 92, 93–94
Sparta 13, 21–25, 30, 54–57, 80–81, 111, 115, 116
status
–in classical Athens 27–30
–of enslaved people 6, 9, 11, 16, 17, 21, 22, 23, 24, 25–26, 44, 56, 58, 64–65, 73, 74, 77–78, 94, 102, 112

–of formerly enslaved people 4, 88, 90, 93–95, 96–99
supply, slave 19–20, 32–36
Tamiolaki, Melina 104, 113
tattooing 52–53, 69, 107
Taylor, Claire 29
teaching slavery VII, 116
Thalmann, William 47–48, 101
therapōn 27
Theseion 57, 78–79
Thessaly 24
Thrace 33, 67, 77
titthēs 17, 47, 51, 62–63, 64
Todd, Stephen 69
Tordoff, Rob 8, 102–103
torture, judicial 29, 51, 53–54
tragedy, Greek 62–63, 89, 102
Van Wees, Hans 24
Vlassopoulos, Kostas 2, 5, 6, 9, 10–11, 14, 28, 29, 33, 47, 48, 73–75, 76, 87, 93
Vlastos, Gregory 112
Vogt, Joseph 47
Walin, Daniel 70
war 2–3, 17, 24–25, 34, 35, 37, 50–51, 56, 66, 69, 78, 84–85, 103, 104, 105, 108, 110–111
Watson, James L. 44
wet-nurses 17, 47, 51, 62–63, 64
whipping 50, 51–52, 53, 54, 57, 69
Wiedemann, Thomas 7
Winterer, Caroline 114–115
woikeus 25
Wood, Ellen M. 39
Wrenhaven, Kelly 3, 66, 102, 107–108
Zanovello, Sara 4, 89–91, 93
Zelnick-Abramovitz, Rachel 4, 86–87, 93, 96, 98

www.ingramcontent.com/pod-product-compliance
Lightning Source LLC
Chambersburg PA
CBHW030656230426
43665CB00011B/1126